RELIGIOUS TELEVISION
What to Do and How

Other books by
EVERETT C. PARKER

RELIGIOUS RADIO, What to Do
and How (with Elinor Inman and
Ross Snyder)

THE TELEVISION-RADIO AUDIENCE
AND RELIGION (with David W.
Barry and Dallas W. Smythe)

RELIGIOUS TELEVISION

WHAT TO DO AND HOW

Everett C. Parker

Harper & Brothers, Publishers, New York

To Truman B. Douglass in appreciation
of his friendship and of his leadership
in communicating the Christian Gospel
through television, radio, the press, and
the pulpit

CONTENTS

Introduction

The modern revolution in communication which began with the advent of mass circulation newspapers and magazines and has reached its zenith with television has brought about swift and profound changes in the habits and thinking of people the world over. During the course of this revolution, work loads have lessened for the average individual and leisure time has increased, to be spent in large part in passive observation of whatever the mass media of communication have chosen to disseminate. Community activities have been drastically affected, especially those concerned with the use of leisure time. Congregate assemblies—in theaters, lecture halls, and churches— have declined in importance to be replaced by individuals or small groups attending to mass media programs in the home.

The almost universal experiencing of particular ideas, methods, tastes, and standards from a single communications source has had a leveling effect, tending to blur local and regional differences and to override folk thought, art, and customs. The obliteration of distinctions between the rural and urban mind and tastes has been particularly marked, with urban standards of thought and living becoming dominant. Even the practice of politics and the functioning of government have been altered to accord with mass media methodology.

Television, in particular, has become a potent force for influencing communities, nations, even the world, in courses of action; in universalizing particular tastes and standards; and in dominating the use of leisure time. It is an instrumentality that cannot be ignored by any institution that is concerned with how the minds and wills of people are being affected.

Christianity and Judaism are enmeshed in a clash of faiths that is world-wide, and it is one in which they need ask no quarter for none will be granted. It is the decisive struggle for the soul of modern man. Its outcome will influence the human intellect for centuries to come.

This struggle requires that the ministry and the Evangel take on new dimensions. The religious fellowship, just to survive, needs to make the power of its faith felt outside its own membership. No longer can the church be gathered only within the four walls of one building. No longer can the clergyman fulfill the role of pastor just to those persons listed on his membership rolls. Television affords one major opportunity for the church to abandon exclusiveness and to penetrate the surrounding life of the community and of the whole culture. This is a calling from God, uniquely pertinent to the needs of our present times, and one which the church will neglect or resist or shy away from only to its mortal peril.

This book is a manual which presents a theory and practical methods for employing television for a ministry to the whole public, and for applying the moral principles of the Judaeo-Christian tradition to the secular aspects of television broadcasting. It is written for students who are interested in the ethical aspects of mass communication and the role of religion in television; and, more importantly, as a comprehensive guide for clergymen and lay men and women who are (a) engaged in the planning and production of religious television programs over local stations and (b) desirous of improving the artistic and moral standards of all television broadcasting.

The theoretical views and judgments expounded here stem from a Protestant rootage, but the broadcasting techniques and program ideas should be equally useful to Protestants, Roman Catholics, and Jews who are actively engaged in television production. There is no claim that the ideas presented here about religion, television, or the relationship between the two are exhaustive, but they do represent a distillation of more than twenty years of experience in writing, directing, and producing radio and television programs and of intimate relationship with a majority of the leading Protestant religious programs that have been on the air in that time. I hope that my experience may help a new generation of religious broadcasters prepare and produce sensitive, imaginative programs that will make the Word of God explicit for millions of persons who need it, hunger for it, and may, through television, have their longing fulfilled.

I am grateful for aid given to me in the preparation of this book by Professor John W. Bachman, who read and criticized the manuscript, Warren Johnson, who drew the figures and charts included in the text, and Dr. Milton Mazer, who provided definitions of psychological terminology.

EVERETT C. PARKER

White Plains, New York
March 1, 1961

CHAPTER I   What Do We Need to Know about the Process of Communication?

Communication is "the fundamental human fact."—Roger Mehl

The wonderful technological system we call television has greatly furthered the revolution in *methods* of communication that is one of the hallmarks of modern culture. Yet the essential *process* of communication has not been altered greatly under the impact of television and the other mass media.

Communication is always a complex affair, but it is never an abstract act. Communication takes place only through encounter. There are numberless varieties of encounter, from the most flitting and superficial to the deep, enduring relations between husband and wife, parent and child, master and student. The forms of communication are equally varied; but encounter and communication blend only when there is a clash of mind on mind.

Language is the coin of communication, but communication transcends language. It is more than a transmission of symbols from a communicator to an auditor; there is need for mutuality, for attentiveness on both sides. Listening is as important as speaking. Expression is futile unless it elicits a response from "the other."

Communication is not necessarily constructive. There is not always a spontaneous meeting of minds, an agreement, a friendly relationship. Expression may be used for the studied purpose of destroying the other. Language may be used to conceal rather than to clarify.

Hendrik Kraemer has pointed up the polarity that is possible in communication: "The act of communication can mean . . . a combat, an effort to defeat the other, to prove that one is in the

1

right; or it can mean a recognition of the other, in which there is a real I-Thou encounter."[1]

Communication that terminates in understanding depends upon mutuality in the encounter. There need not be friendship, nor even trust; but there must be a mutual desire for contact, followed by an exchange from mind to mind and from heart to heart. There must also be something offered that is worth communicating; therefore worth listening to and, more importantly, worth reacting to. Kraemer says the ideal situation "presupposes a *common* universe of discourse" which begins in recognition of one for the other and is then grounded on mutually acceptable "presuppositions and assumptions, and on the same imponderable but very 'ponderous,' spontaneous reactions to the totality of life."[2] This ideal encounter "is the true meaning and intended aim of communication," but Kraemer admits, ruefully, it "is in fact a rare occurrence among men, and a priceless experience."[3]

The normative situation is far from the ideal. We live most of the time in the theological atmosphere of the Tower of Babel, longing for one simple, universal intelligibility; but condemned to separateness and disunity by our inability to relate to each other in dialogue. The breakdown of communication is one of the fundamental facts of our time. Christians see this breakdown occurring between the church and the world. In fact it is much more widespread. Great communication gulfs exist in and between all the levels of secular society. Communication has hard sledding where there is no community. Our society, for all its delicate balance and organization, lacks the common aims, attitudes, understandings, and values that make for community. It is both disintegrated and overspecialized. We are especially handicapped by our inability to harness impersonal scientific and technological developments to social and ethical policies that will benefit rather than harm society. In our pursuit of excellence and exactness, especially in scientific endeavor, we have subdivided knowledge and vocation to the point

[1] Hendrik Kraemer, *The Communication of the Christian Faith* (Philadelphia: The Westminster Press, 1956), p. 73.

[2] *Ibid.*, p. 73 f.

[3] *Ibid.*, p. 58.

where one man knows so much about so little that he has not the capacity to know about the whole. Nor can he easily establish I-Thou relationships outside his segregated vocational group. Others have no acquaintance with his specialty and its vocabulary, nor he with theirs. Even a common language does not bridge the gap between distinct vocations with their distinct attitudes toward life. Not only is the specialist unable to break out of his particularized niche, he is virtually incapable of planning for the complex of which his specialty is a part; even less is he capable of planning in a wider area. Planning and policy making—which perforce shape social courses—are no longer the province of a single informed, creative mind that is steeped in the ethical traditions of the culture and seeks to perpetuate them. The stodgy and unimaginative committee of specialists sits in its place. In these committees where our political, economic, scientific, educational, even religious decisions are taken, the parts do not add up to a rounded whole. Inevitably, there are few "spontaneous reactions to the totality of life." With no "common universe of discourse" possible, it is also difficult to create a common policy that all may comprehend and support. It is virtually impossible to communicate such a policy to the public at large.

THE MASS MEDIA AND THE PROCESS OF COMMUNICATION

Since the mass media of communication—television, radio, cinema, and mass-distributed printed publications—are so all-pervading and garner such large audiences, it might be expected that they would be the great mediators, breaking down the barriers between the inarticulate specialties and creating a commonality of feeling and understanding that is the essence of community. In point of fact, they do no such thing. They are levelers; but the mutuality they engender has to do only with the surface aspects of the culture. These media do seek a "common universe of discourse"; but in working for this end, they are subjected to even more vicissitudes than plague face-to-face communication in our segmented society. Since the media aim to speak to everybody, they are always in a quandary over whose idiom they should employ. And while these instrumentalities do strive earnestly to draw large numbers of people into a common feeling and understanding, the psychological condition they engender is not compounded of an I-Thou encounter on an ethical basis. Rather, the commercial drive of the media consciously seeks to create passiveness in the audience that will tolerate uncritical acceptance of the message that is transmitted.

The *process* of communication, as it operates in the mass media, has many similarities to face-to-face encounter. It is working simultaneously at several levels of consciousness. Both the communicator and the audience members contribute to its thrust. The ingredients are the same in both kinds of interchange: There is a communicator who has something to declare and transmit. There is an audience. (In television, it is made up of individuals, separated in space and motivated by all manner of attitudes and predispositions.) There is the link between communicator and audience—the content of the communication.

Content is transmitted and received as a flow of representations. Both the meanings and the methods by which meanings are sent and received operate on many levels and have many dimensions. There are all the layers of meaning conveyed by visual perception— bodily action, facial expression, clothes, background, the shape and size of physical objects. There are the words, ambiguous by themselves in isolation, becoming meaningful within the totality of transmission made up of syntax, melody, force, time, and pitch used in their expression.

Dallas W. Smythe has likened the process of communication in the mass media to the movement of a conveyor belt. The belt carries many different materials to the members of the audience. They, in turn, approach the conveyor with the widest possible variety of tastes and needs. The communicator gives them what he will; they take what they wish. What they take, what use they make of his communication, how they reshape it to their own ends, are factors in the communication process as diverse as are the dynamics of the personalities and life situations of the individuals involved.

The obvious difference between mass media and face-to-face communication is the absence in each of the mass media of feedback, the give-and-take of a personal relationship between communicator and auditors. The television communicator, of course, hopes that the audience will take all of the material he offers and use it within his context of meaning. On the one hand, he is not overdisturbed at the absence of the feedback of face-to-face encounter, since he is normally engaged in selling something, and the last thing he wants is to have his auditors question the validity of his statements. On the other hand, he has no way to assess impact, to correct misconceptions, to bolster weaknesses, to reply to objections. He can transmit his message only on a take-it-or-leave-it basis. Hence, the frantic effort of the commercial broadcaster to dress it up, water it down, pound it home! His salient purpose is to reduce, and if possible to eliminate, the element of choice.

The religious communicator cannot be satisfied with take-it-or-leave-it transmission or with passive reception of whatever is said. Religious programs are not analogous to shows designed to sell salad oil. The religious communicator, be he Jew or Christian, cannot even be content with the schoolmaster's judgment of successful communication: transmission and proof, through testing, that the message has been received and assimilated. The goal of religious communication, whatever the method used, is the creation of a complex situation in which communicator and auditor react upon each other in such a way that they become involved together in a long-term course of action that goes beyond the communication itself and its meaning. For the Christian, the intercourse between communicator and auditor takes place always in the presence of a "third person" who is both the source of the communication and the objective of the action sought. The communication will be deemed to have failed if both communicator and auditor have not been drawn into involvement with Christ.

Mass Communication and the Culture

Every television program, whether or not it intends to do so, is espousing a viewpoint, some interpretation of life. No program exists in a vacuum. Each one speaks within and to a particular cultural milieu, while at the same time it has acquired its presuppositions from the very culture it is addressing. There is danger that such communication will be circular; that it will be solely a process in which the culture reiterates to itself what it already believes. It is all too easy to predicate programs, wittingly or unwittingly, on the predilections and prejudices that exist in the audience, thus merely feeding back to audience members their prevailing attitudes. A concomitant danger is that the built-in bias of the culture will operate in such a manner as to have the program say by chance what it would not say purposely. That is, the audience members will interpret what they see and hear in such a way that beliefs they already hold will be strengthened, even when the material being transmitted actually runs counter to such beliefs.

When we communicate, we are not speaking to individuals isolated from all influences other than the communication itself. We actually speak to a person-in-culture. Or, we speak to culture in a "personal" package.

Culture as used here is not synonymous with institutions, the society, civilization itself. It refers to the world of meanings in which people live, the valued mode of existence, the experiences that are treasured at the cores of our personalities. Unlike institutions, experiences, meanings, and values are not transitory.[4] They endure

[4] *Meaning* concerns the significance, the sense, the import of what is said. It is that which is intended to be expressed or indicated. It may differ somewhat from what is actually said, as in Paul's Letter to the Corinthians: "Where is the wise man? Where is the scribe? Where is the debater of this age? Has not God made foolish the wisdom of the world? For since, in the wisdom of God, the world did not know God through wisdom, it pleased God through the folly of what we preach to save those who believe" (I Cor. 1:20-21).

Values are principles by which one believes his life is guided. A value is believed by the person who holds it to have intrinsic worth, to be worthy of esteem for its own sake. Once a value has been accepted, it lodges deep in the ego, and it is difficult to alter or dislodge it. Though values are believed by the individual holders to be universal concepts, they are, in fact, related to culture, to a large part are determined by culture (the Anglo-American cherishing of freedom of speech and press, for example); but they also characteristically cross the boundaries of both culture and time. Loyalty and courage have been honored from the most primitive to the most advanced cultures in all ages. Honesty (though its definition varies from culture to culture) is a virtue that is universally lauded. Values are closely tied to both ethics and behavior. They are prone to develop institutional support. Institutions may engage, with public approval, in activities which in themselves are repugnant to society if the acts are associated in the public mind with a widely held value. (Attempts at censorship in the name of patriotism are a case in point.) Institutions are also the chief exponents and transmitters of values. In American culture, the family, churches, schools and colleges, the law, and vocations devote great concern and energy to the communication of values. Values may be professed but not practiced. Thus, thrift is lauded in the American culture, but Americans are the most conspicuous spenders in the world.

from generation to generation, and they can be communicated from person to person.

Imagery and the American Culture

Every culture has social images, both physical and psychological. These images represent valued modes of existence. They may truthfully portray the values and functions of the culture, or they may be partially or wholly false; their validity has virtually no effect on their influence. This influence is very great; in fact, the images are the masters of the culture. They exert social pressure, drawing persons to their service. They become the focal points around which subcultures develop. The individual takes his place in one—or more—of these subcultures, using it to mirror his image of self-in-the-world.

Americans have a great many social images which have blossomed into subcultures that are cherished and nurtured. The subcultures that exist as physical groupings of individuals may be identified in sociological terms. Other subcultures are psychological. Their members often are separated spatially. They may, therefore, be drawn from several social classes and from differing races, nationalities, and religions and still hold like views without the embarrassment that might occur with propinquity. Without individual members

---

Attitudes are the premises upon which people act. They are the conscious expression of values held by the individual. Attitudes are the immediate positions people take in response to the events which impinge upon them. They are the ways people apply values. Opposition to the admission of Red China to the United Nations is expression of an attitude. So is any other venturing of an opinion. Some physical acts, such as blushing under raillery, also exemplify attitudes. Attitudes resist change. Attitudes are functional. They form a *Gestalt* that (1) enables the individual to organize the myriad of stimuli with which he is constantly being bombarded, and (2) gives him the basis for reacting in a manner consistent with his self-image. While attitudes are triggered by stimuli, they are not altered by the stimuli. Rather, they help the personality respond to each stimulus while protecting its core structure from the impact of the outside force. It may be seen, therefore, why attitudes are hard to change. They perform vital functions in helping the person maintain his sense of self.

A *belief* is a state or habit of mind and requires intellectual assent. Beliefs are, therefore, more amenable to change through persuasion and logical argument than are attitudes and values. Belief should not be equated with *faith*. The two are often used interchangeably but there is an important distinction between them. Belief may or may not imply certitude, but it is assumed to be based upon empirical evidence. *Faith* always implies certitude, which may exist without evidence or proof.

necessarily being aware that there are others in a like state, these groupings are readily identifiable because of the similarity among the members in their emotional reactions, prestige standards, mobility and power drives, sentiments and tastes. These psychological subcultures often cluster around communications organs; indeed, as will be seen below, many of them have been brought into being by these media. All forms of the mass media are deeply interested in both the sociological and the psychological subcultures as actual or potential audiences.

Subcultures and their Imagery

Anyone who would influence the dynamic structure of American culture needs to identify and analyze the groupings in which people, knowingly or unknowingly, take up their abode. The standards of these groups shape values and attitudes, and influence actions. The images which are acceptable in these subcultures are the stuff upon which American culture feeds. They are the faces Americans turn toward the world. Whether or not they are the *real* faces is one of the crisis questions of American culture. This question makes a crisis demand upon the community of the Christian faith. It is incumbent upon Christians to study the cultural images, to determine which ones are true and which are false, then to go behind the images to find the real persons in the real culture and to speak to them the saving Word.

Among the most readily identifiable and seemingly most acceptable sociological subcultures in America are rural "folks" living in the open country and in small towns, the "sophisticated" middle- and upper-class city dwellers, and the suburbanites with their high standard of living. The image of the friendly, honest, thrifty, unsophisticated country dweller is the oldest and most persistent in American culture. It is now matched in importance by the imagery attached to city and suburban living. A majority of Americans seems to aspire to membership in these three subcultures; and the imagery connected with them illustrates a popular concept of "the American way of life."

Three of the most important subcultures are the religious faiths: Protestant, Roman Catholic, and Jewish. Within each of the faiths are numerous groupings, some commanding more prestige than others. Religious subcultures have a twofold range. They are easily measurable in sociological terms, but their communication is on a psychological level and they operate in all of the areas of the psychological subgroups.

There are other clear-cut sociological subcultures such as racial and nationality groups, laborers in industry, and agricultural migrants. They do not exert powerful social influence, nor do they fulfill the acceptable self-image of the American way.

Psychological subcultures may be based upon status, interests, prejudices, beliefs, or upon a combination of several such factors. The professions are status groups. Medicine, for example, has a social image of integrity, sacrifice, dependability, service, community leadership, and prestige. This image is broad enough to permit research scientists, Park Avenue specialists, small-town general practitioners, and the doctors of the city slums to identify with it and to feel that they "belong." Nonprofessional vocations also have imagery and standards that foster a sense of kinship among their practitioners.

Religious sects, patrons of the arts, sports-car enthusiasts, stamp collectors, white-citizens councils, political liberals and conservatives, college alumni, and bird watchers are among the uncounted typological cultural subgroups that have imagery, objectives, standards, identity signals, and even specialized vocabularies, recognizable by the initiates and vital to their self-interest and self-image.

The Mass Media and Cultural Imagery

The mass media have assiduously fostered psychological subgroups whose interests and loyalties may be turned to the advantage of the various media organs. The adolescent girls who feed on the celebrity magazines and worship the celebrity gods comprise one such group. *Playboy Magazine* has developed its peculiar social image for young men (not adolescents) of a "valued mode of existence" revolving around owning flashy cars, drinking good whisky, smoking cigarettes, dressing in a particular style, and patronizing certain forms of art and literature. The confession magazines have abstracted their own particular subculture of middle-aged women whom Ross Snyder characterizes as being frustrated in marriage and in the handling of life situations generally, viewing life as brutal and inevitably tragic, engaged in a hopeless round of futile experience, and confirming and strengthening their fears and frustrations by their magazine reading.[5]

The mass media are engaged in a grim and determined competition with each other to capture the various subcultures and deliver them to their advertisers for exploitation. They engage in continuous, widespread research to determine just how and why people clump together, physically and psychologically. They probe for the well-springs of individual motivation. The deep desires of each valued mode of existence are dissected and analyzed. Loves, hopes, ambitions, and fears are tabbed and categorized for usefulness in future manipulation for product consumption. Groups with mutual feelings, values, and purposes are herded out of the mass, their peculiar outlook is cultivated, their views flattered. Then the instrumentality that has succeeded in cutting out and coalescing this small substratum of the culture says triumphantly to the advertiser: "We can deliver this market." If enough of these subcultures can be corralled by a single organ of communication, the consequence may be a *Life* magazine or an Ed Sullivan show.

The mass media of communication have superimposed upon the traditional culture of mind, taste, and manners what Dallas W. Smythe terms a "cultural industry" which deliberately manufactures subcultures for delivery to advertisers. The products sold then help to uphold the valued mode of existence created by the cultural industry stylists, and the circle is closed. Advertising interests seem to be attempting to build an American culture from the roots up to foster product consumption. It is a daring scheme and a revolutionary one in a democratic society. It remains to be seen to what extent the materialistic satisfactions offered by this popularized mass culture may overcome the traditional American resistance to manipulation.

The Study Commission on the Role of Radio, Television and Films in Religion, sponsored by the National Council of the Churches of Christ in the U.S.A., reported "there is much in the

---

[5] Ross Snyder, unpublished lecture to the Religious Communications Workshop, Columbus, Ohio, 1959.

mass media to expand man's horizons, deepen his sympathies and increase his dignity"; but, the members concluded, "the potential of these media for good is balanced by a disturbing potential for the degradation of man, his manipulation and his education in false systems of value." The Commission found the image of man disseminated by the media to be "often poles apart from Christian understanding of man and his purpose." Not only is there "pathological preoccupation with sex and violence," there is "the assumption in both the content of the media and the policies that govern them that man's end is material advantage, power and pleasure, to be achieved through competing with, manipulating and exploiting his fellow man."[6]

The Commission recognized that the practices of the mass media are "symptomatic of a moral disease in our society," and noted that "the churches themselves share in the responsibility" for this disease. The churches may not limit themselves "to the expression of concern over specific mass media programs that are harmful," but must "take positive steps to help like-minded persons and groups to be wise stewards for the public good of these instruments which God has made available."[7]

It seems apparent that the individual sorely needs friends who hold other standards than those of the market place, persons who will speak through the mass media of communication to point out insistently the fact that there are higher cultures than the subcultures of consumption. It is not surprising that large numbers of persons need help in discovering this fact. Life forces many people along at too dizzy a pace for them ever to stop and contemplate what it is doing to them. A multiplicity of persons and movements in addition to the mass media are bombarding people in the hope of influencing their thinking and of capturing their allegiance. At the same time, the people are struggling with a range and depth of problems never before faced by mankind.

This is the first generation to find its fortunes and its fate and those of its children inextricably bound to the destinies of persons

[6] *The Church and the Mass Media*, Report of the Study Commission on the Role of Radio, Television and Films in Religion (New York: The National Council of the Churches of Christ in the U.S.A., 1960), p. 6.

[7] *Ibid.*

far distant in every direction. It is a frightening experience. Never before have people faced the frustration of being so largely dependent upon the decisions and actions of persons they do not know and who will never know them. Inevitably, fear is a dominant force in the dealing of man with man, nation with nation, race with race.

In spite of the impersonality of much of modern living, individual choice and individual initiative are not wholly submerged. Indeed, when it comes to choice, modern men face a bewildering array of possibilities. Our organs of communication employ countless eyes, ears, and minds in the continuous task of probing into all parts of life and its meaning and of reporting back. Virtually everyone in the world now has access to this reporting by the mass media. In America, it would be a rare person who could escape it. Reporting and interpreting are services of the mass media that help to expand intellectual horizons, but they are not an unmixed blessing. People are presented daily with a staggering array of facts and opinions, without having adequate resources to evaluate them. The knowledge and experience they are asked to digest are so complex that they are beyond the capacity of most of us. People wonder whether they can stomach such a mutiplicity of ideas and images; or if they do, whether they can retain their personal dignity in the process. Knowing so much more than previous generations have known, men today are in despair about what to do.

Finding Dependable Meanings

If the individual is to maintain the dignity in which God has clothed him, if he is to hold his own against the blandishments of the market place, he needs a source of dependable meanings and interpretations upon which he may base his choices. He needs contact with people who can be trusted and who have the stability, the knowledge, and the experience to judge the ongoing scene and evaluate it in terms he can comprehend. He needs access to more than one opinion or one interpreter. He needs to understand how ideas are tested and worked out, and to participate in examining them; so, ultimately, he will be his own interpreter.

The role of friendly and dependable interpreter to common humanity is not alien to the Judaeo-Christian tradition. Prophetic religion sees in the tangled events of history and the frustrations of the daily round the sickness and evil of spirit that bring disaster; but beyond the abyss it sees the city which has foundations whose builder and maker is God. It has this great vision to match against the imagery of the market place.

A primary aim of religious broadcasting should be to relate this vision of prophetic religion to the realities of people living in community—*your* people in *your* community. The gospel itself is concrete, pure, absolute. But it never has been and never can be preached in a vacuum. Jesus spoke to Jews in terms that Jews could understand. Paul on Mars Hill, facing an alien Gentile culture, seized upon the thoughts and ideas of Greeks to reveal God's will and presence. So, today, the thrust of the gospel cannot be divorced from the culture in which the gospel is being communicated. The Christian faith is a live, vital thing only as it functions in relation to persons in culture and, paradoxically, only as it is also in tension with the objectives of the culture.

The Christian broadcaster, therefore, needs to be concerned with both the individual and society. He must take sides on the moral and social questions of the day. He must constantly jog the consciences of people, calling attention to spiritual issues and helping them to identify the built-in gods of the culture that are interposed between them and the living God. He must provide information and insight; he must show how a Christian sees the world and what goes on within it, what is the Christian judgment of the culture. Christian communication should offer people an alternative choice to the values of synthetic mass culture. The choice should be theirs to make, and this fact should be made plain to them; so there will be no mistaking by either audience or communicator of the service motive for religious broadcasting.

Persuasion versus Manipulation

If religion on television is to undertake an interpretive role, great sophistication in our handling of the medium will be needed. We are working in an environment where manipulation of people is practiced as a matter of course and as a matter of policy in behalf of the purposes of the sponsor. Some of the most successful television techniques are those designed for the calculated motivation of audiences for purposes that all too seldom are made explicit to them. Without subscribing to the mass communication psychology of manipulation, religious groups may find themselves practicing it unwittingly, compromising their fundamental principles when they believe they are only adapting professional communication techniques to the service of the gospel. One example of a relatively harmless practice will suffice as illustration. This is the use of a "hook" at the opening of a program, a dramatic incident or provocative statement that will catch audience attention and will at the same time disguise the sponsorship of the program until interest has been aroused by its content.

Let us hasten to admit that all blame does not lie with the television industry. Church people, on and off television, are not by reason of their affiliation necessarily free of the temptation to exploit people for reasons remote from the service of the gospel. Indeed, it is possible for churchmen, in their concern for souls, to believe that people ought to be manipulated for their own best interests. Even if one rejects this viewpoint, he will find, as we explain in detail in Chapter 2, that he will have to walk an extremely narrow path if he is determined to be both faithful to God and faithful to the role of friendly interpreter to men.

Since religious broadcasting is concerned with meanings, values, beliefs, and attitudes, it is necessary that the message be persuasive in order to be effective. And since persuasion—in the form of "the sell"—is the basic ingredient in the manipulative practices of commercial broadcasting, there needs to be a clear understanding of how this technique can be used with integrity to achieve aims that will advantage the audience members.

Aristotle, in explaining the motivation for human behavior, said: "Thus all the acts of men are necessarily done from seven causes: chance, nature, compulsion, habit, *reason*, passion, desire."[8] Modern psychology has added little to his insight. But there is a marked tendency, especially in motivational-research circles, to emphasize the

---

[8] Lane Cooper (trans.), Aristotle's *The Rhetoric* (New York: D. Appleton and Co., 1932), p. 57. Emphasis added.

power of emotional factors in shaping behavior and to downgrade the role of reason almost to the vanishing point.

It is all too apparent that men can be induced to act solely by means of appeal to the emotions. (How could mankind be prevailed upon, *reasonably*, to permit the channeling of so much of the world's industrial productivity into armaments?) Television is always playing on the emotions to prompt action. At the end of an absorbing drama, the glittering star opens the door of the glittering car that is being advertised. The camera brings her into intimate close-up; she smiles, speaks: "My friends and I all drive Dreamboats. We get *twice* as much satisfaction and comfort from the Dreamboat ride." On paper, this kind of motivational appeal looks ridiculous. On television, it sells automobiles.

This technique is not persuasion in the proper sense. It is manipulation.

Persuasion has an intellectual base. It involves a combination and an interplay of logical and psychological forces. Persuasion may be begun by the touching-off of some psychological trigger in the audience member, and it may reach its climax by the turning loose of some powerful psychological drive that will cause the person to think or to do what the communicator is suggesting. A certain amount of emotional involvement is prerequisite to the changing of belief or to the taking of action. But if the purpose of the communication is to engage audience members in a long-term process of responsible decision making, rather than to elicit a single, and usually simple, overt act (Go see our car!), there needs to be a rational exposition of why beliefs should change or actions take place. Most people will act once impulsively; some will regularly act impulsively on unimportant matters; few will base their fundamental modes of living on impulse motivation.

One danger to watch for in using persuasion is the error of mistaking your subjective convictions for persuasive arguments. We are all prone to select materials and arguments that are significant to us, assuming that what will move us will also move the audience. This is not necessarily so. It is important to think objectively, adapting one's approach to the audience to the mental attitudes prevalent there. The experience and mood of the audience will determine what material and techniques—logical and emotional—will best serve that particular group.

The nature of television, especially the shortness of programs and the sporadic contact with audiences, may make persuasion difficult. This condition is especially trying because of the need to present the whole gospel if the gospel is to be understood. Since it is obviously impossible to deal with the whole gospel in a single television program, the best solution is to employ "economy of the gospel," using only that portion that is relevant to a particular audience and subject to achieve a clearly defined purpose, and making sure that the meaning of the gospel segment is made clear.

Segmentation of the gospel in this fashion makes the scriptural message peculiarly vulnerable to the treatment it receives from the communicator. No one would expect a religious broadcaster deliberately to distort the gospel message, but it should be remembered that the latent or absent content of a communication is as important as the manifest content. What is implicit in a television program may be as loaded with value interpretations as is the explicit message. Economy of the gospel should be used, therefore, only as a functional element in a well-thought-out and carefully articulated strategy of broadcasting that will have as its purpose the presentation of the whole gospel, even though circumstances demand it be treated in serial form.

CHAPTER 2   Mass Communication and the Christian Faith

The role of the mass media of communication in American culture, while open to all sorts of argument and speculation, is far less ambiguous than is the role that these instrumentalities play in the efforts of the Christian Church to penetrate and influence the culture. Religious organizations make extensive use of television, radio, movies, and the mass circulation press. Yet the churches never have been able to determine the role to be assigned to these media in the implementation of policy. Exactly what functions do the churches expect television, radio, motion pictures, and the press to perform? This question goes largely unanswered, both nationally and locally. Indeed, it is a question that Protestant policy makers, at least, seem never to have taken seriously.

The Study Commission of the National Council of the Churches of Christ in the U.S.A. ably pinpointed the materialistic tone and manipulative practices of the mass media and the involvement of the churches in the "moral disease" they reflect; and in its report, it was able to suggest positive, attainable means to correct such abuses. Yet, when the Commission turned to the churches' use of the communications organs, its best concluding advice to its constituents was that *"the churches cooperating in the National Council must take a new look at the structure and channels they have set up to conduct their ministries in the mass media both within and between the denominations. . . .* The denominations and the National Council itself are urged to re-examine their present provisions for work in the mass media toward the end that these instrumentalities will become agents of the total mission of the church in the modern world. An ecumenical strategy for the media demands the united involvement of the best minds and talents in the whole life of the church and a primary commitment on the part of the denominations to a vigorous Protestant witness."[1]

CURRENT PROTESTANT STRATEGY

For a time it looked as if television were going to afford the opportunity to develop an ecumenical strategy that might result in "a vigorous Protestant witness." Here was something new that cried aloud for new and creative forms of Protestant co-operation. There were no existing vested institutional interests to stumble over. There were no program forms or indiviual broadcasters that commanded loyal and substantial audiences, such as existed in religious radio. The appeal of the new medium had been demonstrated dramatically in the incredibly short time it took television to cover the nation and revolutionize family and individual habits for the use of leisure time. Church people, along with everyone else, recognized that something important was happening, and that they should have a part in it. They began to experiment cautiously with co-operative programming.

There has always been general agreement among the representatives of most of the major Protestant denominations that their communions should co-operate in television broadcasting. The arguments advanced in favor of co-operation are: (1) time for religious broadcasting on television is at a premium because of the scarcity of outlets and the insistent demands of commercial interests that they be served to the exclusion of all else; (2) television programs are so expensive, even when time is provided free, that few, if any, denominations can, in the long run, afford to go it alone; (3) if religious television is to attract a substantial number of viewers and serve their interests, it must be divorced from narrow institutional concerns.

In spite of the undeniable weight of these arguments and the good will that does exist among denominations interested in television, institutional interests and concern over control of the large sums

---

[1] *The Church and the Mass Media*, report of the Study Commission on the Role of Radio, Television and Films in Religion (New York: The National Council of the Churches of Christ in the U.S.A., 1960), p. 14 f.

necessary for television programming have led to the development of religious television in such a way as to promote denominational loyalty and support on the part of constituents. The extent of co-operation in Protestantism is closely akin to that of men fishing in a common pool with lines firmly attached to denominational poles who agree to stay far enough apart so the lines will not get tangled. The fishermen keep up a pleasant conversation with each other and even exchange samples of their bait. They also maintain a mutually agreeable fiction that any fish that wanders into the particular section of the pool staked out by any one of them is somehow uniquely and permanently metamorphosed, so his only rightful home is in that denominational basket.

There is, of course, legitimacy in the concern of denominations to be identified on television. Christian commitment normally involves relationship to the Christian Church through a local church which is part of a denomination. Were denominational identities to be eliminated and all denominational loyalties wiped out, it is doubtful that organized Protestantism could continue to fulfill its mission. Therefore, denominational emphasis in television is not in itself pernicious. But denominational divisiveness has important damaging influences on programming.

First, it encourages program planning by separate communions, with their individual interests predominating over the good of Protestantism as a whole.

Second, programs are developed not on the basis of their ability to reach a generalized audience, and especially the unreached, but for their salability to a denomination.

Third, broadcast policy is shaped by those groups that can put up the necessary money, which are not necessarily the ones that can develop the most sound and creative ideas.

Fourth, and most important, subordinate sectarian interests are given precedence over the supreme obligation of the church to communicate the gospel to those outside the community of faith.

Sectarian advertising is not only irrelevant to the discharge of this latter obligation; it is massively hostile to it. Research findings show that there are a great many people with whom the Protestant churches can never hope to communicate as long as they are limited to their conventional methods of preaching and teaching which require presence at services and meetings. Yet, strangely, and without the churches really deserving it, these people are present from time to time in the religious television audience. Since, for whatever cause, they have rejected the institutional methods and label of the church, the waving of a denominational banner is one of the things least likely to arouse the interest of such people and to give point and persuasiveness to the Christian message.

Even so, denominational programming might be justified if there were great theological issues dividing the communions or if there were important cleavages over things such as social action. Then it might be necessary and right to expound opposing views under sectarian auspices, so people might make choices in belief and allegiance. Obviously, such a situation does not exist. The vital issues and the cleavages are present, but they transcend denominational lines. They may be churning up internal ferment, but outwardly the denominations and the local churches tend more and more to resemble each other in both their actions and their institutional objectives.

The denominations that distribute television programs nationally appear to recognize this fact. At any event, they refrain from stirring up either intellectual or political conflict along denominational lines. They also minimize distinctive denominational bias in their programs in the belief that by so doing they may garner a maximum audience (an interesting admission), and also because they realize that stations and networks are wary of programs that are narrowly sectarian. Only a few independent, commercial religious programs are frankly sectarian in the views they express.

Interdenominational programs also tend to lack sharpness, clarity, and purpose, probably because they are planned by committees where compromise is essential to consensus.

The effect of this almost universal policy of watering down the doctrinal content of programs has been unfortunate. It has negated the possibility of presenting a unified Protestant theological position vis-à-vis such philosophies as Roman Catholicism, secularism, and Communism. Combined with the anti-intellectual spirit that motivates so much of Protestantism, it has virtually eliminated from programming serious exposition, discussion, criticism, and evaluation of current theological positions.

In criticizing the dominant factors that determine Protestant television strategy, we do not mean to impute charlatanry to the persons who make television policy. Nor should denominations be cast solely in the role of villain and a campaign be started to deprive them of a major voice in policy making. There is no assurance that if all religious television were turned over to councils of churches there would be a perceptible improvement in the thrust and power of the resultant programs. What is needed is a radical change in our point of view about the function of television in relation to religion, for television has fallen victim to two peculiarly American and Protestant beliefs that inevitably make it the handmaiden of institutional objectives.

The first is the belief in salvation by joining. One achieves "togetherness" and fulfillment, one is told, by being identified with some attractive and powerful group than can handle life with a flourish. One then bends one's energies to the task of magnifying the importance of the group, because only if the group is powerful can the individual attain a sense of power. Today, the church often fulfills the function of the institution in which power may be discovered. When this is so, we are confronted with the ecclesiastical equivalent of "what's good for General Motors is good for the country." It is assumed that whatever benefits a denomination or even an individual church automatically advances the Kingdom of God.

The second belief is in salvation by gadget. It greets each new technique that comes along—the every-member canvass, religious movies for Sunday school teaching, the family camp, the lay retreat, lay evangelism, the preaching mission, or what have you—as the new, divinely ordered means of grace, and loads upon it expectations so unrealistic that no one can determine its real worth.

Television has suffered from this predilection for gadgetry. It has been promoted enthusiastically by means of promises that it will perform in behalf of organizational self-interest. We are told it will prick the conscience of the lagging churchgoer. It will return religion to the American home. It will raise money. It will sell "religion in

American life" as slickly as it sells cigarettes. It will make pastoral calls on shut-ins. It will encourage a general attitude of acceptance of religion on the part of the public (i.e., it will perform as a public relations medium for the churches).

Two things are lost sight of in this welter of institutional promotionalism. One is that religious television has never been forthrightly tested against any of these promises or against any other designated aims, nor have the sponsoring churches made their commitments to television contingent upon performance in relation to specific objectives. The second is that the employment of television for the purpose for which the church presumably exists—the communication of the Christian faith to people to whom it comes as something entirely new and fresh—is accidental, sporadic, and diffuse. This central evangelistic and missionary purpose of the church is dissipated by being mixed with all sorts of other objectives. In fact, missions and evangelism generally come far down on the list of interests which the churches attempt to serve through television.

Religious broadcasting, in the negative aspects described here, illustrates what European theologians are fond of calling the "activism" of the American churches. They point to the emphasis on program for its own sake, with a rather myopic faith that what is done, because it is done under church auspices, will contribute toward the "building of the Kingdom." Yet a vigorously active program is constructive, if it is conducted for a purpose that is central to the meaning of the Christian faith. More than any other ingredient, it is this clear *purpose* that is lacking in our broadcasting. Wisdom in church leadership commensurate with the wisdom of the gospel would lead the Protestant churches to develop a common strategy worthy of their common faith, a strategy that would be adequate to confront any level of complexity our culture can produce.

How to Develop a New Strategy

The first step toward effective employment of the mass media in the service of the gospel is to base their use upon a recognizable and inclusive theory about society, community, and personality in our time. Such a theory should deal with religious objectives as they relate to all major social institutions, all functional social groupings, all social levels of individuals. Out of the theory may be developed aims that will link the media directly with the priorities of church concern, making them the servants of policy rather than merely adjuncts to existing programs of church organizations.

Both theory and aims need to be flexible. In a mobile, striving society such as ours with its complex organizational structure and shifting patterns of human dynamics, it would be surprising if top priorities for religion did not differ in degree, if not in kind, from time to time and from community to community. Such shifts in emphasis require that communications policy be kept under continuous review and evaluation. It is essential, however, that at every moment we know clearly what we are about and why we are about it, for only out of such clarity can we expect to develop an effective message (the program content).

The message can never be a simple thing, easily arrived at. It must take into account the personality complexities of the audience it is intended for. Each time it is uttered it must be consciously shaped and directed toward some social group in the population in terms of the values, needs, and states of readiness of the members of the group. In its preparation, there needs to be virtually as much time devoted to the identification of the persons and groups to whom religion intends to speak as there is to the message itself.

This program strategy could not be carried out by a single program type or by a single authority figure representing a community or a denomination or the Church at large. It needs what John W. Bachman calls "a planned diversity of programs, faithfully serving different functions in different ways. The matter of format appears to be less significant than factors such as artistic quality, theological integrity, contagious persuasiveness of personal conviction and local follow-up."[2] What is needed in each community is a congeries of programs with different formats, differing themes and styles, and a variety of performers. Each series should be aimed at a distinctive segment of the total community audience, but all programs should be conceived in relation to each other and to an over-all plan.

[2] John W. Bachman, *The Church in the World of Radio-Television* (New York: Association Press, 1960), p. 146.

It seems apparent that the strategy suggested here cannot be carried out in isolation from either the stresses of our anxiety-driven, class-conditioned society or the concrete actions and pronouncements of the churches. This strategy must also involve the policy makers of the churches, teaming them with persons who understand the potency and potential of television. Between them they need to exercise flexibility and ingenuity that will master the complexity of needs and circumstances that exist in the potential audience.

It is not enough, however, to have a theory, an aim, and a message. They must be cast in a form that can be apperceived by the desired audience. Here is where the creative artist has a part in the strategy.

He should be included as colleague, not employed as a mere technician. "It is a mistake," says Bachman, "to build a program by authorizing a committee to formulate the religious message and then hiring a clever craftsman to deliver the capsule with which to deceive an audience into swallowing the distasteful medicine. The artistic form taken by a program is an integral part of its communicative nature."[3] An important element in a strategy of effective religious broadcasting is to leave the artist free to accomplish the aims by means that satisfy his artistic integrity. Writers and other artists of stature are reluctant to have a part in religious programs when such freedom is not granted.

There is little risk entailed in following such procedure. Responsible artists will feel an obligation to make sure that what they say and do is faithful to the character of the Christian message and to the aims of the organizations they are representing. They will work assiduously to attract viewers, knowing that an audience is a prerequisite to any expected accomplishment, but they will not knowingly distort the message or water down its serious character just to hold viewers before the screen. If they fail in achieving the ends sought more often than they succeed, they should not, therefore, be eyed with suspicion and smothered with criticism. Rather, they should be urged to try again. They should always be judged with charity in the light of the complexity of the medium and the weighty character of the message. How often do ministers fail to communicate "the mystery hidden for ages and generations but now made manifest . . . ?"

[3] *Ibid.*, p. 161.

Toward a New Theory for Religious Broadcasting

It is fondly to be hoped that the churches will take seriously the recommendation of the Study Commission of the National Council of Churches that they "take a new look" at their mass-communications ministries. Once this happens, however, we may hardly expect that the basic theory upon which to base a new broadcasting strategy —especially a strategy acceptable to a majority—will spring full-blown from a single mind, or even that such theory can be developed quickly. It can be expected to grow out of a long process of discussion and of trial and error. It will have to be broad in scope to permit inclusion of distinctive social views and theological conceptions. The focusing of many able minds upon the task of hammering out concrete philosophy and aims for religious broadcasting should contribute mightly to a positive result, for, as R. H. Edwin Espy told leaders of the United Church of Christ, "The expression of the church's unity is not posited on the suppression of the church's diversity. On the contrary the very concept of the wholeness of the Gospel is based on the premise that the Gospel is richer than any single manifestation of it, and that every honest manifestation is to be honored as a part of the whole."[4]

One way to start on a theory for broadcasting would be to attempt to measure the values cherished in American life against the ethical norms of the Judaeo-Christian tradition. A workable process for program planning can be established if one applies the principles and standards of the Judaeo-Christian tradition to concrete problems of practical and personal decisions, seeking to develop programs that will reinforce constructive character patterns, both social and personal, and unmask and criticize destructive forces.[5] In the Communications Research Project of the National Council of Churches, criteria were worked out for judging decision-making and value

[4] R. H. Edwin Espy, unpublished address before the Midwinter Meeting of the Congregational Christian Churches, 1959.

[5] This is not a speculative suggestion. This method of evaluation was used in planning the 1961 series of *Frontiers of Faith* on the subject of decision making. Processes of decision making, such as those of the Negro parents in Little Rock who sent their children to Central High School, were probed and judged in the light of Christian ethics.

systems in American life on the basis of Judaeo-Christian ethics. These criteria bear repeating here.

1. In applying the Judaeo-Christian principles and standards to problems [of decision making and values] the freedom of the individual is to be recognized and the sanctity of the individual personality is to be respected.

2. The Judaeo-Christian belief and faith is that the Will of God is that which is ultimately authoritative. Each person has freedom of choice, but he lives under the responsibility of making choices and acting in accordance with the Will of God.

3. As a corollary, the Judaeo-Christian ethic forces upon the conscience of the individual the necessity of deciding with whom, or with what group he will take a stand, and what image of the desirable person and the desirable society he will defend and uphold. This ethic also requires that decisions be taken in council; that the religious man decides and acts under a mandate of responsibility to a community with standards he is committed to uphold.[6]

Out of such criteria can be developed aims and individual programs that deal with vital issues that are the concern of both the church and the television audience.

Aims and the Message

The objectives of a communication and the message itself are inextricably bound together and may be expected to interact. In the first instance, the aims determine the message, but the latter through both its form and effects may influence the objectives in a number of ways, sometimes even taking their place. We shall, therefore, discuss aims and message as parts of a single communications process, using the criteria from the Communications Research Project as a rough guide line. We shall be especially concerned with the relationship between freedom and responsibility and the necessity for each person to make choices that will determine future conduct. We will attempt here to grapple with the problem of religious television at the theological level, on the supposition that if we do not comprehend *what* we are communicating when we are dealing with

[6] Everett C. Parker, David W. Barry, Dallas W. Smythe, *The Television-Radio Audience and Religion* (New York: Harper & Brothers, 1955), p. xvi.

the Christian faith, the *effort* to devise methods of communication is fruitless.

Religious broadcasting, even in the forms it now takes and the ends it is now seeking, is commited to much more formidable and intricate tasks than are other forms of programming. The commercial advertiser has only one simple aim: to sell. The educator has a more complex task, since he must instruct; but he need not be concerned with the use that is made of what is learned. Even the news commentator, who deals with a great variety of subject matter, may limit himself to the events of a short span of hours; and he, too, need have no concern over what influence his message has.

Christians do not have just news to publish, nor a product to extol, nor facts to expound, nor decisions to announce. The communication of the Christian faith involves all of these things, but it is bigger than their sum. It is the transmission of a way of life within which facts can be assimilated and evaluated and decisions made. It is literally the sharing of a Life and of a way of living based upon that Life. And because the Christian faith is so closely identified with a Person and His course of action, it is best transmitted by persons interacting with other persons. Person-to-person encounter and person-to-person sharing are essential to the communication of the faith.

The primary aim of all Christian communication should be to involve persons in a process that not only will give them the basis for faith but also will require of them the ultimate test of faith— overt action. Through personal interaction with others in a Christian setting, people gain not only knowledge but confidence in themselves and their destinies that may lead to the overcoming of fear, the main barrier to living according to the faith.

From beginning to end, the Bible attests to courageous action as a hallmark of the Judaeo-Christian concept of man's relationship to God. Jesus marked the chasm that fear creates between God and man when he castigated the disciples with the stinging criticism: "Why are you afraid? Have you no faith?"

In both Judaism and Christianity, it has been a self-evident truth that *action* is the test of faith. The lawyer, seeking to test Jesus, asked: "Teacher, what shall I *do* to inherit eternal life?" not "What shall I think?" or "What shall I believe?" Jesus queried him: "What is written in the law?" and he answered: "You shall *love* the Lord your God. . . ." Jesus then said: ". . . *do* this, and you will live."[7]

Both men used only action verbs. They were in agreement on this great truth that is fundamental to our communication: The faith is not just an internal thing. Its presence is revealed by action.

Thus, the first aim of religious communication and the first test of its effectiveness is embodied in this question: Does action take place? Make this question the central issue in your broadcasting and you will quickly come to the realization that the core responsibility of religion in its public communication is evangelism.

Television as a Force in Evangelism. Hendrik Kraemer points out a further truism, that "the core of all true evangelism is communication."[8] Granting this, it behooves us to determine accurately just what part television can play in the evangelistic thrust into contemporary culture. So far, we know little about it.

The fact is that all of us in religious broadcasting have been throwing our bait blindly into the waters and blandly assuring each other that something must be happening down there where the fish live. We have very little data from which to derive a judgment one way or the other, even on the most fundamental question of all: Can television actually be an effective instrument of evangelism? It may well be that material presented on television, because of the form in which it is cast and the circumstances under which it is absorbed by the viewer, can be only a preparation for the direct communication of the gospel. Perhaps this preparation must take the form of asking questions and presenting problems, social and personal, that demand the *answer* of the gospel. If the story of man's life can be told in such a way that its emptiness without the gospel can be portrayed vividly and poignantly, then viewers may be drawn to seek the gospel in the fellowship of the church. If television can do this much, it can qualify as a useful handmaiden of the evangel.

The Christian broadcaster who is seriously concerned with evangelism is faced at the very outset by a dilemma posed by the limitations of his medium. Television programs are short, almost never achieving

[7] Emphasis added. All biblical quotations are from the *Revised Standard Version* unless otherwise noted.

[8] Hendrik Kraemer, *The Communication of the Christian Faith* (Philadelphia: The Westminster Press, 1956), p. 11.

even the length of a church service. They are presented infrequently —typically once a week—and they are subject to abrupt schedule changes at the whim of network or station management. The audiences do not view consistently. Even the most faithful viewers miss favorite programs now and then. The average auditor is typically an in-and-outer. If he sees one out of three broadcasts, he is doing well. Thus, even if the programs are planned systematically with each series forming a unity, the apprehension on the part of the viewer will be selective and episodic. We have already pointed out (Chapter 1) how the character of the medium requires the use of "economy of the gospel" to achieve the end sought at a particular time with a particular audience. Inevitably, there will be a distortion of meaning, for the Christian faith is a totality that is ultimately indivisible. Every part of it—its theology, its apprehension of the meaning of faith, its ethic, its conception and practice of worship—is dependent on every other part. To attempt to expound any part of the faith in isolation from the whole is to try what is finally an impossible task. We cannot explain, for example, Christian ethics, without imparting the whole view to which the Christian ethic organically belongs. We may put this "whole view" in very simple form, but we cannot avoid its wholeness. At its most simple, it probably cannot be encompassed in a single television program any more than it can be compressed into a single sermon; but the preacher has the advantage over the broadcaster in that he can expect his auditors to return again and again for further amplification of his message.

The problem of communication is complicated further by the fact that in the Christian faith the creative, whole-making act is not logical synthesis or discovery, but revelation. Christian understanding comes ultimately not by the informing or the sharpening of the mind but by the renewing of the mind. But how does the Christian spokesman and interpreter create this new mind in persons who, however good church members they may be, are strangers to the gospel? How can he communicate what is involved in this renewal when the very terms of the communication he must use belong to a totality which cannot be understood until the renewal has taken place?

Søren Kierkegaard in his conception of men's relation to Christ

has insights that bear directly upon evangelistic concerns in mass communication, insights that give us clues about the manner in which our calling demands that we speak to modern man in the name of Christ. It is well known, Kierkegaard says, "that Christ constantly uses the expression 'follower'; He never says anything about wanting admirers, admiring worshippers, adherents; and when He uses the expression 'disciples', He always so explains it that we can perceive that followers are meant, that they are not adherents of a doctrine but followers of a life. . . ." Kierkegaard makes a sharp distinction between what might have been required of men if Christ existed "only as on high," as against what is required because He also "existed in lowliness." In the first instance, anything other than worshipful admiration would have been presumptuous. But Christ suffered humiliation. That is decisive. In the face of Christ's lowliness, mere admiration is naked arrogance. Thus it is plain that "His whole life on earth . . . was calculated only to procure 'followers', and calculated to make 'admirers' impossible." The standard of action against which to measure the meaning of Christian communication is clear: "What corresponds to humiliation is a follower."[9]

Here is a measurable aim for evangelism via television. It is difficult to achieve; it is fraught with danger that is inherent not only in mass methods of communication but in the whole evangelistic and missionary thrust of modern Christianity. Kierkegaard pointedly warns us where this danger lies:

'But all the same, was He not an object of admiration?' Yes, undoubtedly; for it is impossible at once and, at the very instant of beginning, to avert the danger called admiration, *which is requisite in one sense in order to get people enlisted.* But when 'the truth', true to itself in being the truth, little by little, more and more definitely, unfolds itself as the truth, the moment comes when no admirer can hold out with it, a moment when it shakes admirers from it as the storm shakes the worm-eaten fruit from the tree. And it is Christ's life precisely which has made it evident, terribly evident, what a dreadful falsehood it is to admire the truth instead of following it. . . .[10]

[9] Walter Lowrie (trans.), Søren Kierkegaard, *Training in Christianity* (Princeton: Princeton University Press, 1947), pp. 231-232.
[10] *Ibid.*, pp. 238-239. Emphasis added.

How pointed this warning is for our time and condition! Is any institution more admired than religion in American society today? Nothing else can match the tremendous outpouring of enthusiasm for religion. People are bombarded with slogans, billboard posters, newspaper and magazine advertisements, radio and television spot announcements urging them to go to church and synagogue—and they go. Will Herberg points out "the enhanced status of religious leaders." No other group—government, Congressional, educational, business or labor—can match ministers in public trust, prestige, and pulling power.[11] Popular ministers are widely read and quoted. Their books make the best-seller lists. They garner audiences on radio and television. The aisles are crowded with "decision makers" at the evangelistic rallies. Church membership rolls go up and up. New churches are built to accommodate new congregations. Benevolence budgets fatten. It is almost unthinkable that a person or family should not claim identity with some religious community, Protestant, Roman Catholic, or Jewish.

Is this the faith? Or is it fraud? It seems obvious that we should not lightly dismiss the current revival in religion as mere "shallow emotionalism," an effort to escape the tragic realities of our generation. Herberg rightly argues that "the people who join the churches, take part in church activities, send their children to church schools, and gladly identify themselves in religious terms are not fools or hypocrites. They are honest, intelligent people who take their religion quite seriously." But, he goes on, religion in America today "has lost much of its authentic Christian (or Jewish) content." Even when people "are thinking, feeling, or acting religiously" they are doing so in secularist terms, unconsciously engaging in a religious revival that has little relation to the faiths they profess. "It is this secularism of a religious people, this religiousness in a secularist framework, that constitutes the problem posed by the contemporary religious situation in America."[12]

We cannot know what will be the resolution of this problem

---

[11] Will Herberg, *Protestant-Catholic-Jew* (Garden City, N.Y., Doubleday & Company, Inc., 1960), p. 51.

[12] *Ibid.*, p. 3.

until a time of testing comes. How will each person act, not when he is happily and safely immersed in the frenetic popular movement, but when he is called upon to venture his all, his life, in witness to Christ?

Such a call may not come to America in this generation. Or, if it comes, it may not even be recognized. "The admirer may die in the illusion that the relationship he assumed was the true one"[13] in this time when there is no danger in taking the name of Christian, when no one need suffer humiliation for the sake of Christ. Today the humiliation is visited upon those who shun the name. They have no self-identification, no social location if they refuse to be identified as part of the religious community.

Nevertheless, the requirement that they be followers, not admirers, is not rescinded; and what is required of followers is set down and may be communicated:

Do not be conformed to this world but be transformed by the renewal of your mind, that you may prove what is the will of God, what is good and acceptable and perfect. . . . Let love be genuine; hate what is evil, hold fast to what is good; love one another with brotherly affection . . . serve the Lord. Rejoice . . . be patient . . . constant in prayer. Contribute to the needs of the saints, practice hospitality. Bless those who persecute you; . . . Live in harmony with one another; . . . Repay no one evil for evil . . . live peaceably . . . never avenge yourselves . . . if your enemy is hungry feed him; . . . Do not be overcome by evil, but overcome evil with good. (Romans 12, *passim*)

A major task of Christian communication is to weed out the admirers from the followers for the good of the souls of the people and for the good of the church which transmits the faith they are now so eager to embrace. This is a task that can be accomplished if communication is carried on not for the sake of sectarian tactics but for the sake of the faith. It is necessary to eschew the glorification of the personal and social advantages and satisfactions to be derived from church affiliation (from being admirers) and to hold up before the people the stark absolutes of the Christian gospel, demanding a commitment that will draw followers into the working, sacrificing fellowship in Christ. They must understand that, even when there

[13] Kierkegaard, *op. cit.*, p. 239.

is no danger to the person, to the inner self, the follower is still required to make a decision that all others can avoid. There is an
absolute demand that exacts an absolute answer. Both the demand
and the resultant action will be a foolishness in the eyes of the
world. The admirer will not endure the resultant public humiliation.
He will quickly fall away in the face of the requirements of the
gospel, however avid he may have been in his support of the popular
religious views and practices.

This is not to say that Christian communication should not deal
with people in culture. It needs to be thoroughly human in its
orientation, to be in touch with the modern world and its problems,
to recognize and speak to what is going on in the interior world of
persons. It will do this best from a biblical base, using the biblical
understanding of man to inquire into the critical questions being
asked by modern man and to formulate fundamental answers. We
cannot expect the Bible to provide us with ready-made answers to
the dilemmas of modern man. "The strange new world within the
Bible" of which Karl Barth speaks is not only strange and new, it is
repellent in its strangeness and novelty. It is a world in which men
discover that they cannot think up for themselves the final and
decisive truths. The finely wrought systems of human logic have no
validity there; for the Bible deals violently, one after another, with
every cherished presupposition by which modern man lives. The
biblical view of man is most repellent to our age in this rejection
of man's pretensions to work out his own destiny. The Bible—
and, as a consequence, the Christian faith—denies the ability of
men to find the final answer to a sequence of progressively more
intelligent questions which they have been learning to ask about their
role in existence and their faith.

It is incumbent upon the evangelist that he show modern men
that it is their answers that are rejected, never their questions; that
faith rejects their desires, never their needs; that only in the faith
as revealed in the Bible can they hope to find the orientation and
the foundation from which to seek God's intention and purpose for
men today.

The Communication Dilemma. This issue of the relationship of
man's ambitions to God's will poses a critical dilemma for Christian

communication. It is the central issue with which the evangelist must continually grapple. On the one side the evangelist knows that nothing less than the whole gospel, in all its drastic newness and revolutionary power, is sufficient for dealing with our human predicament. Only the whole gospel is really *gospel*. On the other side, he knows that the full gospel comes to men as a scandal and an offense. One cannot present the gospel on television, or anywhere else, without giving this offense; yet television is the last place where people may be expected to turn to be scandalized and offended, conditioned as they are by the commercial sponsors to look to this medium to soothe and amuse them, to support and approve their beliefs, prejudices, and behavior.

While the gospel is not ultimately alien to man and his needs, it is alien to the *old* man, the man who is the essential target of our communication. It is alien until this man has been driven to face the questions: Who am I? Where did I come from? What am I here for? The moment a man poses such questions to himself the agony involved in answering them becomes paramount, and the gospel is no longer alien. Its eternal dimensions begin to be apparent.

One of the Amsterdam papers aptly summarizes the acute dilemma of the Christian who assays the use of television for evangelism:

It is obvious that the task of evangelism has its perils. The Church, by loyal faithfulness to what it has received, may make its message meaningless. [On the other hand,] by excessive concern for the contemporary relevance of its utterance, it may be betrayed into unfaithfulness to the Gospel of God's judgment and God's mercy. . . . The problem of evangelism is just the perpetual rediscovery of the narrow way on which alone the Church can be true to its two-fold vocation of faithfulness to God and service to His creatures.[14]

It may be seen from the foregoing that the communication of the Christian faith is a far more subtle and complicated task than most religious broadcasters have, so far, been willing to undertake. There is a serious question whether this task can ever be wholly accomplished through such an instrumentality as television. At best,

[14] *Man's Disorder and God's Design*, Vol. II (New York: Harper & Brothers, 1948), p. 201.

television is undemocratic, operating as it does with one communicator and multiple auditors who have no opportunity to talk back.

This situation poses an ethical problem for religion. It is all too easy to fall in with the accepted practices of the broadcasting industry: Go after a big audience. Entertain them. Don't get them upset. Don't say *anything* that will offend *anybody.*

Granted that we would like to have large audiences for religious programs. We ought to try to attract them. An audience is a prerequisite to any kind of communication. Granted there is advantage in having programs that are wise, witty, intriguing, flawlessly produced—in short, entertaining. Beyond this, religion dare not subscribe to the "something for everybody—no offense" theory. Religious broadcasting is subject to the inflexible qualification that what is communicated shall bear a recognizable relationship to the meaning of the Christian faith and the purposes of the Christian church, and shall be ultimately vital to man and his needs. 1149047

Let us face frankly the fact that our actual communication through television more often than not falls far short of this stern demand. Programs seek to create amorphous "good will," to give viewers vague personal reassurance. The test of their effectiveness is not: Have viewers been shocked into facing the core problems of their existence? Rather, it is: Are they *interested?* (There is something to be said for this!) Are they *convinced,* in the sense of agreeing with what has been said? Have they received *inspiration,* something that makes them feel better? Instead of stirring people to make agonized appraisals and take hard, responsible action, programs have lulled them into "peace of mind," promising the conquest of insecurity and anxiety by solemnly pronouncing the formulas for the abolition of inner conflict; have condoned the shedding of guilt without expiation; have dredged from the Bible the source material for the achievement of a paradise of "normality" and "adjustment."

In this glorification of the other-directed man, the Word of God, the Will of God, and the Grace of God have found little place. In their stead has been offered a sort of gracious adjustment—a spiritual euphoria—an allaying of the pains and vexations of existence. Such programs are themselves basically insecure, substituting as they do formulas of behavior to achieve personal security for the admission of the fundamental insecurity that surrounds all Christian communication. Their fear of offending is all the more distressing in view of the enormity of the offense that real Christian communication inevitably provokes.

If our television broadcasting has fallen short of the demands of the gospel, the failure does not provide an excuse for the church to turn its face away from the mass media of communication. No person or organization can avoid these instrumentalities, for they are the modern tools by which man speaks to his fellow man. The church can seek out better ways by which such media as television may be used to communicate in depth; it can face up to the inevitable failures that will result, and still can try again. We should be able to learn a great deal from our missionaries about the process of communication. When we appear on television, we are in much the same condition they are, separated from those with whom we would communicate by barriers of culture and class, looked upon, as likely as not, as intruders, doomed always to fail more often than we succeed. Faced by the totally new enigma of the non-Christian culture, missionaries must develop a wide variety of communication forms and methods keyed to the mentalities, values, attitudes, and patterns of thought and speech of an equal variety of groups. The important thing is that missionaries *do witness* by setting in motion a process of communication whereby men have revealed to them the reality of their own lives, and through which they become equal and respected collaborators with the communicators.

The communication of the Christian faith transmits a design, a meaning for the present experience of people. The faith does not afford security from physical and material disaster, or freedom from pain, or sure-fire formulas for solving the enigmas of personal life or the conflicts of the world. Far from it! Rather, it binds men to a process of repeated, responsible decision making; but at the same time it opens the door of escape from meaninglessness to the joy of life in Christ, to freedom from fear, to freedom to live responsibly.

Rudolf Bultmann sums up the meaning of the faith as "the courage and the strength, in all the darkness, in all the enigmas, yet to speak the 'even so.' It is the courage and the strength of the believing man, in the loneliness of decision, to take on himself the responsibility for his action. The Christian faith is this courage and this strength because it is trust in God's grace, which called man into life and gives his life a meaning even though he cannot yet see the meaning.[15]

THE OBLIGATION OF PUBLIC COMMUNICATION—A SUMMARY

A Christian fellowship, be it council of churches, denomination, or local church, cannot, in conscience, use the mass media of communication solely to boast of its achievements, or to proclaim the superiority of its beliefs and methods, or even to persuade in behalf of those institutions in which it has placed its own trust.

Our primary task in our public communication is not to serve ourselves but to serve our Lord. We are to proclaim the Word—proclaim it in the conviction that each man is called upon to join in the search for the meaning of that Word; that through freedom to seek and recognize the truth he shall come to his own confrontation with God. Our only justifiable use of the mass media, therefore, is to fulfill the obligation of service to all of God's people. If our goal is to communicate the faith, it must be achieved by leading people to make a full, vigorous, and searching inquiry into their own faith and works in the hope that through the Christian community they will find the security and strength to risk the actions that are the ultimate test of faith. Institutions and programs have a place in such communication only to the extent that they further the principles, ideas, ideals, and possibilities of the Word.

Religious organizations, in pursuit of such weighty ends, are called upon to understand many audiences and their problems and to speak to each one in terms of its values, needs, and readiness for the message of the faith. This kind of strategy places an enormous load of responsibility upon the people who make communication policy. They must continually examine and re-examine their public communication in the light of their own commitment to the gospel, scrutinizing their own motives and methods more closely than those of others, ever seeking "the narrow way" which will keep them faithful to God while they act as servants to His creatures.

[15] Rudolf Bultmann, "Theology for Freedom and Responsibility," *The Christian Century*, Vol. LXXV (August 27, 1958), p. 967.

CHAPTER 3   The Audience

HOW DENSE IS THE MASS?

Every television sponsor hopes—and program producers would have us believe—that when the director throws the opening cue for program X on network Y, he has waiting for him, glued to its television sets, an enormous populace, each member conditioned to respond enthusiastically to the stimuli that have been astutely prepared, pretested, and predigested by the producer's "groupthink team." Fortunately, this Orwellian view of the American public is only a figment of the advertising agency sales talk. The audiences often are large—by anybody's count. They do keep coming back to particular programs. They do buy the products advertised. But the terms "mass communication" and "mass media" deceive us. Investigation of viewers, even by the television industry's oversimplified methods of nose counting, shows that: (1) almost all audiences for individual programs are minorities of the potential audience available at the time of the broadcast; (2) each audience is made up of familiarly heterogeneous human beings, differentiated sociologically by age, sex, education, occupation, religion, place of residence, and similar criteria, and psychologically by a variety of responses to identical stimuli.

It is proper to use the term "mass" as one descriptive characterization of modern general communication that seeks to have a single source reach and influence a large number of auditors who are widely scattered geographically. Insofar as "mass" indicates sameness or homogeneity, however, it must be applied to the medium rather than to the audience for the material being communicated.

The same picture, the same sounds, the same action, the same voices do appear at the same instant in hundreds of thousands of living rooms. They project their messages impersonally and simultaneously to thousands—even millions—of persons. This simultaneous impact of a single communicator upon so large a group of auditors is the new, unprecedented, revolutionary fact in communication. Its effects upon the character and acts of the American people are yet to be assessed. Yet it cannot be overemphasized that the people who simultaneously receive the messages are far from uniform units of personality or taste or position.

How dense is the mass, then? Not very dense at all! Public-service broadcasters should not let themselves be hoodwinked by the television industry shibboleth that the only worthwhile program is one with "mass appeal." The only pertinent question to be asked of a program is concerned not with "mass" but with numbers and quality of audience: What minority can it reach? The size of this minority is not an insignificant factor in judging a program's potential, especially when weighed in relation to production effort and cost and scarcity of time; but the quality of the audience is equally important, since the quality composition largely determines the influence of the message being broadcast.

Audience Analysis Based on Choices and Reactions

Each person has several choices in his use of the mass media which, although limited, are important to him and to the communicator. The individual chooses to listen or not to listen, to read or not to read. In the majority of cases he may also choose to give his attention to one of two or more campeting messages or media.

Choice is also exercised in reacting to a particular message. Even when two or more persons decide to attend to a certain television program or mass-circulation magazine or newspaper, the variation in what they actually see and hear, or how they interpret what they see and hear, is sometimes quite unexpected by the communicator.

Audience analysis, beyond nose counting, is, therefore, a highly complex affair. (Even nose counting is not accomplished easily, because of the large number of viewers available to a single television station, to say nothing of even the minimal audience for a network.) Study of audiences in depth is concerned with discovering and describing the minority of a population ("universe" is the research term applied to whatever group you are working with) who constitute an audience, comparing this minority with the total population, and trying to discover in this process what characteristics the audience has that differentiate it from the rest of the population. If these differentiations reveal a fairly distinct group (i.e., housewives, teen-agers), one may go on cautiously to hypothesize, in terms of the known characteristics of the particular audience, some relationship between the format and content of the program on the one hand and the needs and tastes of the audience on the other.

It is well known that commercial rating firms that test the popularity of television programs greatly influence the programming decisions of stations, networks, and advertisers and their agencies. Ratings are based on a count of listeners. They seldom treat seriously the sociological and psychological factors in audience composition.

All the rating services attempt to determine the viewing practices of a small population sample. Then they project their findings to the population as a whole. The A. C. Nielsen Company, for example, wires an electronic recorder into sets in approximately twelve hundred homes, then projects the data it gathers to the more than forty-five million television households in the United States. Even though such research is based upon a balanced national sample and may accurately record the comparative audiences for competing programs, it cannot take account of the fact that audiences are actually self-limiting on the basis of the cultural status of the individual viewers, even when those viewers are watching a program. The *effects* of a particular communication depend much more upon the cultural characteristics of audience members than they do on audience size. These cultural factors, clustered around social class and religion, of course, operate in differing situations with varying degrees of power. There are complex differences between the transmission of ideas and mere acquaintanceship of the audience member with a mass-produced commodity, such as a cigarette, which, while competitive, is not intrinsically different from its competitors.

However, even in the effort to sell products—which is the major, indeed almost the sole, activity of commercial television and radio— the communication takes place in a social matrix which is a dynamic composite of social class, cultural taste, national origin, race, and religion. Every given audience member occupies a position in this matrix and, in addition, is often in process of changing his position. This class-origin-religion status of each member of the audience will strongly influence his attitude toward the communicator. It will have a similar influence on the interpretation the auditor gives to the content of the message he receives. These forces that motivate response are particularly relevant for consideration in religious communications, since their content deals specifically with values.

One example will suffice. In an urban community, the majority of television viewers will be working class people, and probably will be Roman Catholics. How will the minister of an upper-class Protestant church fare with such an audience, just on the basis of his position in the community and his appearance on the air? What influence will he have with a Roman Catholic factory worker who sees him on the air, and who knows that the factory manager belongs to his church?

This example also points to another complicating factor in the relationship between communicator and auditor. If you would develop effective religious television broadcasting, it is not enough to know just the size and the sociological composition of a potential audience. Wise interpretation of such information, aided by a good working knowledge of tastes and needs, can be helpful. The religious communicator needs to know, in addition, what is going on in the minds of his viewers, what are the hard-core personality traits that may transcend social status, what are the psychological processes by which individuals make up their minds to view or not to view religious television, to accept or to reject what they see and hear, to act or to refrain from acting.

The narrow separation between certainty and uncertainty in forecasting the effects of any communication is too well known to require documentation here. Mass communication in a field as value-loaded as religion is a tremendously complex and many-sided affair in which the position of a viewer in the social structure and his psychological condition have as much to do with his reaction to a religious broadcast as does the content of the program itself. The personality of the viewer is also an important factor in determining whether or not he will look at a religious program. The Communications Research Project discovered that *personality types* may be identified in relation to viewing or nonviewing of religious programs, and that use and nonuse of such programs can be logically related to personality drives and needs.[1]

As a broadcaster, you need to strive constantly to understand the workings of these forces in the audience you are trying to reach. Audience study is a primary requisite for intelligent program planning. From the standpoint of understanding and interpretation, the most satisfactory method is the case study of the type cited in the previous paragraph. A nondirective interview, supplemented by certain details of life history and current status and one or two personality tests, can provide definitive clues to the complex motivation that is associated with television viewing of religion. The interview will not reveal all—or even the most important part—of an individual's motivation, but enough can be learned to project with some assurance the role and effects of religious television in the person's life style and to predict reaction to future exposure to programs.

What Effects Does Television Have on the Audience?

One of the most important research problems in mass communications is posed by the need to know just what people *will* accept, ideationally, from television. What, if any, facts, ideas, and opinions presented on television will influence opinions or change beliefs? Hunches about the power of television to sway opinions range between two extremes. At one pole there is the view that television probably has little, if any, influence on the mass of the people; that its only power to change beliefs lies in its ability to influence established opinion leaders of social groupings such as a church or a woman's club or an informal gathering of shopworkers. These leaders disseminate their views to the rank and file; and through them opinions are formed. At the other pole there is the concept that, in America at least, one must now reckon with a population that has been molded as much by the mass media as by formal schooling. Probably the truth lies somewhere between these views. Our society

---

[1] Everett C. Parker, David W. Barry, Dallas W. Smythe, *The Television-Radio Audience and Religion* (New York: Harper & Brothers, 1955), chaps. xii-xviii.

is so complex that it is hardly conceivable that television alone would be responsible for effecting a major change in a person's beliefs. There would be too many other communication sources working on a matter of really vital importance, such as family, employer, friends, and the opinion leaders whom the person respected. Furthermore, the communication from these latter sources would be on an intimate, face-to-face basis, while the television contact would be largely impersonal.

John W. Bachman points out that "the media are more likely to reinforce than to change attitudes because people tend to choose programs and to pay attention to features within programs which agree with their existing views and interests."[2]

On the other hand, television is so new that its ultimate effects must wait upon future measurements. It is possible that, along with other organs of mass communication, it is gradually influencing people in important ways. This influence may be especially pronounced in children and will appear years or even decades in the future. In the short run, research is showing some measurable effects from television. Bachman warns us not to be misled by small percentages in the statistics. "When it is reported that a certain broadcast has changed the opinions of only 5 per cent of its audience this may sound insignificant until it is remembered that (1) change in attitude is not a common occurrence in any form of communication, including the pulpit and classroom, and 5 per cent may be a perfectly respectable figure; (2) a single network program often attracts 20 million or more viewers, 5 per cent of whom would total a million, a very large number indeed; (3) the effect of the program may be cumulative because the million influenced directly by it may spread the influence among relatives, friends and co-workers, and (4) the 19 million unaffected by one program will be exposed to many other broadcasts in the same week, one of which may have more influence on them."[3]

How does television exercise its influence? The nature of the medium is such that, if there is to be communication, there must be symbol transference from the communicator to the audience,

[2] John W. Bachman, *The Church in the World of Radio-Television* (New York: Association Press, 1960), p. 34.
[3] *Ibid.*, pp. 34-35.

which the latter will receive through empathy and vicariousness. This process need not be employed, as it is in commercial television, solely to draw audience members into identification with products and companies directly, or with performers who stand as symbols for products. It would seem that in television, as in face-to-face confrontation, the communicator should be capable of evoking deep-seated emotional and intellectual responses from the auditors; in contradistinction to the theory that no ideational response to television content will be forthcoming until the group-opinion leader has signaled the acceptable thought course. On the other hand, the Communications Research Project found men—especially some in junior executive positions in large corporations—turning to such programs as that of Bishop Fulton J. Sheen, not for intellectual stimulus or inspiration, but to discover topics it would be "safe" to discuss and opinions it would be "safe" to hold in their vocational peer groups.

Television is an enemy of private-thought processes. Its constant demand for empathy is also a demand that the viewer be "other-centered." The vicarious experience of the viewer, derived without hope of overt reaction to the communicator and the content; the effort of the commercial to convert him, to get him to trade; the sense of being always "in company" with other persons (performers and studio audience) all combine to minimize the rational and heighten the subjective quality of the process of viewing. The "other-directed" facets of the personality are called into play in the watching of television. The medium concentrates on, and reserves its approval for, the public relations elements in the psyche of the viewer.

Your Potential Audience

There are 535 commercial and 45 educational television stations in the United States at this writing. There are slightly more than 52 million households, and 45.2 million of them are estimated to own television sets; with 5.5 million of them having more than one set. By comparison, there are 4,196 AM and FM radio stations, 49 million households with radios, and 139 million radio sets in use.

The majority of television homes (35,945,000: 79 per cent) can receive four or more stations; 18 per cent of the homes (8,190,000) have access to two or three stations; three per cent (1,365,000) are limited to one station. The country is undersupplied with television stations because of the failure of the Federal Communications Commission to discharge its responsibility to provide the necessary channels. The Commission decided to open national television service on the very high frequency band, knowing there were not enough channels available there to provide local communities with competitive service comparable to that among radio stations. Later, when it opened the ultra high frequency band, the Commission refused to designate VHF and UHF areas. Instead, it intermixed the two services, community by community. Since very high frequency was first on the scene, sets were equipped to receive only that service. Viewers were loath to pay the costs of equipping their sets to receive both services, and manufacturers refused to make receivers that would tune in both bands because it would increase costs. Ultra high frequency stations in intermixed communities, having no audiences, were economically unfeasible and were forced from the air. The UHF service has been virtually abandoned, leaving the country woefully short of available channels for stations, a situation much to the liking of the major networks, since it gives them monopolistic control over the limited number of VHF outlets.

The accessibility of two or more stations to 97 per cent of the television homes is a chance result of the urban concentration of United States population. Very high frequency engineering requirements for separation of stations on the same channel and the small number of channels have resulted in a patchwork rather than a grid pattern of station allocations, with high concentration of stations in large cities. New York City, for example, has seven very high frequency stations, which limits nearby New Haven and Hartford to one each and blocks out other communities within a radius of one hundred miles of the city. The small VHF station-to-receiver proportion cuts down sharply on the number of religious, educational, and even commercial programs that can get on the air. It especially limits the potential audience for religion, since religious broadcasting has always depended upon an abundance of local rather than network programs.

Television set ownership tends to be concentrated in the areas of greatest urban development, in part because reception is better there. The highest regional set ownership is in the northeastern states, where 92 per cent of the households have sets. East north-central states have 92 per cent set ownership, west north-central states 86 per cent, and Pacific states 88 per cent, but ownership in southern states is only 80 per cent. The most urbanized counties, such as Cook County in Illinois, which includes Chicago, show 94 per cent set ownership by households. In the most rural counties, set ownership drops to 66 per cent.

Television viewing in the home is estimated to average about six hours a day. Virtually all television homes appear to use their sets sometime during each week. Peak viewing is on weekday nights between 8 P.M. and 10 P.M., when an average of 29 million homes have sets in use. Daytime averages are much smaller, about 12 million sets in the hours from noon to 6:00 P.M. and 4.8 million between 6:00 A.M. and noon. There is virtually no viewing before 8:00 A.M. on weekdays, and use of sets falls off sharply at 11:00 P.M. No one, so far, has found enough audience to count on Sunday mornings, although it is fairly certain that children—but not teen-agers—watch then and on Saturday mornings. Between 12:00 noon and 6:00 P.M. Sundays, 68 per cent of all homes are reported to have their sets on and to watch for long periods at a stretch.[4]

Children aged four to fifteen constitute a specialized audience. They watch television throughout the day, although programs especially *for* children are concentrated in the so-called "children's hours," 5:00 P.M. to 7:00 P.M. on weekdays and from "sign on" to 7:00 P.M. on Saturdays and Sundays. These hours represent about 25 per cent of broadcast time, but programs designed for children seldom exceed 10 per cent of a station's schedule. Children, therefore, watch adult programs most of the time. Teen-agers consider themselves to be adults in their television habits. They watch adult programs.

Most research findings on viewing by children are inexact, but there is general agreement that they watch television a lot. The

---

[4] Figures cited are from the United States Census Bureau, reports of the A. C. Nielsen Co., and other research sources. The 1960 Census will probably show a higher absolute figure for set-owning households, but should not materially change the percentages of set ownership in the various parts of the country.

Foundation for Character Education estimates that children spend twenty to thirty hours a week before television sets.[5] Smaller children may spend ten to twelve hours watching children's shows. The rest of the time is spent looking at adult programs. Except in the most remote rural areas, virtually all children watch television regularly, whether there is a set in the home or not. However, homes where there are minor children are almost certain to have television sets.

THE AUDIENCE FOR RELIGIOUS PROGRAMS

The Communications Research Project found that in New Haven, Connecticut, six out of every ten households regularly watch a religious program on television or listen to one on the radio.[6] A more recent study of a small sample of households in central Illinois tended to confirm these findings. There, sixty-five out of one hundred twenty households (54.2 per cent) reported regular viewing or listening.[7]

The interest evidenced in religion is all the more remarkable in view of the small amount of broadcast time devoted to religious programs. On New York City television stations, one per cent of total time on the air is devoted to religion, and religious programs rank last among program types in the amount of air time made available to them. New York stations lack typicality in relation to the rest of the country only in the fact they may present more religious programs than do stations generally throughout the nation. This condition exists in New York because the three networks own and operate stations there. The network managements require these stations to carry all of the sustaining religious programs that are aired nationally through the networks. Affiliated stations need not carry such programs unless they wish to do so.

The strong audience appeal of religion is all the more apparent in view of the fact that the major religious programs are aired, almost without exception, in the morning, early afternoon, and late at

[5] Thomas R. Carskadon, *et al.*, *Television for Children* (Boston: Foundation for Character Education, n.d.).

[6] Parker, *et al.*, *op. cit.*, p. 201.

[7] Dallas W. Smythe, *Attitudes Toward the Frontiers of Faith "Conversation Piece" TV Series* (Urbana: University of Illinois Institute of Communications Research, 1958), p. 45.

night on Sundays. Having a program available to the audience member at a time when it is convenient for him to watch it is perhaps the most important audience determinant. It should therefore follow that if religion could garner a fair share of evening time, when a really large audience is available, religious programs could hold their own in audience interest against virtually anything else on the air. It is well to remember, though, that convenience to watch is compounded of two elements, time and competition. *Omnibus*, a program with substantial intellectual appeal, was able to amass large audiences, running as high as fifteen million households, on a Sunday afternoon. But during the season *Omnibus* was aired on the American Broadcasting Company network from 9:00 P.M. to 10:30 P.M. Sundays, its rating fell off by more than two-thirds. On Sunday nights, it was competing against such programs as the *Alcoa Playhouse* and the *Loretta Young Show* on the National Broadcasting Company network and *General Electric Theater, Alfred Hitchcock Presents*, and the $64,000 *Challenge* on the Columbia Broadcasting System, all of them programs with more "mass appeal" than *Omnibus*.

Only one religious program, that of Bishop Fulton J. Sheen, has had the opportunity to test itself against the competition of the major nighttime entertainment shows. At first, Bishop Sheen more than held his own against Milton Berle. Then the novelty wore off, and the Bishop faded quickly and went off the air in the face of sustained nighttime competition. Although he has remained as an important figure in religious broadcasting, Bishop Sheen has never been able to recapture his short-lived popularity with evening audiences.

People may be more willing to watch a serious program at an inconvenient time, such as Sunday afternoon when there are few entertainment shows on the air, than they are to tune in during the more convenient night hours when competition from entertainment offerings is keen.

Be that as it may, the general audience for religion is large and covers a cross section of society. The New Haven studies found that the three-fifths of the households regularly watching religious programs are no different in social characteristics than are the two-fifths who do not follow religious programs. Jews and Protestants—

especially upper-class Protestants—are, however, more frequently found in the *nonaudience* for religion than are Roman Catholics and Protestants who are factory and lower-grade white-collar workers.[8]

The whole audience for religion is generalized, but specific program audiences are far from being cross sections of our society. Each program selects its own audience, specialized in both size and social composition. The New Haven studies showed that Protestant programs and the network trifaith presentations (*Frontiers of Faith, Lamp Unto My Feet,* etc.) in a city that size (250,000) have audiences about equal in numbers to a large church congregation. The viewers are more likely than not to be church affiliated. They are almost without exception church oriented, that is, they have a background of religious training and church attendance, even though they may at the moment be using television as a substitute for active church membership.[9]

The format and content of a religious program appear to delimit sharply the audience the program will attract. It should be possible in any community to predict accurately the kind of audience that will be attracted to a particular religious program whose characteristics are known, providing the social class and religious composition of the population also are known in detail.

Religious broadcasters err in failing to take into account this predilection of their programs to be self-selective of audiences. Queried about their target audiences, spokesmen for religion almost invariably specify all-inclusive groups: "all the unchurched," "all families," "all adults," "the unsaved." They think that when they go on the air their audiences are as universal as the gospel itself, that they are speaking to everybody. They make the mistake of believing that because television is a universal medium, it automatically delivers an audience that is representative of universality.

The truth is that duplication of pulpit material or of in-church discussions—which is what most religious broadcasts do—will draw only the same class of audience the communicator will get in his church. Furthermore, the magic of television which attracts so many millions to spend the bulk of their leisure time before their sets

[8] Parker, *et al., op. cit.,* pp. 202-206.
[9] *Ibid.,* pp. 207-219.

will not automatically rub off on an amateur performer; nor will it make a man who cannot inspire in the pulpit inspire on the air. He who would use television successfully must undergo the discipline of becoming as much a professional in broadcasting as he is in religion. He must also give professional consideration to the needs and dimensions of audiences and to their readiness to absorb a religious message.

WHAT AUDIENCE SHOULD YOU SEEK?

It should now be apparent that television audiences develop and remain in being through the operation and interplay of a complicated cluster of personality factors, including sex, age, class consciousness, religion, occupation, education, interests, tastes, even sheer inability to find a more satisfying way to pass time. In their responses, these audiences are self-limiting on the basis of their psychological relationships to the program material being offered. The tendencies to resist the communication, to avoid active response —even though there is general agreement with the communicator's views—are much stronger in the case of programs that dig into ideas and values than they are when shows seek only to sell commodities by means of entertainment designed *not* to disturb existing mind sets or to offend emotional bias.

Religious broadcasting, since it consciously seeks to bring about fundamental life changes, must be prepared to serve the largest number and variety of audiences it is possible to reach. There is scarcely a subject or an interest that cannot legitimately be brought under the scrutiny of religious interpretation. The fact that a stand on an issue is unpopular or that a potential audience is a small minority, should not deter the religious broadcaster—as it does the commercial advertiser—from treating the one or aiming at the other from time to time. Yet there is a factor of diminishing returns that operates in the division and subdivision of audiences ad infinitum. Good stewardship requires that program potential be weighed against audience potential to determine how to get the most out of the resources available. How much money must be spent for a particular program or series? What are the available talent and facilities? What time and effort must be spent on production? What results may be expected in relation to audience impressions? What is the certain need of a particular audience for a particular program? What is the audience's readiness to receive it?

We should apply certain criteria to our choices of audiences, just as we do in choosing program content and formats: What audiences are most readily available to our programs? Which ones have needs that religious broadcasting should be able to meet? Which ones will get the most out of a particular presentation? Which audiences may be more open to receiving religious communication through television than might other potential groups?

None of the foregoing questions is more determinative than the others in making judgments about potential audiences. Yet they point up the fact that the religious broadcaster, like the advertiser of cake mix, has certain people who are more likely to listen to what he has to say, *broadcast via television,* than will certain others. The religious broadcaster, in addition, has certain audiences that he ought to face up to and try to influence, even though they are not openly willing to listen or may even be hostile. We shall term these various classes of viewers the "prime" audiences for religion, by which we mean those audiences at whom we should aim the bulk of our religious broadcasting. These prime audiences fall naturally into broad, general groupings that leave wide latitude for the choice of program format and content. There are so many potential viewers in each group that a broadcaster may confidently expect to find an audience among them.

Women

The most important of the prime audiences for religion is made up of women, especially those between the ages of twenty-five and fifty-five. This group ranks first in size, availabality, and homogeneity.

Whatever program may be on the air at whatever time of the day or night, with the exception of sports, there will be more women than men in the audience. Moreover, women spend more gross time viewing television than do men.

Most adult religious programs that manage to escape television's Sunday morning ghetto are assigned daytime weekday periods when women viewers vastly predominate. For this reason alone, women constitute a primary audience for religion. But it is the widespread homogeneity in outlook, interests, problems, and activities that characterizes the women of twenty-five to fifty-five in our society that makes them the prime target audience of every user of mass communication.

In the first place, these women are bound together by a sense of equality—if not of kinship—that does not exist in most societies outside America. About three out of four of them share a common vocation, wife and mother; but the equality relationship is deeper than this. American women of middle and late middle age, of all social classes, maintain a physical vigor and attractiveness and a range of interests and activities that keep them on a firm competitive footing with younger women. On the other hand, younger women, buttressed by education and early assumption of economic and marital responsibilities, quickly attain a poise and a maturity that permit them to move with sureness in the face of older women's greater experience. The lines between generations—even between mother and daughter—are no longer sharply drawn. There can be common interests and common actions; there is keen competition between as well as within generations.

Second, there is the commonality of interests. Topping them all is the necessity to keep up successfully with the constantly changing pattern of relations between husband and wife. There is the need to adjust to the coming of children and their growing up, to economic conditions, to vocational success or failure of the husband, to changes in moods and emotions and all other facets of personal relationships between husband and wife, to the thousand and one other concerns a woman faces in her marriage.

Equally of common interest are matters relating to children—in all stages of their growth and development. America's population explosion coupled with the drastic lowering of the general marriage age has widened the age distribution of children, both within and between adult generations. It is becoming common to find infants in homes of older parents, teen-agers in homes where the parents are in their thirties. All but the ultra-sophisticated social gatherings are dominated by talk of children. And why should they not be?

What is there more important to think about, wish about, talk about, learn about than children?

Where can mothers turn for wise, dependable counsel on how to guide their children toward their destinies? He who can develop an I-Thou relationship with America's wives and mothers based upon their concerns over relations with their husbands and the nurturing of their children will have the ready attention of the most comprehensive of all television audiences.

There are other, but less important, commonalities of interest among women that can become the bases of television programs. They include matters of personal relationships outside the home, especially problems of social conformity and social acceptance; interest in vocations; intellectual pursuits; good stewardship of time and money; and a host of others in which religious interpretation of the subject is relevant.

A third reason for the importance of women as audience is the tremendous influence they wield in our society. They have acquired social, economic, and political power. Analysis of our economic life, in particular, demonstrates that product design, packaging, marketing and consumer services are oriented largely to the needs and desires of women. Politically, while bloc voting by sex is not demonstrable, the influence of women in shaping the policies of administrative agencies of government is considerable. Women dominate public-school affairs. They exercise a large measure of control over both policies and practices of welfare, charitable, cultural, and other community agencies.

A fourth reason for aiming religious broadcasts at women is that they may be more open to the reception of ideas and more flexible in responding to the need for social action than are other audiences. In dealing with community affairs, especially with school problems, women will work together across class and racial lines. Women's organizations also tend to be nonpartisan when they work on community problems that their members consider to be vital to the public welfare, such as the provision of adequate schools or enforcement of housing, zoning, and traffic laws. They can be appealed to on the basis of issues rather than on their relations to the various power blocs.

Finally, remember that the church is an important institution to women. Probably a majority of women today are active in the church. Those who are not active recognize its role in the lives of the others and may be willing to listen when a respresentative of the church speaks on issues that they feel are relevant to them.

Men

Communication with men who are in the vigorous youthful and middle years, corresponding to the twenty-five to fifty-five year old women's audience, should also be a primary objective of religious broadcasting. But the difficulty of catching men, holding them, and influencing them with programs that deal with ideas and values is formidable.

Men fall into fewer homogeneous groupings than do women. Vocational interests are a good illustration. A program dealing with religious values in a particular vocation, such as "Ethics in Selling," would appeal only to a limited male audience, in contrast to a similar vocational topic, "Ethics in Motherhood," which, theoretically at least, would appeal to almost the whole female audience.

Men are further segmented by age and by the vocational competition between generations. Even within individual vocations there are wide variations in attitudes and in vocational interests among men, depending upon their positions in the vocational hierarchy.

Viewing habits also may influence attitudes toward religious programs. Men do not usually find themselves exposed to television programs that deal with ideas and issues, simply because such programs are not often broadcast during the peak-viewing evening hours, when men are most likely to be in the audience. The television industry, by choice, has virtually denied itself the opportunity to influence male thought, except in the limited area of product acceptance or rejection. Men must look to other communications media for opinion leadership. Television consumption by men is primarily for purposes of entertainment. The majority do not expect anything else from television. It is questionable whether the occasional religious program that seriously concerns itself with ideas can successfully buck the preponderant viewing habits of the male audience.

Religious programs designed to reach men must take into account all of the foregoing, and the general effects of television described earlier. Whatever your purpose may be, you need to recognize the fact that the average man views television for pleasure. Pleasure is not necessarily synonymous with escapism. He may find keen pleasure in programs that make him do hard intellectual work, if they will also help liberate him from his group pressures and mores and emotions, allowing him to contemplate alternative responses and to try out new emotions.

Such programs will need to be something other than platitudinous discussions of current problems or homilies with happy endings, cast in dramatic form. They should cut sharply and deeply into the myriad layers of anxiety and conformity under which we all hide. They should frankly confront the viewer with the unpleasant knowledge that every human act is potentially a step toward tragedy. They should refrain from presenting religion as a formula for solving problems, or the church as an institution where one can take ones troubles to shrug them off. Programs that deal with problems should apply the test of Christian conscience to the solutions offered, stripping away the hypocrisy that is inherent in most human attempts at resolution. Programs that treat of human troubles need to recognize that some, if not most, human ills—sickness and suffering, for example—cannot be shaken off by the application of religion; but that religious faith is the force that will surmount them.

Mature religious programming directed at men will follow the example of the gospel itself, eschewing trivia and grappling with the fundamental issues of being and belonging. Such programs will consciously have to violate commercial television's taboo and appeal not to a "mass audience" but to specialized tastes and minority interests.

Families

Television viewing by families reaches a peak in the watching of the popular evening entertainment shows. In fact, a rather frequent cause of dissension in families is the conflicting demands over what programs shall be watched by the whole group. Some market research has been devoted to the question Who decides what to watch? on the theory that the person who gets his way on choice of program is the strongest character in the family and therefore the one most likely to influence purchasing decisions.

Families will always constitute an important grouping in the television audience, in spite of the fact that multiple set-owning homes are increasing rapidly. For the religious broadcaster, families with minor children, especially couples in the first ten to fifteen years of their married life, should be another prime target audience.

The New Haven Communications Research Project found that married couples in the vigorous youthful and early middle years can be attracted to religious programs that they feel are treating problems relevant to their needs. Seventy per cent of the audience for *This Is the Life* and 69 per cent of the audience for Bishop Fulton J. Sheen consisted of households in which there were husband, wife, and minor children. These percentages were 15 per cent higher than the ratio of such households in the whole New Haven population.[10]

Both of these programs deal directly with family affairs and give precise directives for family living. Programs by Bishop Sheen which this writer has analyzed have given specific instructions on such things as the role of the mother and of children in the family, the role of the family in God's scheme of things, the meaning and function of sex, where authority rests in the family, how to teach children, what to teach them, and numerous other family topics. *This Is the Life* treats familiar, universal, and recognizable human problems in the context of a believable family and community situation. Workable solutions are presented for the problems that most families face. There is a believable representation of the role of the church and its pastor in the family and in the community.

Both of these programs attract lower-middle-class and working-class families—people who are seldom the objective of religious broadcasts. However, both programs are likely to be of most help to persons who will unanalytically accept a voice of authority giving directions as to proper conduct, since both offer authoritarian definitions and solutions for problems. *This Is the Life* is far less authoritarian and more benevolent than is Sheen. Its solutions are not manipulative. However, its appeal to thinking people is weakened

[10] *Ibid.*, p. 218.

by the transparency of some of its plots, the contrived nature of some of the situations it depicts, and its use of sterotyped characters.

There is a place in any community for programs that can interpret family living. There is also apparent interest in such programs on the part of the most vigorous group in the community, the parents of small children. Protestant agencies need to expand their programming in this field, experimenting and testing as *Talkback* has done.[11] This series, with its drama-discussion format, has some exciting treatments of family problems. The dramatic skits are sound scientifically and are written and produced in an entertaining manner. *Talkback* depends for its dénouement on a discussion panel of local persons. This panel may not always be as lively as the dramatic skit that precedes it, but it has two important merits. First, it permits local participation. Second, where the panel does a good job, the localized flavor of its discussion is far more interesting and vital than a filmed discussion by a panel of outside "experts" would be.

The production of "family life" programs is probably beyond the talent and financial resources of the average local community, since the experience of *This Is the Life* and similar programs has shown the desirability of drama for this purpose. Here is a type of program that could well be produced nationally on film or on tape and distributed for local scheduling and sponsorship. It is the sort of program that local churches should urge upon their parent denominations as a co-operative project of the National Council of Churches. Its financing, at the highest level of artistic accomplishment, would not be an undue strain if the major denominations co-operated wholeheartedly in the production.

Children

Preschool children do not now constitute an important audience for religious broadcasting. Little, if anything, is known of their ability to absorb religious meanings from television. Other types of television programs than religious primarily fulfill the functions of a

[11] *Talkback* is available free for broadcasting locally. Order from the Broadcasting and Film Commission, the National Council of the Churches of Christ in the U. S. A., 475 Riverside Drive, New York 27, N. Y.

baby sitter for these youngsters, even such excellent programs as those of Shari Lewis and Captain Kangaroo. Yet preschool children make up a large and constantly increasing audience for television, and they are engaged in a continuous process of learning and of adjustments to new experiences of life. If religion has anything to say to them at all, it might well be said on the air, where they are much more readily available than they are in church schools. Some experiments seem to be in order. One that might be tried would be to use religious nursery-school curriculum material for story telling and simple dramatization. The excellent new nursery-department books by Phoebe Anderson are one such source.[12]

Children in the fourth through ninth grades are, perhaps, the most important audience of all for religious television. Like the preschoolers, they are engaged in a constant process of testing and learning. Every experience is grist for their mills of experimentation, acceptance, rejection, and synthesis as they develop characters and points of view. All of them watch television; although the amount of viewing varies from that of the addicts who spend more than half their waking hours outside of school looking at television to that of the indifferent who see only a handful of programs each week. (Viewing is greatly dependent upon intelligence and maturity. The more intelligent and the more intellectually mature children do the least viewing.)

Younger children (eight to ten years) like action and have little interest in ideas. They understand and appreciate only clear-cut issues (the "good guys" versus the "bad guys"). They comprehend plots only vaguely, and they respond to incidental action rather than to complete stories.

By age eleven, children are ready to absorb values about life from television. They begin to accept the television concept of the social structure of our culture. This attention to values heightens with age. It is especially keen in early adolescence, when children readily accept and respond to televised representations of personal relationships and adult life in general. These new concepts are not derived from educational programs designed to transmit them pedagogically. The children get their ideas of what adult life is like and what is accept-

[12] Published by the United Church Press, Philadelphia.

able adult behavior from watching the general run of commercial adult entertainment programs, especially "life" dramas and "problem" dramas. Children watch adult shows regularly. For the most part, they prefer them to children's programs. Girls, especially of junior high school age, seem to be more responsive to the social and personal values enunciated in adult television programs and are more often influenced by television generally than are boys.

Most scientific studies of children and television show that the popular concept of children glued to their television sets avidly watching whatever comes over the air is false. Children show about as wide a variation in television tastes as do their elders. Where selectivity is possible, they turn from what they do not like to something they do like. However, this selectivity seldom, if ever, dictates the choice of an educational program over an entertainment show. When the decision, as in one-channel communities or under parental control, is between watching an educational program or not viewing television, children will watch and even enjoy the educational show. But given a choice of programs, they seldom will discover such fare for themselves.

Children have never wholly succumbed to the wiles of television. They have too many other interests. They are too intelligent ever to rate television as high in importance as school, and only infrequently do they rate it as high in interest as outdoor sports. Different children use television in different ways. Only a minority views so much television that there is provable danger to personality and intellectual development. Yet, to the vast majority of children, television bulks large, both as a consumer of their leisure time and as a force that influences social intercourse with their peers.[13]

This extensive use of television makes children, all unwittingly, a prime target for the merchandisers of products and the exponents of commodity-centered social theories. The "social engineers" have their eyes on our children. They would consciously and gladly turn them into "custom-made" men and women, existing primarily to

[13] Anyone who is contemplating religious programs for children should read Hilde T. Himmelweit, et al., Television and the Child (New York: Oxford University Press, 1958). This report of television viewing by children in Britain is the most comprehensive, scientific study of the subject made to date.

be manipulated for the sale of products. It is not too far-fetched to conceive that an unrelieved diet of television standards of taste and behavior may turn our children into the "packaged souls" that Vance Packard envisions.[14] Children are not sophisticated enough to weigh and judge the validity of the other-directed, group living, consumption-centered standards that television projects as the norm for adult behavior. They badly need some guide lines for moral human behavior, presented through the medium that is so assiduously trying to cultivate them.

Through the years, religious broadcasting has virtually ignored children. Yet they are an audience readily available to religion; the only sure audience during the Sunday morning hours when most religious programs are on the air. They are used to formal teaching and learning through television; the schools, with their closed circuit systems, have made this routine. They are receiving thirty to forty-five minutes of indifferent instruction in religion per week in church school, as against many hours of indoctrination, via television, in principles and practices that are directly opposed to Judaeo-Christian teaching.

The late Albert Crews of the National Council of Churches had a great vision of a daily program for children that would teach the Bible, church history, missions, and all the other subjects taught in church school. He was never able to surmount difficulties of choice of curriculum, the chief obstacle to the development of a national Christian education program for children. But the achievement of such a program need not wait on national action. A local community could develop a rounded television curriculum if a group of able teachers would give the necessary time and energy to the production of the programs and the necessary follow-up in homes.

Teen-agers

Here is the least predictable of the prime audiences for religious television. We know pretty well when children, housewives, and working men and women can be expected to be watching television; but the teen-ager lives an erratic life, following a haphazard schedule.

[14] Vance Packard, *The Hidden Persuaders* (New York: David McKay, 1957), chap. xxi.

Furthermore, teen-agers do not like to be singled out for special attention; it smacks too much of the status of being a problem group. In their use of television (but not of radio), they identify themselves with adults and they view adult programs. This is a form of upgrading, but it is also a recognition of the fact that their most important objective is to come to grips with adult life. They are shy and wary, shunning the paternalistic, the traditional, the cliché, the pat solution. They sense that there are no easy answers to their questions.

A marketing study by Eugene Gilbert shows that 70.2 per cent of teen-agers consider television to be the most entertaining of the media in which they encounter advertising regularly (magazines, newspapers, radio, television); and that 31.8 per cent think it would be the hardest mass medium to do without. (Radio scored first here by an eyelash: 32.1 per cent.) The teen-agers like serious plays (44.6 per cent) and comedies (17.4 per cent) best, and quizzes (5.0 per cent) and educational shows (4.4 per cent) least among program types. They pay little attention to television news (4.7 per cent), believing newspapers to be more reliable and informative.[15]

My own more recent study of leisure-time habits of a small sample of teen-agers (132)[16] tends to confirm Gilbert's findings concerning preference for program types. These youngsters have catholic television tastes, with no outstanding program favorites or choice of types; but they enjoy dramas and comedies more than they do other kinds of programs. They show little or no discrimination in viewing, and will watch anything that is on when they turn to the television set—"Whatever is most interesting when I can watch." (All members of the sample had access to three or more channels.) They would rather see "real-life drama" than westerns. They show a remarkable interest in serious plays, with evidence that they are familiar with content. They do not watch disk jockeys, educational or religious programs, or news on television. They listen to popular music on radio or records and listen to some national and international news on radio. They seldom look at metropolitan newspapers, but do read community and school papers for local news and

[15] See Eugene Gilbert, "Do Your Ads Sell Youngsters?" *Printers' Ink*, Vol. 259, No. 11, June 14, 1957, pp. 31 ff., and Gilbert, *Advertising and Marketing to Young People* (Pleasantville, N. Y.: Printers' Ink Books, 1957).

[16] Unpublished. Conducted January-April, 1960.

features such as the Ann Landers newspaper column of advice on manners and morals.

More significant than program tastes is the place of television in the leisure-time programs of these young people. The teen-agers studied could identify six major leisure-time activities. All of them engage in all six at one time or another. These activities were ranked in two categories: (1) what the young people *like* to do with their leisure time; (2) what they *actually* do with their leisure.

RANK ORDER OF LEISURE TIME ACTIVITIES OF TEEN-AGERS

Activity	Rank in which the Activity is Preferred	Rank of Actual Engagement in Activity
"Hacking around" (visiting, driving, walking, shopping, etc., with peers)	1	1
Group activities (clubs, choirs, fraternities, etc.)	2	3
Going to movies with peers	3	6
Reading and listening to radio or records	4	2
Watching television	5	4
Listening to records or radio	6	5

Notice that the preferred activities take place in groups. Teen-agers are not loners. Nor are they patient spectators. Few of the young people queried watch discussion shows, but many are eager to appear on such programs, especially on *College Bowl*. When ideas are being bandied about, young people want to try out their own thoughts, not just listen to others.

None of the youngsters in the sample watches religious programs. (None watches television on Sunday mornings.) On the other hand, a majority (89) ranks religion high among things considered to be important and interesting in life. (The sample is a cross section of

Protestant, Roman Catholic, and Jewish subjects.) Make religion lively, interesting, and vital on television, they agree, and they will tune in.

What do they think would be lively, interesting, and vital? They had four worthwhile program ideas: (1) real life dramas that deal with religious issues; (2) visits with people who are doing important things and can explain the meaning of what they are doing; similar visits by teen-agers to see different vocations and to have their spiritual meaning explained; (3) talks between teen-agers and "live" adults about "real life problems" such as jobs, college, sex, the meaning of Communism, etc. (No programs wanted on relations with parents!); (4) a missionary education program that would introduce teen-agers to various peoples and cultures, showing how they live, what they think, and what their religions are.

In view of the teen-age interests revealed above, it is nothing short of tragic that the Columbia Broadcasting System airs *Look Up and Live* early Sunday mornings when there is little audience for the program. The Protestant segment of *Look Up and Live* has been engaged in some lively experimentation in "indirect evangelism" for teen-agers, which deserves to be presented on the air before a large teen-age audience. Every week an attempt is made "to communicate theological meanings in non-theological or existential ways, to sense the function of television to prod, to confront, to focus in such a way that youth senses the church and the gospel can be relevant to his situation."[17] In this kind of programming, nothing is automatically excluded. There is no divorcement of the sacred from the secular. Nothing which the teen-ager may experience is untouchable. His interests and, especially, his curiosities are treated with respect but subjected to rigorous examination in relation to the gospel.

The producers of *Look Up and Live* have recognized that programs for teen-agers must begin with teen-age interests. Therefore, church services and hortatory addresses are excluded. Teen-agers think they have heard all that before. *Look Up and Live* finds a common meet-

---

[17] From an unpublished critique of *Look Up and Live* by Edward A. Powers, General Secretary of the Division of Christian Education, Board of Home Missions of the Congregational Christian Churches. The author is indebted to Mr. Powers for assistance in analyzing teen-age television habits and interests.

ing ground with its target audience in the context of popular culture —jazz, folk music, modern dancing, "real life" drama. A serious attempt has been made to interpret life from the Christian viewpoint in the idiom of life the teen-ager understands. There is some evidence from the reaction of teen-age groups to kinescopes of the program that *Look Up and Live* has discovered how to communicate the urgency and relevancy of the gospel in a fresh, live way.

Much more experimental programming is needed to help us learn how to communicate religion to teen-agers via television. The development and testing of such programs locally would be an important service both to the audience of youth and to religious television.

How About Your Audience Rating?

If it is good, rejoice in it and be suspicious of the depth of your program content. If it is bad, do somethng to find out why. But do not let the rating tail wag the program dog!

Almost nobody really believes a rating. And nobody can tell you for certain what it means. About the best a rating can do is provide a highly questionable estimate of the number of viewers into which an advertiser can divide his program costs to guess at how much he is spending per viewer. Thus he calculates a program's "efficiency." But he still does not know whether or not a single person with money in his jeans and a yen for the product watched the commercial, or if he did watch it, whether he will buy.

Bulk ratings are an even greater absurdity when applied to test the effectiveness of religious programs, unless you broadcast on the theory that if you can entice enough people into the hall you are bound to convert a sufficient number to make the meeting worthwhile. The true measurement of the effectiveness of a religious program is not how many watched but what happened to those who did watch. This measurement cannot be determined by bulk statistics. Here is one of the most telling arguments in favor of locally sponsored religious programming. The local program can be so contrived that direct contact can be made with a substantial portion of the audience. Personal interviews with the respondents can then be employed to serve a twofold purpose: to test the effectiveness of the program and as personal evangelism. Nationally distributed programs can also be used for these purposes if they are so designed that audience responses are elicited and local organizations then conduct follow-up visits.

If religious television broadcasting is to be worthwhile, it is essential that there be scientific evaluation of the effectiveness of our programs. No other form of public communication essayed by church and synagogue costs as much in time and effort of personnel and in money as does television. Admittedly, religious broadcasters must share the anxieties of the commercial sponsors over the fact that no matter what kind of a rating system is used, one can never be sure of just what has happened as the result of a program or series of programs. But good stewardship demands that we employ the most enlightening measures available to judge the results of our efforts.

One of the most disturbing things about the church's use of television is the fact that the organizations that sponsor the programs have little or no scientific data about the size and composition of audiences or the effects the programs are having. Some programs remain on the air year after year without anybody knowing with any degree of certainty whether they have any business being there.

No council of churches, and certainly no denomination that has the money to produce television programs, is so impoverished of funds and talent that it could not conduct audience studies on a small scale. At the very least, there can be a telephone survey made while a program is on the air. It can be done by volunteers calling every tenth name in the directory.

Something more than this minimal survey work is needed, though, if we are to be proper stewards of our work in mass communications. There is need for a continuing program of research, both nationally and in every community in which religious broadcasting goes on. It should go much deeper than a mere statistical determination of audience size. We know virtually nothing of how the communication of values takes place in our society now that the mass media play so large and influential a role. We have never assessed the emotional involvement of viewers in religious programs which they watch. We do not know if, once a person becomes interested in a religious television program, there is a way to transfer that interest to a local church. We are not even sure whether religious television benefits the church, hurts it, or fails to affect it at all.

These random examples merely scratch the surface of items the churches should be seeking data on from communications research. The religious broadcaster is in a position roughly analogous to that of the pastor of a church. The minister needs to have intimate knowledge of every member of his church if he expects to fulfill his pastoral function. There may be some things withheld from him, there may be others he cannot fathom; but the one thing his congregation will not forgive is for him to fail in his pastoral duties because he neglected to try to find out. Religious broadcasters have not tried to find out. How long may they expect to be tolerated in their ignorance?

CHAPTER 4

Program Types and Program
Planning

Television program types have become virtually standardized in
something less than a decade and a half of the life of the medium.
No other major field of art has permitted its forms and methods
of expression to become fixed and repetitious to the degree television
programs are. Most television experimentation, most new program
developments—even those that at first sight seem to be creative
and clever—eventually develop into mere variations of the prevailing
show types.

Some years ago, Dallas W. Symthe in his studies of television content established a typology for adult television programs.[1] The same
program types that he identified then continue to dominate American
television today. Television is like politics, the faces change but the
methods go on forever.

It is well to be familiar with the standard program types and with
what each may be expected to accomplish in the "playing" (i.e., the
transmittal) of content. In the Table which follows, the program
types are classified roughly in the order of their importance in station and network scheduling, first by general category (e.g., entertainment), then by rank order within the category.

These dominant program types have three common characteristics:
(1) they account for virtually every program on the commercial
television stations; (2) each type commands approximately the same
proportion of broadcast time from station to station; (3) they are
aired at the same time of day from market to market. Presumably,
these program types represent to a large degree continuing tastes of

[1] Dallas W. Smythe, *Three Years of New York Television* (Urbana, Ill.:
National Association of Educational Broadcasters, 1953), pp. 15-16.

Program Types and Examples

Program Type	Examples
Entertainment	
Western drama	*Gunsmoke*
Sports	Baseball
Variety	*Ed Sullivan Show*
Crime drama	*Alfred Hitchcock Presents*
Personalities	*Person to Person*
Comedy drama	*Ozzie and Harriet*
General drama	*Play of the Week*
Domestic drama	*Leave It to Beaver*
Quiz and stunts	*What's My Line?*
Music	*Telephone Hour*
Information	
News reports	Station and network news bulletins
News commentaries	Chet Huntley-Dave Brinkley
General information	*C.B.S. Reports*
Domestic information	Various homemaker shows, mostly local in origin
Orientation	
Public issues and events	*Meet the Press*
Education	*Continental Classroom*
Cultural analysis and appreciation	*Camera 3*
Religion	*Frontiers of Faith, Look Up and Live*

the television audience. Certainly, they represent the continuing tastes of the commercial sponsors. But no one has even come forward with data proving that the staying power of these types is related to program preferences of the public.

Within each program type there is keen competition between shows for the favor of the audience. Every year, for instance, there is competition between Ed Sullivan and a rival variety show on the National Broadcasting Company network, spotted against Sullivan in the hope of luring his audience away.

The program types are themselves also in competition with each other. They do not all enjoy the same degree of exposure to potential audiences; that is, they cannot all garner equal percentages of the broadcast time or a share of the choice evening hours. Some are barred from the peak viewing times, even if they have a sponsor.

Informational and orientational programs, like religious programs, are customarily assigned to oblivion by being scheduled at times that cannot be sold, such as early Sunday morning.

The more prolific entertainment types tend to seesaw up and down the popularity scale in network and station scheduling. Witness the demise of big money, give-away quiz programs and the concomitant meteoric rise of the adult western to the top program spot. The quizzes, of course, were discontinued because of public disgust over the evidence of widespread rigging and payola. But the public was not consulted whether it wanted so large a slice of its viewing time filled with westerns. The whole process of program placement and program balance represents solely the wishes of the commercial sponsors and the networks.

RELATION OF FORMAT TO CONTENT[2]

Format is a term borrowed from printing and means "the shape, size and general make-up of a publication." Applied to a television program, format is descriptive of the method used to transmit the content. It is how you play what you have to say.

The format is secondary in importance to the purpose and content of the program. Some shows, like *What's My Line?*, develop a format that becomes their identifying signature. Even so, the format is only a vehicle for the transmission of the content; it does not make the show what it is.

Format is only loosely tied to program typology. It can be markedly different between shows of the same type. The *Jack Paar Show*,

[2] In discussing and describing program types and individual programs, both religious and secular, we will treat only national programs, network or distributed on film, that readers of this book might reasonably be expected to see and study.

Person to Person and *Open End* all center on conversation by "celebrities." Both Paar and *Open End* use static staging with participants seated in a studio. Yet the grouping of performers, the sets, the lighting, and the handling of cameras are so different on the two shows as to constitute two kinds of format. *Person to Person* is radically different from either of the others. It interviews persons in their homes, roving from room to room during the conversation, showing the subjects in their natural habitat, as it were.

The treatment of subject matter determines the format a program will assume on the air. If the Broadway play *The Andersonville Trial* should ever be presented on television, it might be adapted for the medium, but it would still be a play. However, the subject of the work, the trial of Henry Wirz, could also be treated in lecture form— by either a historian or a lawyer; in a discussion; or by means of an interview with someone who is an authority on the trial.

It is true, of course, that programs may be designed on the basis of format, and content subordinated to form. *Playhouse 90* was drama. Only plays were acceptable program content; but it should be noted that this limitation did not circumscribe the subjects a playwright could write about. *Continental Classroom* is always a lecture, *Meet the Press* a group interviewing an individual. In neither case is there a limitation on what may be said about the subject at hand. Westerns, too, are based on format. In addition, content is inflexibly confined to a single formula plot, and characters are stereotypes.

Format in Religious Programs

Some of the better-known religious programs consciously subordinate format to content. *Frontiers of Faith* uses a dramatic form when it wants to tell stories of human conflict that illustrate religious truths. At times it may present leading religious thinkers talking about vital issues. Sometimes it is a documentary, showing people at work in church and community. For a part of each broadcast season, it is a discussion program. Sometimes it uses a variety format to present religious music and dance.

Look Up and Live runs the gamut from problem drama to pure variety. It is closely akin to *Omnibus* in the range of its intellectual interest and its flexibility in both content and format. Series by series, and even week by week, *Look Up and Live* adopts whatever format suits its immediate purpose.

Off to Adventure[3] is a documentary. It shows people living and working in their own environments. The fact that it is shot on location and presents people and events as they are limits the possibilities for variety in format. However, the treatment of subject matter does vary from program to program, depending upon the situations being filmed.

Among programs in which format is paramount, and content must be shaped to suit it, are *The Eternal Light, This Is the Life, Talkback*, and the talks by Bishop Fulton J. Sheen. The first two are dramas. *Talkback* uses two formats in a single program, a dramatic skit followed by discussion. Bishop Sheen never varies his performance. He stands before the camera in his robes and talks directly to the audience, but he employs a varied and formidable array of persuasive techniques to influence his viewers.

Religious programs aim at communicating ideas and values more frequently than they do at illustrating situations and behavior. Therefore, it is well to develop objectives and content before determining what format will be used in performances. Once you know what you want to do, format will follow in due course, with the decision hinging on the question of what type of program will best communicate the chosen message to the desired audience.

All too often, religious programs are planned the other way around. A station offers a council of churches a spot for a "devotional" program, meaning a rotation of speakers with church music for filler. Automatically, the offer is accepted and the speakers begin to appear and to speak their unconnected pieces without serious consideration having been given to (1) what such a program will mean to the religious life of the community; (2) what *ought* to be said on the particular station at the time being offered; (3) what audience the program will reach—if any. Another method of programming that is in vogue is for a council program committee to decide Jones

---

[3] *Off to Adventure* is available free for broadcasting locally. Order from the Broadcasting and Film Commission, National Council of the Churches of Christ in the U. S. A., 475 Riverside Drive, New York 27, N. Y.

would make a good interviewer. The not-too-unwilling Jones then finds himself interviewing on television without anyone having asked the fundamental question: Interviewer of whom, for what purpose?

How to Decide What Needs to Be Done

Do not go on the air for the prestige it will give to your church or to your council or to certain selected clergymen; nor because the station offers time so it may report to the Federal Communications Commission that it is presenting religion as a public service. Broadcast only if you have something worthwhile to say to the people of your community and if you can say it in terms that the people will listen to and understand. That does not mean that you reach for the lowest intellectual plateau among your viewers, as do the mass-audience entertainment shows. It does require that you may have to modify your idea of what is "good for the audience" to conform with what the audience thinks is "good," a compromise that is always necessary in the communication of ideas, since we can enter the consciousness of the audience member only through reference to his experience.

The Program Committee

The television program committee for a council of churches should be made up of persons who are broadly representative of the interests of the community. It should include laymen and laywomen as well as clergymen. (The Broadcasting and Film Commission of the National Council of Churches finds it advantageous to have clergy and laity in about equal numbers on program committees.) Once organized, this committee needs to address itself to seven tasks. It should: (1) study the needs and interests of the people of the particular community, determining what is going on in their lives that religion can and should speak to via television; (2) set the goals for Protestant broadcasting in that community; (3) audition proposed programs (whether initiated by themselves or others), considering them in the light of the agreed goals; (4) decide how many programs of what type should be broadcast under the auspices of the council; (5) make general plans for each series of programs, leaving the preparation and production of individual broadcasts to a qualified producer; (6) approve the producer's budget for each program and supervise its expenditure; (7) conduct policy relations with stations, leaving performance arrangement to be handled by program producers.

The detailed analysis of programming suggested above and in other sections of this chapter is a first step toward effective broadcasting. The second step is to work out a clear, written agreement with the station delineating the responsibilities of both parties in the production, promotion, and evaluation of any programs that are to be aired. This is the only defensible method of conducting station relations. It will help to avoid misunderstandings that may lead to recriminations. More important, it will place control of programming where it belongs, in the hands of the religious bodies of the community rather than under the oversight of the station. The station will almost certainly be more inclined to have religious programs deal in trivia that have what it considers to be mass audience appeal than to have a faithful presentation of the gospel that may be counted upon to offend some segment of viewers.

It is unnecessary and inadvisable to conform to the view that religious programs should be designed to reach the largest possible audience at all times. Bowing to this dictum of the industry may win the temporary success of getting on the air, but its long-range effects will be disastrous. First, it is a surrender to the viewpoint that places the church in the position of condoning the use of television primarily for mass appeal entertainment. Second, it gives station managers who may know nothing about Christianity and the church the power to decide the standards and methods under which the message of the church shall be presented. Third, it is a betrayal of the many audiences—perhaps a majority of the people—who would like to detach themselves from the mass, who would be pleased to receive from television something they are not now getting, something that can be measured in qualitative rather than in quantitative terms.

We want, by all means, to be on friendly terms with the management of the stations through which we broadcast. We want also to work with them on terms of mutual respect. We can hardly respect ourselves if we abandon responsibility for presenting faithfully the message of the gospel by allowing secular agencies to gain control of what the church is to say. Most station managers will, naturally, suggest that religious programs conform to the standards and practices of the commercial shows. Few will resist if they are confronted by opposition from religious organizations that is coupled with a lively, imaginative program plan. None will have respect for the religious group that meekly knuckles under and distorts its own message just for the sake of getting on the air.

Analysis of the Community

The periodic community analyses made by the program committee need to be specific and to originate in "grass roots" testimony. The committtee should have before it the issues and ideas that are agitating other units of the council. The committee members should call upon responsible persons in all walks of life to help them determine the particular pressures, problems, and religious needs of the various people in the community as of a particular year, month, and week. The pressing ideas and events that are "in motion" in the community are the raw material from which to shape religious telecasts.

Assuming the broadcast season to run from September to June, a yearly analysis and the concomitant program planning can best be done in a planning institute of at least two days in length, held in the early spring. All of the next season's broadcasting, except special events, should be blocked out that far in advance in order to allow for adequate preparation of the individual programs.

Setting Goals

Goals should be concrete: "To emphasize the sanctity of the human personality." "How to deal with the frustrations and loneliness of the 'middle years.'" "To interpret adolescent development in terms of the Christian gospel." "To help our children understand children of other cultures, so they may not think them strange and hostile." "To develop emotional identification between audience members and Christian missionaries and thus foster support of missions."

All of the foregoing have been used as statements of purpose for religious programs. Note that all of these goals are broad enough to permit differing theological viewpoints to take their particular positions and to make their specific witnesses. It is essential to Protestant broadcasting to give the opportunity for a variety of interpretations of beliefs, ideas, and issues; but this is no excuse for the objectives of our programming to stray from the fundamental truths on which all Christians agree. The ultimate goal of all our broadcasting is the communication of the content of the gospel. This content is the good news that "God was in Christ reconciling the world unto himself." Out of this affirmation have come the moving ideas of Christian life. God "reconciling the world" is something that has happened, that is still happening. It is the point of contact between the divine and everything human. Christ crucified—and risen; that is always the central message, but it is not esoteric. In the word of reconciliation it comes into force in everyday life. God is dealing with "the world"; the gospel is directed to the stuff of human existence. The revelation, the judgment, justification, transformation by grace are a part of human experience, not set over against it. Therefore, no human experiences or aspirations are taboo for analysis and interpretation in our broadcasting if we seek their meaning in relation to God's reconciling will.

This kind of delineation of the underlying viewpoint, faith, and method of Christianity is necessary as a guide for any sustained television and radio ministry in a community. The program committee members should be continually seeking a fresh grasp of the philosophy of life and faith that they hope to have grow in the minds and hearts of their audience. What are those things held precious by Christians? What are the central experiences of the Christian life? What are the major strategies of Christianity that need to be communicated? What is the Christian interpretation of the events that are rushing at people; the Christian judgment of the decisions people are making? These are a few of the major questions worthy of consideration as the committee seeks the means to awaken faith in the viewers and to deepen their commitment and witness to the faith.

Programming to Achieve Your Goals

Once the fundamentals have been agreed to, the committee is ready to proceed to the next step, the choice of programs that will carry out basic objectives. These programs may originate locally, they may enter the community via a network, as does *Frontiers of Faith*, or they may be filmed series, as are *Off to Adventure* and *Talk-back*. Whatever their source, they should be aired in your community only if they fulfill the aims laid down by the program committee. Do not let outsiders do your programming for you. However wise and skillful they may be, they do not know your community and its needs. By all means use good outside resources, such as the programs distributed by the National Council of Churches, when you can. They will lighten your work. Sometimes they will be of a type or a quality that is beyond your local resources. But do not use outside programs automatically, just because they are easily obtainable.

How can you be reasonably sure a series will help you achieve your objectives? First, by writing out a simple statement of the specific purpose of each series of programs and of each individual program. Second, by planning the programs in accordance with the purposes. If you are using filmed programs, examine each one before broadcast to make sure it is suitable for your ends. Find out from the source what is going to be on network shows you are endorsing. If you are producing your own series, the ideational content of each program within the series should be described for the guidance of the production staff. This kind of planning can take place even before the format for the programs has been chosen.

Following are the preliminary statements of purpose proposed by the *Look Up and Live* planning committee for the programs in the series, "The Seeking Years." The objective of the series was to apply the criteria of the gospel to the struggle of youth to attain maturity. These statements were first discussed by the committee members. Then they were turned over to writers to be used as guide lines in the preparation of script treatments. Notice that the statements are in the form of *ideas*; they are not concerned with the specifics of format and scripts. Even in Statement 2, the committee—which must have had some thoughts on the matter—rightly left the choice of "specific struggle" to the writer, who must develop it out of the personalities of his characters.

1. The struggle of a Negro youth whether to follow a path of non-violent or militant action in the fight for integration. Various conflicting

pressures, fears, and problems confronting persons involved in this decision should be explored.

Theologically, there should be involved in this portrayal the themes of crucifixion and resurrection. Resurrection lies beyond crucifixion. A person is involved in crucifixion, that is the betrayal of God's love and action, whichever course he is to follow. He is torn among self-righteousness, idolatry, escape, and self-centeredness. The affirmation that resurrection lies beyond crucifixion should be involved, which is that victory comes as the result of God's initiative, not simply because a person makes the right choices. (The foregoing statement became the basis of James Benjamin's drama of segregation in the church, which Jack Gould, television critic of the *New York Times,* called "a small masterpiece in its searching understanding of race relations, in its shining integrity and compassion, in its absorbing challenge to the conscience of anyone who professes a religious faith.")

2. The struggle of a teen-ager for independence and maturity in the face of overprotective parents. A specific struggle should be explored, not necessarily resolved, in giving an answer to the problem. The tensions, guilt feelings, and escapes should be illuminated through the program.

Theologically, this program should explore the relationship of persons to each other and to God. The child's destiny is not ultimately in the hands of parents, but in the hands of God. Parents are not the final object of faith of the child. Rather, the child and the parents are to trust each other to God.

3. The struggle of a youth over a conflict in values between what he is taught and what he observes (the double standard). How are decisions to be made—by what is taught or by what is observed as practice? What are the struggles which arise when the duplicity is detected? The program should suggest an understanding of the nature of man through which the conflict is to be handled.

Theologically, the program should deal with the recognition that the youth also stands in need of forgiveness for his self-righteousness. A new level of awareness of his own self-righteousness which enables him to handle duplicity without condoning it will be presented. The real loyalty is to persons rather than to principles. Above all, loyalty is to Christ as Person rather than as principle. The hope is that in this loyalty one can be freed of both duplicity and self-righteousness.

4. The struggle over handling sins and limitations. Is it to forget the past, to assume everybody else is doing the same thing (Kinsey), by

feeling unworthy in the presence of "good" people? Or is it by knowing the reality of forgiveness from God? A specific illustration of wrong should be explored, concentrating not so much on the specific act as on the manifestations of shame, guilt, and failure. A struggle through the problem of sin to know the reality of forgiveness and restored relationships should be portrayed.

Theologically, the parable of the prodigal son theme would be the base, not simply as a story but as it deals with human problems.

Notice how closely the proposed content of the *Look Up and Live* programs is linked to the audience sought—teen-agers. There has been criticism of *Look Up and Live*—by adults only—because the planners have insisted upon dealing with teen-age problems in teen-age idiom. Such is the fate of a program that is really successful in reaching the audience it seeks; other audiences are turned away. On the other hand, it is questionable whether the program that reaches a multiplicity of audiences can leave any ideas of significance with any of them.

Your programs "as broadcast" should grow out of a careful appraisal of the interrelationships between your goals, the audience to be reached, and what needs to be said to reach that audience. The committee should consider questions such as these: What does the audience know about the subject chosen? What more does it need to know? How much can the audience assimilate of what we want to say? What must be done to prepare them for the viewpoint to be presented? What belief do we want to change; what action do we want the audience members to take? How can the action be most clearly defined? What is the most vivid means of presenting the subject matter?

Here, at last, is the place where the committee, in consultation with the producer, picks a format.

PROGRAM FORMS

The complexities of television production plus the reluctance of local stations to provide adequate time for camera rehearsals usually make it necessary for religious programs to use simple formats. This limitation is not necessarily a handicap. Programs that are not overloaded with production frills give the individuals who are participating a chance to shine, and it is personalities that are the life-blood of television. One can fill a page with the names of well-known television personalities for every one listing of a program like *Playhouse 90* or *Play of the Week* that has gained fame as a *production* rather than as a showcase for a performer. Even when programs are identified in the public mind by titles rather than by the names of stars, they generally owe their popularity to one or more performers. What would *What's My Line?* be worth without the clever members of the panel who appear week after week and give the show its character? Or *Today* without Garroway? Or *Meet the Press* without an endless supply of willing politicians?

The entertainment and sports worlds quickly developed television personalities. So, too, did politics, education, the press, and even the bar, albeit more slowly. Medicine alone has failed to provide starters in the television-personality sweepstakes. Religion, in spite of its concern with public communication by minister, priest, and rabbi, has fallen sadly behind. Only Bishop Fulton J. Sheen, Bishop James A. Pike, and Billy Graham have been able to attain national recognition as television personalities.

Persons are just as important in local programming as they are on the networks. They can be featured in many types of programs. A personality shines brightest and probably has the greatest impact on a one-man show. Furthermore, a one-man program is the least expensive, easiest, and most foolproof production you can put on— if you have the man! There's the rub, of course. It takes great skill to do a one-man show, plus the dedication to give the necessary ten to fifteen hours of preparation and rehearsal required for each appearance. But—if you have the man—the field is wide open for adult Christian education.

Types of Programs

We will describe only those programs which are feasible for a council of churches to produce at small cost and with the talent apt to be available.

Lecture-Demonstration Programs. The first serious attempt to present college-level courses in religion via television was made by the Washington (D.C.) Church Federation. For several years they have presented a one-hour course in New Testament on Saturdays, garnering a weekly audience estimated at 85,000 persons. The instructor is Edward Bauman, chaplain of American University. College credit is available and a small number of viewers have registered for it. The program takes the form of a lecture before a class in the studio. Bauman uses usual classroom demonstration aids, such as a blackboard. Sometimes he has a guest teacher whom he interviews.

There is no reason why other communities should not follow the example of Washington with equal or even better success. We suggest that adult religious educational programs be thirty minutes long, as are *Continental Classroom* and *Sunrise Semester*. A one-hour lecture is too long in the classroom; it is excessively long on television.

Educational programs should be conducted by professional teachers who know their subjects well and who will take the pains necessary to give a *course*, not just a series of talks. Washington Church Federation has the ideal arrangement, a co-operative venture between the council of churches and an accredited college or university. Courses can then be offered for credit. But if your community does not have a college, why not turn to a public school teacher or to a director of religious education who is skilled in teaching adults to lead the program? Your council might also issue a certificate for completion of required work.

Adults enroll by the thousands in courses in Bible, church history, social action, religion and personality, and similar topics, taught in churches, often with amateur leadership. There should be an audience available in almost any community for such courses taught on television by professionals.

Interviews. The interview is a simple program to produce, but it is not simple to prepare. It can be vividly exciting or deadly dull, all depending upon the people who participate.

A good interviewer is a rare jewel, indeed. He must understand people. He must like them. He must like to talk to them. He must be able to draw out comparative strangers on short notice. His sensitivity to his audience needs to be equal to his sensitivity to the person he is interviewing. He must know what in the person being interviewed will interest the audience, what will bore them, what will shock them, what will offend them. He must be willing to be self-effacing, always subordinating himself to his subject. He must be able to frame questions that will (1) draw his guest out and (2) give his guest the greatest possible scope for his answer. There is nothing worse than the interviewer who says: "Let's see, Dr. Brown, you took charge of the mission hospital at X in 1938 when two out of three people there suffered from malaria and you have spent most of your career since then developing methods of malaria control until now almost nobody gets that disease. Isn't that right?" The rueful doctor can then grind his teeth and mutter, "Right."

An interview needs to be carefully prepared for but not rehearsed, otherwise it will lose its spontaneity. The interviewer should have in mind the questions he wants to ask, but he need not reveal them to his subject. It will do no harm for the interviewer to have notes which he can refer to from time to time to remind him of issues he wants to raise, as Mike Wallace does; but such notes should be used sparingly. Under no circumstances should the interviewee be permitted to read prepared answers or even to work from notes. It will destroy the sense of an encounter between two persons and will make the program stale and flat. Some people may argue that it is necessary for the person being interviewed to have notes in order to quote facts accurately. Not so! If the interviewee knows his subject, he will be exact enough in his answers. Many people think they must be absolutely accurate in such things as the quoting of figures in order to prove their competence. Actually, overexactitude gets in the way of comprehension by the audience. Tell the audience that 67.43 per cent of the population of Y are illiterate and they will not even hear the figure, much less remember it. But say, "About seven out of every ten people can't read"; they will hear and remember that.

If the interviewee is given the questions in advance, he will show it, and spoil the naturalness of the conversation. Of course, the questions should be about things he can be expected to be able to discuss. Within that restriction, the more surprised he is by a question, the better his performance is likely to be. To watch a man think, grope for an answer, and finally get it is an absorbing experience for the viewer. The interviewer should not try to trap his companion, nor need he reveal his own erudition. It is his job to ask the "dumb" questions, things he may be expected to know but which the audience members will be curious about because they have not met the interviewee. Having learned everything he can about his guest, the interviewer will do well, when he gets on the air, to visualize himself as having casually encountered a stranger in a hotel lobby and of being in the process of sounding the person out as to who he is, what he does, and what his interests are.

The interviewer should be careful not to hold the floor for long periods. The person being interviewed should be allowed to talk within the first fifteen to twenty seconds after the interview is under way. The interviewee should be given ample opportunity, commensurate with the importance of the question, to reply to each query, but care should be taken that he does not make speeches. Then it will no longer be an interview.

A simple set without intruding props or busy backgrounds is best for an interview. The person being interviewed should be placed full face to the close-up camera and should be on the screen the majority of the time. The interviewer can be back to camera, can sit unobtrusively in profile to the camera, or can even be off camera. One of the better interview setups is that used by Mike Wallace. One camera is on the person being interviewed and can range from medium shots to tight close-ups. Another camera can do the same for Wallace to show him asking questions or reacting to what is being said. This setup will also permit a two shot on either camera, if only two cameras are used.

The inexperienced interviewer is liable to make two mistakes, either one of which can be fatal to the program. He may fail to prepare himself fully on his respondent's background, experiences, personality traits, tastes, and other pertinent things, and thus be unable to ask the right questions. Second, he may fail to narrow the subject matter to a compass that can be handled in the time available. In our imaginary example of Dr. Brown, an interviewer might draw from him vivid details about what malaria does to people and how the disease is controlled, other information about the doctor and his life being subordinated or disregarded. Or, if the scientific material is dull or too complicated, it might be confined to one or two questions and the bulk of the interview given over to discovering Dr. Brown's beliefs and revealing the facets of his personality.

Interviews usually have one of two purposes. An interview may be documentary in character, designed to present authoritative facts and records of experiences through the testimony of a person who has firsthand knowledge of them. Such interviews are interpretative, reportorial in character: "I was there." "I saw what happened." "I know the people." "I have a part in the event." Facts are the *raison d'être* of this kind of interview, but its success still depends upon the vitality and intrinsic interestingness of the person being interviewed.

A second type of interview is all personality. Its purpose is to introduce the viewer to a Christian who is accomplishing things in the arena of life. Distinguished visitors to the community are obvious subjects for this type of interview. The person interviewed need not be famous. A school teacher who has the respect and love of her pupils, a carpenter who sees his trade as a Christian vocation, a wise and loving mother who appreciates the trials and rewards of family living—people like these teamed with a skilled interviewer can fascinate the audience. Such interviews are personal witness adapted to the mass media.

Sometimes, but rarely, the two types of interview can be combined if the respondent is a person who has interesting factual material to report and who can also make a vivid personal witness to the meaning of Christianity. An interview with Albert Schweitzer would epitomize an opportunity of this sort.

Discussions. There are three elements that are vital for a successful discussion program: (1) a good topic that deals with a problem that is important to the audience; (2) interesting people who know what they are talking about and who can conduct an intelligent, spirited conversation; (3) a clash of viewpoints, not in the sense of a debate where positions are fixed and unalterable, but a bringing to bear on the problem all important shades and differences of opinion.

One mistake frequently made in discussions is to pick a "best" solution and point all of the argument and interpretation toward it. If you are talking about a vital issue, seldom can you expect to solve it in thirty minutes of conversation that includes a variety of views. The best that can be expected is to have the participants point up the problems, define the terms of meeting them, and suggest some possible and *important* solutions and the means to attain them. Such an "open-ended" procedure is best for the viewer, too. It gives him the opportunity to exercise his judgment, find his own truth. If, infrequently, there is an open-and-shut solution that the participants can agree upon, it should, of course, be presented to the audience.

The procedure for planning and managing discussion programs is described in detail in the example of *Frontiers of Faith* in Chapter 5. Kinescopes of the programs may be obtained from the National Council of Churches' Broadcasting and Film Commission for study. After you have outlined a series of discussion programs, and before you go into production, do three things: (1) Sample a few people in your target audience to make sure you have chosen subjects that are important to the viewers; they may have only institutional importance to your organization. (2) Make a list of the basic issues to be raised under each topic, again to make sure they are important enough to sustain a discussion. (3) Try to set down the terms and concepts that may come up in the discussions that will need to be defined and explained for the benefit of the audience. Be sure these definitions are included in the background papers, so all the participants may be in agreement on terms.

Discussion programs should be played in severely simple sets; so the attention of the viewer will be centered on the participants. Group the performers so they will seem, when seen by the camera, to be in the informal array usually assumed by persons in conversation with each other. Do not put them in a straight line and pan across them, or in a V shape, even though these settings make camera coverage easy. Do not put them on a judge's bench with name plates in front of them, or hide them behind bouquets or potted plants. Be sure the camera follows the conversation and that it does not fall into a rotating pattern of long shot, medium shot, close-up. Do not stay in close-up all the time, either. It is a good idea to use two shots and three shots for variation and to show the whole group in a wide shot from time to time to keep the audience aware of the participants as a group.

Documentaries. The term "documentary" is used loosely to describe any kind of program, other than a news broadcast, that conveys information about human problems or activities. This is a mistaken use of the term. A documentary is based upon facts—persons in action, documents, events, ways of living. Usually, a documentary is reportorial; it deals with its material at the source, i.e., movies of migrants herded into substandard housing on a farm. This reporting, though, is not in the form of an impartial news summary. The documentary lets the people involved in the action it is covering speak for themselves; it shows action instead of talking about it. This does not mean that the good documentary is necessarily partisan. Like the good news story, it can tell both—or many—sides. It may not seek to persuade, may merely expound and let the viewer make up his mind. On the other hand, a documentary may be frankly persuasive, may represent the passionate beliefs of its producer, and it may still be a good documentary. The important things about a documentary are that it shall deal honestly with whatever situations come to hand and shall have a theme that gives the program unity. Usually, this theme is a great problem or a great achievement that will touch people both emotionally and intellectually. The objective of the program is to involve viewers in the issues being interpreted, so they will participate actively in the working out of solutions.

Before attempting to produce documentaries yourself, study some of the better ones on the air. Many stations are still carrying *Victory at Sea.* One of the best, Edward R. Murrow's *See It Now,* is off the air, but you can rent prints of many of the programs from your local film library. A good *See It Now* for study is the story of Clinton, Tennessee. The American Broadcasting Company series for Bell and Howell has some exciting new techniques that may become standard documentary procedure. They are worthy of study. There are also many documentary motion pictures not made for television that may be studied to learn good and bad methods of documentary production. Some good ones are *Nanook of the North, Louisiana Story, The Plow That Broke the Plains, The City, The River,* and *The Procession.*

Do not be discouraged when you look at a program like *See It Now* and realize the enormous cost and effort that went into producing the most simple interview. Of course, you cannot duplicate Edward R. Murrow's resources, but you can reach for his sensitive understanding of his subjects and you can duplicate his rigorous standards of truthful reporting.

With a little imagination and a lot of hard work, you can assemble documentary material on your own community. Where Murrow had to take his cameras to his subjects, you can bring your subjects to the studio. Perhaps you cannot take motion pictures of the sites and actions you want to document, but by using good still pictures or slides taken especially for the program and moving them in rapid succession, you can get some illusion of action. There are all the visual devices listed in Chapters 5, 6, and 8 to help you; and you can probably invent more that will fit your needs.

Admittedly, the documentary is probably the most ambitious and complicated program a council of churches should attempt. For instance, you must have a written script. You must rehearse until every part has fallen perfectly into place. You must do extensive research. You must have money to spend for preparation. Yet, if you want to lay bare a sore spot in your community and bring it under Christian judgment, if you want to show the church in action, if you want to treat a social issue in depth, if you want to give people the chance to talk directly to people, you will find the documentary one of the most effective programs in your repertoire.

Musical Programs. A choir standing in formation and singing for long or short periods is about as dull a video program as a religious organization can present. Programs of religious music are something else. They can be entertaining, instructive, inspirational. They should be designed around soloists and small instrumental and choral groups. A large group number is permissible here and there. There should be a great deal of movement with quick changes from number to number, set to set, person to person. Musical programs can be heightened in effect by the use of dramatic lighting and imaginative sets and costumes. Watch some of the better musical variety shows for production ideas.

The quality of the performers and of the music played and sung is the ultimate test of this kind of program. If you do not have top-notch performers who have been well rehearsed for television, stay away from this type of program. You may be tempted, too, to get time after the local hillbilly show for a rousing gospel hymn sing. Resist it! Do not represent the gospel with shoddy music any more than you would with shoddy ideas in a sermon.

Variety Programs. A variety show is one in which a series of more or less interconnected "acts" follow each other in sequence. Usually each episode has music in it or is opened and closed by music. The musical program discussed above is, technically, a variety program. A program of religious dance interspersed with readings would be variety.

A formal service of worship falls in the variety category. We do not advocate the transference of church services to the television screen. They are for corporate participation, not for spectator viewing. No one has yet developed a "form" whereby a person may worship via television, and many of us are doubtful whether the sacramental experience that is the beginning of worship can take place before a television screen. On the other hand, if we believe that God is not only the object but the initiator of worship, that our souls respond to His promptings, then we cannot deny that television may become one of the sacramental vehicles through which He reveals Himself. We have few words of wisdom about how worship can be experienced through television, except to advise you to seek out the men of faith in your community who can at least interpret the *meaning* of worship. Give them the opportunity to experiment and to exchange notes with others who are experimenting, too. Let them put all the symbols and forms and words and acts we use in worship under the closest scrutiny and severest test. They may well discover that television defeats worship. But unless many of us inquire and experiment and alter old forms to fit new conditions we find in this new art, we shall never know with what power God chooses to move through this medium to seize upon our hearts.

Other Program Types. Drama is too well known as a form to need explanation here. You will need script, a competent cast and director, and much rehearsal to produce it well. Even then it may not have the impact of first-person witness.

Religious news has been largely neglected on television. There should be room for authoritative commentaries modeled on the better general news commentaries.

Spot announcements may be used effectively for the promotion of such community-wide programs as One Great Hour of Sharing, and Share Our Surplus, or to advertise events of general community interest. The most effective spots combine visual and audio content. Spots may be ten seconds, twenty seconds or a minute long, depending upon time availability.

Children's Programs

Any religious program for children would be expected to have an educational objective. First and foremost, though, it must be entertaining. An adult, if he thinks the subject is important enough, may stay with a program that begins to sag in interest; children never will. They require a high level of attention-compelling interest at all times.

Although children will watch adult shows indiscriminately, when it comes to programs at their own level, they are selective. Fifteen-year-olds will turn away from material pitched at a twelve-year mentality; young children will become bored with material that is over their heads and will leave. There is no such thing as an across-the-boards, mass-appeal children's show. Each series will self-select an age and intellectual level, whether it is meant to or not.

The children's program needs three basic elements: an idea or concept fitted to a particular age; a pleasant, lively, likable performer (or performers) who understands children of that age; pacing that is correct for the intellectual ability of the target audience. A knowledge of language contexts and vocabulary peculiar to the audience age is also essential. In all this, it is better to aim a little above the group level than to talk down to the children. The audience that thinks it is being patronized melts away fast.

Children will be satisfied with simple forms of programming if they are learning something new. They learn best when you combine something familiar with something new, using the former to lead into the latter.

For several years, this writer has produced *Off to Adventure*, a series of fifteen-minute missionary education programs on film. The program seeks to familiarize fourth, fifth, and sixth grade children in Canada and the United States with children of other cultures and with their customs. The twin themes of the series are (1) that all persons are brothers in the eyes of God and should be in their own minds and hearts, and (2) that Christians the world over believe, think, and act much alike, and strive for the same ends. In spite of meticulous attention given to details that will guarantee the authenticity of ideas, settings and action, it is not easy to accomplish the aims of *Off to Adventure* through programs shot on location in such widely separated places as Japan, Hawaii, Alaska, rural Quebec Province in Canada, New York City, Puerto Rico, Trinidad, Ghana, Angola, the Congo, and South Africa. Nearly every program presents people and situations that are new, strange, even bizarre from the standpoint of the majority of the children in the audience.

We use children as the common meeting ground, the something familiar. Children of the locality being studied are featured in almost all the programs. Sometimes a child from North America is introduced as a visitor to give contrast and to show how easily one may make friends with persons of unfamiliar cultures. We are careful to include other familiar things, such as schools, churches and Sunday schools, well-known sports and games, and families going about their everyday affairs. These things are our bridges to the unfamiliar.

We have learned to pace our programs much more slowly than is usual for entertainment shows. Sometimes adults complain about this slowness of movement and the fact that each program is relatively simple and is not overloaded with content—especially abstract ideas and concepts; but testing of children who view *Off to Adventure* shows that these techniques help them understand what is being shown and said.

We also repeat and repeat and repeat, both in the visual and the audio. The hardest thing to gauge is just how much explaining to do and when to let the action carry the story without amplification. In the effort to make the religious message explicit, we tend to err on the side of explaining too much rather than too little. Yet wherever possible we try to stimulate the children to use their own imaginations, to work out for themselves the implications for their own lives of what they are seeing and hearing. We attempt to have the participants in the programs be relaxed and natural in their action and speech and to point their performances at the individual child viewer.

These educational principles and the production techniques used to achieve them can be applied to advantage in any series of children's programs. *Off to Adventure* has used them successfully to explain such complicated things as Buddhism, Shinto, why we have missions to Eskimos and Africans, and the meaning of Christian brotherhood.

STATION RELATIONS AND PROGRAMMING

The owners of the broadcasting facilities—the transmitters, the studios, and the equipment—do not own the right to broadcast or to use the frequencies assigned to their stations. Under the Federal Communications Act, they are licensed by the Government to broadcast in "the public interest, convenience or necessity." They enjoy the privilege of being on the air and of making a profit from their operations at the sufferance of the people of the United States. When the people who control the stations and networks give over virtually all the broadcast time to the presentation of commercial entertainment shows and fail to schedule public service programs representative of the civic and cultural interests of their communities, or schedule such programs only in undesirable time segments, they literally disobey the law.

On the other hand, there is a phase of this matter of the provision and use of public service time that should not be neglected either by the stations or by civic organizations such as councils of churches. This is the responsibility of stations and networks to maintain programming standards that will not permit the debasement either of public taste or of television as a form of art. Ideally, such standards should be applied to *all* programs. In fact, except to screen out the obscene, the salacious, and material offensive to the sponsor, they are not applied to commercial programs. It does not follow, however, that because stations err in judging the suitability of commercial shows, they should also sin in regard to public service programs.

No community organization, however prominent, has a *right* to time on the air simply because it desires it and asks for it. No station manager is justified in granting time for programs that have trivial aims or that are planned in haphazard fashion. He owes it to his audience to demand programs that are interesting, that present a valid viewpoint, that will be produced skillfully. Only those organizations that are able and willing to offer the audience something worth looking at should have the privilege of using the people's air.

Therefore, the cardinal principle in station relationships is to come to the station with something worth putting on the air. The best way to convince a station manager that you can fulfill this requirement is to present him with a detailed plan for a series of programs that will be of interest and service to a specific audience. Include the purpose, audience to be reached, number and description of the programs, production plans, rehearsal requirements, sets, promotion plans, and at least one sample script.

Don't just tell him about it! Put your plan on paper. Don't mail it! Take it in and sit with him while he reads it. The station representative will have some questions in mind about any program. Here is a plan for presenting program proposals, together with the questions it should answer for the station manager or the program director:

Information About the Program	Questions It Should Answer for the Station
The Idea	
State it briefly, in one page if possible.	Is this a *program* idea? Can it be translated into shows?
Title	
Make it catchy, no more than four words long, so it will fit into newspaper listings.	
Audience	
State it specifically: "Families in first ten years of married life." Suggest a broadcast day and time.	What audience do they have in mind? Will the program fit the audience? How big an audience? What time?

State your *purpose*—what you want to accomplish with the audience. Tell what viewers will gain from watching the program. Tell *why* you think they will watch.

Will the programs interest our viewers?

Format

Describe the format or formats.

Do they have an effective way to present their idea on the air?

Individual Programs

List the title and central idea and give a brief description of each program. Ask for a specific number of programs—for example, a twenty-six week series—not for an indefinite assignment of time. State the program length—fifteen minutes, thirty minutes. Tell how many times a week you want to be on the air.

Are there enough program ideas to sustain a series? How long are the programs? How long is the series?

Production

Describe sets, props, visuals, etc., that will be needed. Indicate who should be responsible for providing them.

What will be their physical needs? Who will provide sets? How elaborate must they be? Will the sets and the production fit the studio limitations?

Describe any special production needs and problems, such as shooting of motion picture footage or taking of still pictures on location.

What production problems will there be?

Propose a rehearsal schedule, including necessary camera rehearsal. Designate number of cameras needed.

How much studio and crew time will each show require? How will rehearsals fit into the crew schedule? Will they require overtime?

Personnel

List the producer and all persons who will work under him in behalf of your organization. Suggest the director you will like to have the station assign to the series.

Who will be responsible for the planning and production of the programs? Is this group reliable? Do they know their jobs? Which director will work best with them?

Promotion

Outline your promotion plans for the series, including what use you intend to make of each publicity medium available to you, such as TV spots, newspapers, posters, church bulletins, etc. Detail any help you expect from the station publicity department. Name the person who will be in charge of promotion for you.

What will they do to create an audience for the series? Will their publicity plans gear in with the station's promotional program?

Evaluation

Detail your plans for securing audience response. Will you offer a premium to persons who write in? Will you make an audience survey? Content analysis? Other research?

How will the station know who is listening? What methods will be used to discover weak spots in the programs and to correct them?

Budget

State the things you are willing to pay for and what you expect the station to finance. You do not need to set a dollar figure, but you must be clear on how costs are to be met. Actual sums can be negotiated after the program has been accepted by the station.

How much will these programs cost the station?

A Summary to Guide Program Policies

All available research findings indicate that there are large potential audiences interested in watching religious television and that the people are widely varied in their personality, sociological status, interests, and beliefs. Reaching such a multidimensional audience requires imagination coupled with a detailed knowledge of each audience sought and the aims the programs are intended to serve. There is no limit to the diversity in programming that may be employed. Drama, discussion, teaching, reporting, interviewing, and every other program form may be expected to draw an audience as long as the subject matter is vital to the viewer and production is skillful and content interesting. In fact, without such variety in programming, religion will deprive itself of the opportunity to speak to a maximum number of people. Religion should aim to communicate with a diverse number of audiences, each of which must be attracted and held by a particular program aimed at its particular interests and needs.

Whatever programs religious organizations attempt, they should rationalize what they are doing. There should be an over-all strategy, and each program should have a clear reason for existence within the generalized framework of theory and purposes. Each program should also have a specific task to perform, one that can be written down in a statement of policy which defines exactly what the program is attempting to do and how its producers intend to go about it. Only through such detailed planning can the sponsoring agency have a yardstick against which to measure the program's results.

CHAPTER 5　Writing for Television

One of the prime weaknesses of locally produced television programs is that, however well thought out they may be, they are seldom written out. Yet the quality of any television program is never one iota better than the program's written content.[1]

Content that will communicate requires, first, the marshaling *on paper* of ideas about the program. These ideas then need to be translated by a writer into a combination of visual and auditory symbols (actions, words, sounds, music) that can be assimilated by a director and his cast and, in turn, transmitted by them to an audience. The director cannot be expected to determine *how* a particular program should play unless a writer first shows him *what* is to be said and done. Unless the director and the performers have clear, concise instructions about what to say and do, they cannot be expected to give a workmanlike performance. A script is essential to their grasp of their responsibilities.

WRITING WITH PICTURES AND WORDS

When you write a television program, you must bear in mind every moment that you are working in a visual medium. Words and sounds are no less important than they are in any other form of communication; but they cannot alone communicate meaning as they do in radio, or as words do on the printed page. They must be linked to visible *action* to form a totality of expression such as occurs in every real-life encounter.

Since most amateurs are not accustomed to working out this audio-

---

[1] This statement applies, also, for discussion programs, which should have a written outline made at some point in the preparation of the program.

visual totality in the form of a script which can, in turn, be translated into people-to-people communication, it will be good practice
for you to test each of your ideas in visual terms. If you cannot visualize a line of action, the idea might better be abandoned and
something else substituted. A good way to prepare a first draft of a
television script is to work out a visual impression of each element
of the program in your mind, writing down a short description of
each mental picture as it develops.

This procedure is not as difficult as it seems. Most of us think in
pictorial terms. We use pictorial words to describe ideas. It is easier for
people to deal with concrete elements of experience than with abstract
principles. Probably no two people ever had the same abstract
thought. Yet, it is usually easy to find a semantic meeting ground in a
concrete illustration. If you doubt this, consider the method Jesus
used. The Parables illustrate the most profound philosophical truths
in pictorial terms that are readily understandable to the most simple-
minded men of all ages. Moreover, the Parables will *play* well. They
can be acted out successfully by Sunday school children. Jesus' use of
the bread and wine in the Last Supper was pictorially symbolic and
continues to be so to this day. He communicated abstract truths by
painting word pictures—really by relating little plays, e.g., the illustration of the salt, the lamp hid under a bushel, the woman searching for her lost coin, the sower at work, and many others.

A purist in visual methods might argue that the ideal television
program would require no words or sounds at all. The entire story
would be told in pictures that would communicate their meaning
beyond peradventure. The truth is, though, that words and sounds
—and, less frequently, music—are essential for the conveyance of
meaning, even in the presence of pictures. But they should be used
in relation to the pictures, doing what the picture cannot do alone in
a given situation. It is neither justifiable nor effective to use words
in place of a picture in a visual medium, nor to torture a picture
into doing something that words can do better.

How Words Are Used in Television

Words are an integral part of the image derived from any person-to-person confrontation, whether it be informal conversation, a

speech, interview, or discussion. In television programs where the visual element is dominant, words will be needed in most cases to supplement the picture, explaining the action, objects, or processes that are being shown. Words have three functions in a television script. They may *define, interpret,* or *extend* the pictorial image.

Definition is used when the audience may not be familiar with what is shown on the screen. For example, in a program on "God in Nature," beamed at children who live in the inner city and have never visited the country, it would be good practice to show a cow and have a narrator say, "This is a Jersey cow."

When and how to use definition is one of the thorniest problems a script writer faces. If you define in words something that is immediately intelligible to the viewer from the picture, he will feel you are talking down to him, will be annoyed and offended and may tune out. On the other hand, except for simple and generally known things, you cannot safely assume that the viewer has your knowledge of the objects or situations you are showing to him. This warning is especially pertinent for religious broadcasters. Terms, symbols, objects, and concepts that are commonly used in religious circles may be wrongly interpreted by the general television viewer or may have no meaning for him at all. It is a mistake to assume that the average viewer will recognize such objects as communion vessels, vestments, elements of worship, even so well known a ceremony as a service of baptism; or that he will be familiar with such terms as *the gospel, the church, redemption, salvation, sacrament, evangelism, mission*—even the generally understood word, *sin.*

Fortunately, because of the video element in television, its writers have a distinct advantage over writers for radio and public speech. People are much better able to comprehend the meaning of the unfamiliar if they see a picture of it than if they merely hear it explained. The ear is a notorious prevaricator, the eye less so.

Interpretation is used to give meaning to what is seen on the screen, in the context of the objectives of the particular program. Thus, in the example already cited, let us assume the children viewing the program know what a cow is. Then: Why this particular cow? If the story being told was that of how a 4-H clubber raises prize cattle as a project, the interpretation of the picture might be: "John's cow was his pride and joy."

Almost all pictorial material will benefit from interpretative supplementation, especially in religious programs, where the viewer, even though he thinks he understands what he is seeing, may doubt his ability to make a valid interpretation. On the other hand, you must take care that the audio does not fight the video, offering an interpretation that is not instantly apparent from the picture itself or, worse still, presenting some idea that is not in the picture at all. If the audio and video do not agree, the viewer will believe what he sees. He will reject spoken interpretations, concepts, and ideas that run counter to the picture.

By the same token, the viewer will accept as fact things that may not be true, if he thinks he sees them in a picture or if they are there but are not explained. Some years ago an aircraft carrier and a destroyer escort collided in the Atlantic. The bow of the carrier was damaged. The destroyer was sunk. A television news broadcast showed the carrier being warped into drydock at Brooklyn Navy Yard for repair. The narrator described how the carrier was damaged by being stuck by the destroyer, without explaining theories about the cause of the accident. Subsequent interviews with audience members revealed they were unanimously convinced that the commander of the destroyer had disobeyed orders and so run into the carrier. Actually, there was widespread speculation in newspapers that big ships in fleet maneuvers often disregard their smaller companions, and that the carrier may have crossed the designated path of the destroyer.

Carelessness or lack of responsibility in editing, suppression of pertinent pictorial material, or failure to give proper interpretation through the audio may distort the meaning of a picture story to the same degree that written text is subject to misinterpretation.

Words are used to *extend* the meaning of a picture or series of pictures through conversation between the characters, explaining action. Extension occurs in the conversation in discussion programs. In drama, this form of writing is known as dialogue. It is used in all forms of dramatic writing, be it for television, motion pictures, or the stage. Dialogue is pertinent when the action itself will not alone convey the meaning intended.

Relations between people are meaningful at two levels: (1) through the actions of one person toward another or toward a group, or the actions of a group toward a person, and (2) through what the person says as he acts or talks about his actions. Actions and words often belie each other in human encounter. They can do the same in drama, either purposely or because of ineptness in relating writing and action. The truism "actions speak louder than words" operates in public performance as well as in real life. What is done, or what the recipient of the action *thinks* is being done, has more influence upon the subject than do the words spoken. In the same vein, but vicariously through the actors, the viewer is influenced by his conception of the relationship of action to words as the program he is watching develops.

Sometimes it is instructive and entertaining just to watch somebody doing something without explanation. But most human actions where public communication is the aim would be meaningless, or would have their meaning distorted, if the characters did not explain themselves as they went along. Try to dramatize the biblical story of David and Goliath in pantomime and you will see how essential dialogue is to action. The scene where Saul offers his armor to David and the latter rejects it could not be understood by an audience without dialogue similar to this:

SAUL (*offering armor to* DAVID): Take my armor. It has protected me well in many a battle.

DAVID: No, my king.

SAUL (*angry*): There is no better in all Israel. Do you fear it is not stout enough? Then do not go to fight Goliath.

DAVID: I cannot go with these; for I am not used to them.[2]

Sound always accompanies action; is, in fact, a part of action. You should indicate to a director what sounds you want used. He will decide whether or not it is feasible to produce them. Sounds that tend to drown out dialogue, such as noise of machinery, may best be omitted, even though they add reality to a scene.

[2] I Sam. 17:39.

Be chary of writing *musical sequences* into your scripts. Music, at best, is a device to do something you did not have the ingenuity to accomplish with pictorial action and words. "Mood music" will seldom—if ever—arouse emotions in the viewer. They must be sparked by words and actions.

Music may be useful for thematic purposes, to introduce or close a program. It can be effective as background for pictorial sequences that do not require words. Quiet music can reinforce the serene beauty of a ship sailing a calm sea, and turbulent passages can quicken the reaction to a storm scene. The right quality of music, properly cued, can be used under dissolves from scene to scene to indicate passage of time or change of locale.

It is difficult to find music that is exactly right for a given purpose and to fit it into the production. It is not enough for you as the writer to indicate from time to time "background music" or "music bridge" and to leave the rest to the director. He should be told what you hope to achieve through music at a given point, what kind of music is needed, how it should be used. Better still, go to the music library and choose your own material. Then you can be reasonably sure it will meet your requirements.

We should not lose sight of the fact that the exigencies of religious broadcasting make it inevitable that many programs will not be prepared by a writer starting from scratch. They will be primarily talks or discussions. They will not require full scripts. But a writer is just as essential as for any other type of program.

In the first place, the performer cannot be expected to prepare his own program beyond what he is actually to say. Someone must then help him reorganize his material in a style suitable for television. Visualization must be developed that will legitimately fit the ideas being expressed. A format must be established and the program content fitted into the available time. Finally, the blueprint must be reduced to paper in script form for the guidance of the director.

In preparing such a program, you must remember that even the most dynamic speaker cannot be expected to hold an audience on television for long periods with a straight talk. It is well to keep in mind the question: What are they seeing now? Strive for interestings bits of action by the speaker that fit what he is saying. Have him use a blackboard to write down salient points and to keep them in the minds of the viewers. Look for visual devices: still pictures, motion picture clips, objects that will help tell the speaker's story. Remember that the face of the person presenting the program can be dramatically exciting and write in changes of expression and posture and other action that will help the story move. Even though you do not write what is finally to be said, it is still your function as script writer to think up what the viewers are to see. If you can develop a pictorial line of action, the director will catch it in his cameras.

WRITING THROUGH THE CAMERA'S EYES

Not only must you write in pictures for television; the pictures must be of a sort that can be picked up by the lenses of the camera and projected on the television screen. Space is a sharply limiting factor in television. The size of the studio determines size of sets, the working space available for action, and the variety and scope of camera movement. More importantly, the small, home television screen places limitations on the number of persons that should appear in a scene, the area the camera can cover, the depth of field, and the amount of detail that can be handled. Television is an "intimate" medium because the screen reproduces best intimate scenes. Figures that bulk large in brilliant detail on the big screen in a movie theater look like peas on the face of the tube in the living room. Television is small, not because the camera is more limited than the movie camera, but because the screen is small.

This size limitation is of transcendent importance in script writing. You must keep constantly in mind not only *what* the camera will see and transmit, but the *perspective* and *range* of the picture. The content of each picture or sequence must be of sufficient size to ensure instantaneous recognition by the viewer. You should have a definite purpose in mind for each picture, and you should compose the picture to accomplish that purpose. It is better television technique to concentrate on a small area where details will be clear than to cover a larger area where details may be lost.

Warning: Do not visualize pictures that have important subject matter in the outer 10 to 15 per cent of the frame area. Most receivers cut off this portion of the picture, even though it is visible in the camera finder.

WRONG COMPOSITION   CORRECT COMPOSITION

The elements of camera composition are discussed in detail in Chapter 8.

THE SETTING OF THE SHOW

Another responsibility of the writer is to provide the setting in which action takes place.

Everyone who has attended a play knows that when the curtain goes up, before a word is spoken each audience member experiences a definite intellectual and emotional reaction to the stage setting. The decor literally sets a mood that may have a major influence on the reception of the dialogue and action. So it is, also, with a television program.

The set will have a large part in determining what you call attention to in your picture. If you want to concentrate on a person or an object, you will require a neutral background with little identifiable detail. In contrast, you can then focus sharply on objects, persons, and action in the foreground. Or, perhaps you may wish to create an emotional climate or arouse cultural feelings. Your subjects must then be blended into suitable backgrounds and costumes; as, for example, a period room where every detail will be accurate. Ideas and the process of conception can be advanced by the use of abstract sets: decorative backgrounds composed of angles, planes, and other geometric designs; draperies; architectural figures, geometric units or artistic designs or figures in a pleasing composition that does not strive for realism in a recognizable locale.

The set is your "location." But in television it is something more than just the place where action goes on. The television camera is capable of moving in to explore every nook and cranny of the set; therefore, the audience member is not limited to an over-all, general view of the location, as he would be in a stage presentation. In the hands of skillful television writers and directors, the set ceases to be just background and becomes an integral factor in the action. Careful planning can people the set with objects that, at the right moment, can be brought into camera focus to provide dramatic impact.

To achieve this purpose, set planning should be a fluid process. The set will come into being as the script progresses, taking shape around and within the developing pattern of action. This method of making the set an organism that grows as plot unfolds is especially suited to dramatic writing; but it can be equally useful in the writing of other types of programs, even where the action is relatively static, as in talks and discussions.

Writing the Script

Almost anyone who can write well can learn to write for television!

We have already shown that new techniques must be mastered, new principles must be followed. For television is different from any other medium of communication. It has its limitations for the writer in contrast to radio with its opportunities to range to the farthest boundaries of thought, of time, and of situation without the handicap of visual setting or of stereotyped format; or of live drama or public speech where audience reaction is immediately apparent and corrective procedures are possible to overcome hostile or indifferent attitudes.

Television is the most complicated and mechanized of any means of communication, requiring intricate and expensive equipment for both transmission and reception. It is exceedingly expensive, even in its simplest manifestations. It never is a one-man, or even two- or three-man, affair. Any television program is the result of the combined talent and actions of a large group of workers of many crafts, of whom the three key leaders are the producer, the writer, and the director. The script is but one link in the complicated chain that must be strung together to bring a program to the air. Yet the writer is television's lifeline. Poor directors, casts, cameramen, can spoil a good script, but even the greatest of them can seldom turn a bad script into a good production. Television already has outstripped all other mass media in its hold on the American people. Its immediacy and the intensity of its impact give it vast power to attract and hold large audiences. But its artistic qualities and possibilities have scarcely begun to be realized. It is largely through good writing that television will gain the necessary resources to fulfill its potential destiny as a medium for informing, educating, and entertaining.

If you are a good writer, you do your hardest work before you ever sit down to your typewriter. You labor in your mind—thinking, analyzing, and probing themes and situations in search of a *fresh idea*. It need not be soul-shaking in importance, but it must be original and pertinent to the readiness state of the audience you are trying to reach. You may deal with an age-old theme. (What theme is wholly new?) You must put it in a new setting, invent a new complication, develop a new character, look at it from a different-than-usual point of view, find a fresh resolution for a stale conflict. This is something deeper than the trade tricks of finding a gimmick to attract interest, or a twist in development to gloss over the jaded "good guy versus bad guy" plot, or a surprise snapper for the ending.

A good writer first has something to say that is both *informing* and *entertaining*. Then he says it effectively, in interesting, attractive fashion, expressing his idea in terms that are understandable to his auditors.

And, if you are a good writer, you will treat your idea honestly, no matter where that treatment leads you. The curse of religious broadcasting is the story—and it is legion—that does not ring true. The ending is apparent before the beginning is well under way; the characters are stereotypes, existing not for themselves but for the ends of the writer; the plot is a house of straw, set up only to be knocked down; and the resolution is not the inexorable working out of deadly conflict, but an omniscient directive handed down by the omnipotent "pastor" who is not himself involved in the travail of the struggle. Such programs do little for the viewer but take up his time.

It is not necessary for every religious program to point a moral or to teach a lesson. As a writer, your hope and your job is to communicate. You will be successful only as the audience understands your meaning, is involved in your struggle, and is moved by your solution. Your impact on the viewer—and his openness to the impact of the Christian gospel—will be far greater if you can get him to cry out, "Oh God, that might have been me," than if you leave him as merely an impassive observer of the triumph of Christian virtue.

Furthermore, television demands honesty because it speaks to the viewer in a situation where his emotions are not easily aroused. He watches in the privacy of his own home where he is not subject to the mass reaction of a theater audience or of a church congregation. In this intimate situation, he will react only if he is deeply moved. By himself, he is quick to spot and reject the shoddy, the superficial, the moralistic.

This is not to say he will not react to the old, the common, the familiar. No theme that deals with reality is so hackneyed, no realistic story is so trite that you cannot make it come alive when you deal with it as if it were fresh to you, when you probe it for the kernel of truth that is in it. Only the superficial is trite; the depths of any life situation, where the truth lies, are always new. So it is with themes and characters. The well-worn theme raised to a new level of interpretation takes on new meaning. The stock figure becomes clothed in reality when his motives, thoughts, and emotions are explored in depth. He takes on individuality when the stereotyped surface layers are peeled away.

Finding a Fresh Idea

Where do fresh ideas come from? Only you can say for yourself. But it is probably safe to assume that you will not get fresh ideas just from sitting down at a typewriter and waiting for "inspiration"; nor can you always count on taking episodes directly from life. Because a thing is true, it is not necessarily a good medium for communicating ideas. "It really happened" is not a talisman that ensures usefulness in a television script. A fresh idea usually springs from a combination of past experience and observation wedded to a theme of interest and importance. It must then be developed through exciting, original illustrations or characters, created especially to motivate the action of a particular program.

Creative writing begins in the piling up and the interpretation of two kinds of experience: (1) of the people to whom you are writing, and their store of meanings and experiences; and (2) of the meaning you are writing about.

Pile Up Experiences of People. How do you enlarge your experience of people? Take an interest in all people—of all classes, creeds, and races—and in all things, especially in all things that people feel.

Your goal is not just number of experiences, but vigor and depth of understanding. Unless such experience of people has emotional impact and striking, unforgettable significance for you, you will have no basis for making it become live and vital for others through your writing.

The experience of people acquires depth and intensity to the extent that we are involved in situations of crisis. The trusted pastor who has personally lived through the struggles, defeats, and victories of a community of people into which he has so woven his life that his people's crises are his crises has the advantage here. Perhaps more than anyone else, the pastor has the opportunity to build up a personal reservoir of the critical events in all lives: birth, death, triumph, despair, defeat by a hated competitor, loss of a job, the breakup of a marriage, the wondering how a child should be nurtured, the endurance of the revealing moment when the inner motives of a person are suddenly stripped bare.

Any methods and interpretations that will make you more sensitive, more able to feel deeply into the human situation will help your writing. For example, your own experiences thoughtfully evaluated may be important tools for understanding the depth of the experiences of others. Likewise, the interpretations of others, as expressed in theology, psychology, poetry, literature, drama, television programs, may give insight.

Further, any man who has within him something of human kindness and a love of persons has advantages in deepening his experience of people. Love is essential for the discovery of the real nature of persons. Love is more than just a general amiability and skill at establishing contact. Love requires a persistent drive to maintain relationships, to intercommunicate, to understand, to establish those conditions which will enable the other to be most fully a person. Essentially, this is the attitude that the Judaeo-Christian religion has always advocated for relations between people.

You prepare yourself for writing by relating yourself vigorously to other people, by seeking to probe their innermost meanings. Then you let these people be active in you as you write. By necessity, every television program is indigenous. What happens within the viewer, rather than what is broadcast, is the program that goes on in the world of affairs. You will do better writing for television if in the back regions of your imagination there are lively and particular people who are working out some universal problem which is to be the subject of a particular broadcast.

The first guide to effective writing is, therefore: How many people, in what situations, and with what meanings, have you taken into your mind and emotions? The exploration of character is the backbone of all good writing.

Fresh Experience of Meaning. The other side of the preparatory coin is the storing up of fresh and enlivened experiences of the meanings you wish to communicate. A minister who can find no new significance in the gospel during the week will preach a stale sermon on Sunday. Until a new vigor exists in his mind, none can exist in the sermon, and certainly none in his listeners.

Faith, meaning, and ideas are alive only at their moment of birth. They must be continually reborn in some new manner, in a situation new in some respect. An upsetting experience must occur. We must be shattered, or at least loosened, from our usual way of responding to a person or situation. We must realize that the accustomed way will not handle the event.

The essential thing is that our ideas and meanings shall not remain anchored in complacency. The creative act depends upon energies and emotions *in motion*. Something must happen to set them in motion. If we are fortunate, something compelling hits us; we reach out toward its power and lure; we work furiously to handle it. Fresh experiences and energy-on-the-loose are created.

One way to freshen meaning is to go places and do things. Get into situations different from those you have been in before. Do something different from your usual routine. A layman recently went to Australia to help establish a home missions board and came home a television "natural." People like to hear from someone who has "been there," who can say, "I've seen how interesting the other fellow is."

Get into conversation with someone who is alive with ideas, who will challenge your accepted structure of meanings. Try to meet his arguments. Learn from him and pass it on in your writing.

Or read modern poetry or an article or a book interpreting how it stands with man today. As Henry James observed, the moral significance of a writing depends upon the amount of felt life that has gone into it. Put your creative abilities to work in creative criticism.

In summary, to prepare for creative writing, pile up the resources of creative experiences into two germinal clusters—experiences of people and experiences of meaning. Let them interact on each other. When they mesh, something new will be born and will begin to develop.

But, you say, this is nothing new. This is what any minister, priest, or rabbi worth his salt does in preparation for his weekly sermons, and for any other writing. Right! You are first a writer, then a writer practicing in television.

The Framework of the Script

Once your idea is developed, it must be fitted into the framework of elements that govern all television script writing, the combinations of *sight* and *sound* that are peculiarly suited to television production. Speech, music, and sound effects are the tools you will use in writing the auditory portion of your script. Visually, you will be concerned with the set and details of its usage in story development; with the actions and the expressions of your cast and their stage business; and with use of the camera to convey impressions. These visual writing elements occur in *all* television shows, from the most complicated drama to the simplest instructional talk. Their smooth blending determines in large part the potential quality of a production.

Your writing will always be circumscribed by television's four rigid limitations:

1. Space. Few local studios are spacious. You will probably be limited to small interior sets and minimal camera mobility. Almost never will you have more than two cameras for your program.

2. Number of characters. We have already warned you about the smallness of the television screen. Four persons are about the maximum that can be handled in any one scene. Three persons are better; two or one, best. There should be no such thing as a mob scene on television.

3. The time limit. The stringent time limit on programs is even more of an artificial checkrein on creativity in television than it is in radio. You will have to develop a time sense that can overcome this limitation. This time sense can be learned. Without it you will find your climaxes occurring in the last thirty seconds or near the first third of your program.

4. Continuous performance. Not only must you work in a predetermined time, you must do it without interruption. There are no intermissions for set and costume changes, no chances to cut and splice as in a motion-picture film. The who, what, where, and how of storytelling must be fitted into a largely artificial time-space situation, yet move fluidly from start to finish without pause.

Structure

Erik Barnouw once wrote of radio, its "peculiarities commit it forever to the quick start, the simple plot, the unprecedented concentration on plot essentials."[3] He could as well have been writing of television.

The bugaboo of time, even in an hour-long drama, forces a television program to start more quickly, to have a more arresting opening, and to move more rapidly than does a stage play, a public speech, or a motion picture. The theater playwright purposely delays

[3] Erik Barnouw, *Handbook of Radio Writing* (Boston: Little, Brown and Company, 1947), p. 25.

important events until his audience is settled and his preliminary byplay has attracted its attention and aroused its interest. Only then does he introduce his main character. A skillful public speaker frequently follows the same plan, using his introduction to gather up the loose ends of audience attention. In television, there is no time for preliminary fencing before the central issue begins to unfold. The plot or problem or thesis must be posed, the main theme or characters established, and the action well under way within the first thirty seconds to a minute.

Your story, your thesis, your argument must be compressed. A half-hour drama has to start almost at the crisis point, an argument with the issue. There is little time to develop the background of either. Thus, a discussion on the subject "Church and City" would not have time to develop the historical pattern of city-church life or the reasons for urban expansion. It might well begin with the blunt statement that urban culture is dominant in American life, support the assertion with a few major facts (preferably visualized), and then go on to point out what the churches ought to be doing to meet the demands of urbanization.

The problem of compression is not as difficult as it may seem to be, because of the great versatility possible with the camera. It can assume and quickly discharge the bulk of the responsibility for exposition and explanation.

For example, a close-up of a street sign, followed by a shot of Michigan Avenue in Chicago showing the bridge, the Wrigley building, the Tribune Tower, an apartment building, followed by a cut to the interior of an apartment immediately establishes locale (Chicago's Gold Coast) and the class of people involved in the action (upper-middle class).

Maps, still pictures, film clips, objects, costumes of the characters, miniature sets that appear life size on the screen (for instance a model of a church) and from which the camera can dissolve to the actual set, close-ups of signs (such as book titles or a name on a desk) are only a few of the devices that can communicate information to the audience quickly, and often more interestingly than could words.

Following is the opening which this writer once used for a simple story-telling program for children in which it was necessary to establish quickly that the action takes place in a jungle village in Angola:

Video	*Audio*
LONG SHOT OF LARGE WALL MAP OF AFRICA.	(MUSIC: JUNGLE DRUMS THEME)
DOLLY IN FOR CLOSE-UP OF ANGOLA.	
CUT TO CLOSE-UP OF PLACE NAMES.	
PAN DOWN TO "VILLAGE-BY-THE-FORD." HOLD.	
DISSOLVE TO STILL PICTURE OF VILLAGE.	
PULL TO SHOW PICTURE #2, CLUSTER OF HOUSES	
DOLLY IN TO CLOSE-UP OF HEAD MAN'S HOUSE.	(*MUSIC: FADE OUT*)
DISSOLVE TO NARRATOR	NARRATOR
	The home of the head man is always the best house in an African village.
DISSOLVE TO CLOSE-UP OF HEAD MAN'S HOUSE	NARRATOR
	This is the home of Nyanga's grandfather, the head man of the Village-by-the-Ford. See how it . . . (etc.)

The opening scene in any type of television program has one distinct purpose, to *set the scene* in time and place. Within itself it must carry all the information that might be found in the program notes for a play or in the introduction to a speech.

Once started, the television production must move rapidly, maintaining at all times a high level of attention-compelling interest. Let the movement lag for only a few moments, let the details of plot development or the line of argument become even slightly obscure and the viewer will tune out. Your task is to progress smoothly from one scene or action to another (in drama this progression is conflict, crisis, climax, resolution), keeping your audience always oriented to the correct sequence of movement. Transitions are of major importance in carrying your audience with you. They must be written into the script in terms of pictures the camera is to transmit and words the participants are to say. For instance, to show passage of time on a railway journey, you might have two characters talking together, then cut to the exterior to show several station signs, returning to the interior of the coach to show one character reading, the other asleep. In a discussion, the transition from one idea to another could be shown by cutting to a close-up of one participant who would introduce the new material.

The concentrated movement of a television program allows for treatment of one strong, central idea, and one only. There must be a clear relationship between the factors in the idea pattern. There is no place for elaborate subplots (*Hamlet* cannot be done well in a one-hour television program), for extraneous illustrations or details, or even for an unessential picture or sentence that may lead viewers to deviate from the direct story line. Any television program—from an hour-long drama to a five-minute sermonette—needs to be structured in three parts, beginning, middle, and end, with smooth transitions between them. This is the framework of the television script. The content is governed by the sets, the participants, and the time available.

Visual Writing

We have already said that the essence of the television program is the picture. The secret in using words is to make sure that everything that is said will advance your argument or story; i.e., reveal such things as the background, education, and occupation of your participants, explain action, and prepare the viewer for the next sequence or idea pattern. Dialogue, for example, should sound like ordinary conversation. But it has to be more than that. It has to provide information that will move your story ahead; so you plant leading questions to elicit facts that cannot be acted out; you mention present and past activities; you invent key words and phrases that will delineate character. This kind of writing is also useful in purely expository programs.

Style. Television requires a brisker, sharper, more simple style of writing than you may use in literary composition. Sentence structure should be simple. Avoid qualifying phrases and clauses. Make your sentence style and vocabulary intelligible to the least common denominator of your audience. But never make the mistake of writing down to your viewer. You will write badly.

Be concise. Be simple. Write in the viewer's terms, not your own. This means use plain talk and, at all costs, avoid professional jargon. Remember that unfamiliar words which might be recognized in print may escape the ear on television and result in loss of interest and attention from the viewer.

Preciseness and aptness are basic requirements of television writing. Three words may be precise in expressing your meaning. Only one of them will be apt.

Strive constantly for accuracy in transmitting your meanings to the minds of viewers. Accuracy may be obtained:

1. By having an exact knowledge of the end you wish to achieve in presenting a particular topic to a particular, recognizable audience within the time available and through the format chosen. Analyze all of these factors. Spell them out, in writing, before you attack your script.

2. By a clear, precise statement of your central idea, couched in terms of the experience of your particular target audience. Try to write your central idea in a single sentence that can be communicated to your viewers.

3. Through a well-considered, logical outline that will be apparent to your viewers when your program is finally on the air.

4. Through paying constant attention, while you are writing, to the meaning and context of the pictures and words you are using. Remember that words are constantly shifting in meaning; and that some people are consciously attempting to shift meanings, as in the case of the use by Communists of the word "democracy" in such contexts as "Peoples' Democratic Republics." Furthermore, we cannot all agree on one meaning for the words and terms we use freely. "Right to work" means one thing to labor, another to manage-

ment. Meanings depend upon contexts. A listener may know the dictionary definition of a word, but he has no knowledge of your *meaning* in using it until it is uttered in the *context* of your presentation. Therefore, you, as a writer, must examine your contexts critically to bring them as nearly as possible into conformance with the experience and understanding of your viewers. *This practice is a basic principle of the art of communication. The audience is always the determinative of what you say and how you say it.*

5. By *defining* whenever there is the slightest chance you will be misunderstood.

ANALYZING YOUR WRITING

The ability to analyze his work critically is the acid test of any writer. Even with the most vital, exciting idea, the greatest possible writing skill, and an inspired production, you can never be sure you will catch, interest, and hold your target television audience. Television is art, and art is tricky. Its end product can never be forecast with any confident degree of certainty. Nevertheless, there are criteria you can apply to determine if there is a reasonable chance your work will do the job you want it to accomplish.

As you write, and particularly after you have completed your first draft of the script, ask yourself some critical questions. Be honest about the answers! If there are too many "nos," scrap your project and start afresh.

Here are a few key questions. You can add your own to complete a set of standards for script evaluation.

First, examine the *idea*.

1. Now that you have seen it in print, is your idea a real bill of goods? Is it sound? Freshly conceived? Dramatic? Does it interest *you*? Do you have conviction about it?

2. Will your idea interest the audience? Which audience? Why do you think it will appeal to a specific audience?

3. Is it a rifle shot? That is, do you present one clear idea; does it tell a single story? Have you chosen a precise purpose that you can achieve with the audience in the time available?

4. Will your idea make people respond, both emotionally and in-

tellectually? Will it appeal to impelling motives which cause people to act: to their desires for self-preservation, for emotional acceptance and fulfillment, for the recognition of the Self as something that counts in the scheme of things; to their love of family, friends, and common humanity, and to their desire to contribute to the welfare of those persons, institutions, and traditions they hold dear; to their sentiments and tastes?

5. Is the idea big enough for a series of programs? How many? Of what type? Requiring what participants?

Now turn to your *treatment* of the idea. The format, the pattern of movement of the theme, the participants in the production, the locale—all play a decisive part in making your idea a success or a failure.

1. Is the treatment you have conceived original? Is it both entertaining and dramatic?

2. Does your script have a true beginning? Does it start from a definite, recognizable point and begin to move immediately toward the conclusion? Are the very first pictures, words, and sounds pertinent to the story? Do they set the scene, give vital information or argument, lead directly into the action?

a. Does the program open with an arresting incident that is related to the action and that will catch the attention of the viewer? Does it open fast, without extraneous announcements, music, descriptions—pictorial or verbal? (Religious programs often waste time and lose viewers by employing long, explanatory introductions or credits.)

b. Does the opening enchant and captivate the viewer, enlist his sympathy? Will he care about what is going to happen, the choices that will be made? Does it pique his intellect, making him think, "How does it come out?"

c. Will the viewer immediately conclude that the persons who planned the program understand him and his needs, and are interested in him?

Here is an example of an opening for a religious program that meets most of these tests (A Glossary of Television Terms will be found on page 223):

MODERATOR (OFF SCENE)
. . . Let's look in at this anxious father . . .

(CUT TO MCU OF FATHER. HE SITS IN EASY CHAIR
AGAINST LIMBO BACKGROUND READING A BOOK.
WE CANNOT SEE ITS TITLE.

MODERATOR (CONT'D)
. . . and this equally anxious son.

(WIDEN SHOT TO INCLUDE TEEN-AGE BOY
CURLED UP IN ANOTHER EASY CHAIR ACROSS
FROM THE FATHER. THE FATHER TURNS A
PAGE IN HIS BOOK, LOOKS AT THE PASSAGE
HE IS READING AGAIN, GRUNTS AND LOOKS
OVER AT THE BOY)

FATHER
(CLEARS HIS THROAT)
What're you reading, son?

BOY
Aw, nothing . . .

FATHER
Not one of those comic books, I hope?
You know the kind I mean. The kind
that——

BOY
Nah, those're for squares.

FATHER
Hmm. You know, son, it seems to me
you and I don't have any little talks
any more.

BOY
(LOOKS UP) Did we ever?

FATHER
Oh. Well, what I mean is . . . I think we
should have talks.

BOY
About what?

FATHER
Well—something may be bothering you.

BOY
Something bothering *you*, dad?

FATHER
No-oo. I just—well, I just—
(TRIES A DIFFERENT TACK)
I want you to know there's nothing you
can't talk to me about. You know that,
don't you?

BOY
You think I been . . . *doing* somethin', is
that it?

FATHER
Of course not.
(LOOKS AT THE BOY SUSPICIOUSLY)
You . . . *haven't* been *doing* anything . . .
have you?

BOY
Like what? Gee, dad, sometimes a guy
feels like a *criminal* around here! When
I come home mom wants t'know where I've
been—who I've been with—

FATHER
(GROWING MORE SUSPICIOUS)
Well, who *have* you been with?

BOY
Nobody! Gee whiz! I could ask you the
same thing!

FATHER
Just what do you mean by *that*?

BOY
I don't mean anything. I just mean—

well—how would you like it if somebody
was always yammering about where
you've been and who with and—

FATHER
I have nothing to hide, young man!

BOY
Well, neither've I!

FATHER
Don't yell. And it seems to me that
if you're afraid to talk to your own
father, then something's mighty wrong,
young man!

BOY
Gee, I don't dig this at all. *You're*
the one that wanted to talk!

FATHER
Well, I just thought there might be
something on your mind.
(WANTING TO WRIGGLE OUT OF THIS)
Look—I know you're a good boy, son.
I trust you implicitly.

BOY
Me, too, dad. I mean, you're okay.

FATHER
(BEAMS) You see—nothing like a
little father and son talk, eh?
(LOOKS AT HIS WATCH) Well, they
said they'd have the car ready
about now.

BOY
Yeah. And I gotta meet Peggy. So
long, dad . . .

FATHER
So long, son.
(THE SON EXITS. THE FATHER SCRATCHES
HIS HEAD AND MUMBLES)

FATHER
Hmm. Wonder who Peggy is? Oh, well . . .

(HE EXITS)
(THE TWO BOOKS THAT THE FATHER AND SON
WERE READING HAVE BEEN PLACED ON A SMALL
TABLE BETWEEN THE TWO CHAIRS. WE COME
IN FOR A CLOSE UP OF THE BOOKS. THE
TITLES: "UNDERSTANDING BOYS" AND
"UNDERSTANDING YOUR PARENTS".)
(BLACKOUT)
CU OF MODERATOR
DISCUSSION FOLLOWS[4]

"The Tyranny of the Teen-Ager" was a discussion program. This dramatic "teaser" opening served to arouse interest, to help the viewer identify with the issue, and to set the scene for the discussion that followed.

3. Does the script have a development? It must have some place to go once it is underway, and the viewer must be made to understand that the writer has a purpose in mind and is in control of the means to accomplish it.

a. Does the story march? Do complications occur that will hold audience interest? Is the viewer led to think, "What could possibly set this mess aright?"

b. Are the characters real people, living real lives? Are the ideas existential? The essence of a play or a story is the evolution of a character in a continued and changing situation. The essence of a discussion or talk is the application of the same process to an idea. When you write drama, for instance, every character must be a real person to you. Each must speak and act in character at all times. If your lines might just as well be read by character A as by character B, you have not created real people who will be convincing to the audience.

Both characters and ideas must be honest personalities. That is, conclusions reached must be consistent with the facts and arguments

[4] From "The Tyranny of the Teen-ager," a *Frontiers of Faith* program presented by the National Council of the Churches of Christ in the U.S.A. Skit by Gene Hurley.

presented; characters must be consistent in their decisions and actions. If characters change, it must be because their kind might be expected to change under the particular stress your story places on them. To reform an unreformable character just to illustrate a moral principle is dishonest drama. Few things will alienate viewers more quickly.

c. How is character revealed? It should unfold through deeds not speeches. The deeds result from choices made when the characters are placed in situations of crisis. Fred Eastman has stated: "Drama becomes great in direct proportion as the characters shown are people worth knowing, the struggle shown is intense, the choices presented important and the decisions made embodied in great deeds."[5]

d. Are the episodes carefully delineated? Does each stand out from the others as a separate unit? An episode is one incident. (It corresponds to the paragraph in writing.) All programs are episodic. Your responsibility is to see that the episodes do not just occur, that they are planned in sequence. Each one should be designed to accomplish a single purpose—establish a point, reveal a character trait, arouse some emotion in the audience, advance the plot or argument one step. An episode may be long or short, but as soon as its single purpose is accomplished, it should be dropped and the next episode begun. A change in episode involves a shift in scene, entrance or exit of a character, or introduction of a new thought. In television, episode change *always* requires a camera change.

e. Does the development of your script lead up to one big scene or assertion—the climax? If you are writing a drama, is the conflict— between the protagonist (hero) and the antagonist (villain)—leading up to the climax adequate to the climax? Does the conflict reflect a struggle common to the experience or observation of the audience? Otherwise, it will not be believed.

f. Does the climax center on the making of an important choice by the characters—to have or have not—a choice that will be believable to the audience? (Hamlet's "To be or not to be . . ." is an example of an important choice.) Are the inner souls of the characters stripped bare by the choices they have to make?

4. Does your script have an ending? Does it end as it began—at

[5] From the author's class notes.

the proper place? Your script should end where the story ends. You should not go on to preach a sermon or to point a moral. If the spiritual values are not clearly evident in the story itself, no amount of commentary will get them over to the audience.

a. Does your story have a "pay off"—a satisfying denouement? Is the conflict resolved in a convincing manner, so the audience may be willing to accept the argument you are advancing? (Fantasy is an exception; the denouement need not be convincing, but should have emotional impact.)

b. Is your point established? Can the viewer understand what you mean; or is the important central idea still in your mind?

Before you leave your writing, ask these questions.

1. Has your script actually said something to the viewer that is important to him? Will it help him to live a better, more useful life; to endure misfortune; to struggle against human weakness as an earnest of his duty to God? A television program is religious only as it leads the viewer to confront the Judaeo-Christian imperative.

2. Will your program help the viewer to think creatively? The best kind of writing is so suspense-filled, so compelling that the audience member becomes an active collaborator in the development of the story or argument. He anticipates, plots ahead of you, saying, "This is what is going to happen next." It makes no difference whether he is right or wrong in his speculation. The important thing is that he has projected himself into your train of thinking and has himself become creative. Then you have achieved the essence of communication!

THE SCRIPT FORMAT

There is no universally accepted format for a television script. Your station may favor one format, the station in the next town another. In the form used for "The Tyranny of the Teen-ager," all of the writer's dialogue and stage directions are placed in a column on the left hand side of the page, leaving the right side for the director to pencil in his notes. Some directors prefer the standard motion picture script form where all video material—camera directions, set description, action, and stage directions and business—is on the left, and the audio material—dialogue, directions for the interpretation of lines, sound effects and music cues—is on the right.

Camera, set, and stage directions; instructions to performers for action and interpretation; music titles and cues; and sound instructions and cues are written in capital letters in both script forms. Dialogue, narration, and other speech are written in upper and lower case. There are minor variations in usage. Some producers underline camera instructions, others do not. Music and sound directions are sometimes put in parentheses. Sometimes character names, such as JOHN, are underlined.

One of the most important things for you, as writer, to remember is that the director *directs* the show. By all means tell him in your script in the clearest possible manner *what* you want the cameras to transmit, the *kind* of action, reaction, and interpretation you want from the cast; but do not tell him *how* to do it. That is his prerogative. He is supposedly competent to instruct and rehearse his cast, position his cameras, and determine the length and order of scenes and shots. On the other hand, you should be thoroughly familiar with his problems so you will not demand the impossible of him.

A Sample Script

Printed below is a portion of a dramatic script which has been broken down by the director into numbered scenes. He has expanded the writer's instructions concerning decor and action into detailed descriptions of the effects he hopes to achieve.

FADE IN TO:
INTERIOR DAY
1. MS PARLOR. IN BG THE DINING
ROOM. Like the outside of the
house, the INT., including the
furniture, is heavy, reflecting
LAUBER'S values. We see massive
mahogany furniture, overstuffed
chairs, prints in ornate frames,
a big round dining room table.

LIGHTING SHOULD REFLECT THIS
HEAVINESS.
EMILY moves into frame while
taking off her gloves. As she
puts her hat and purse on a
table, she turns to the direction she has come from.

EMILY
I'll have dinner on the table in a
few minutes, Papa.

EMILY moves off and out of
picture as LAUBER steps into
frame in a MCU. He nods ab-
stractedly. He picks up a
ledger and we see him carry it
to dining room table.

CUT TO:

2. MS LAUBER FROM ACROSS DINING
ROOM TABLE. He puts down ledger.
He pulls out chair to sit down. IN
BG we see through doorway EMILY mov-
ing here and there in kitchen.

3. LAUBER'S hands grip the chair back.
He does not sit. Instead moves slowly
pensively to mantle as CAMERA PANS
WITH HIM. LAUBER leans forward to the
pictures.

SOUND OF EMILY SCRAPING
OUT POT IN BG.

CUT TO:

4. CU FAMILY PICTURE of Mrs. Lauber
with four small children, three boys
and a girl.

5. CU LAUBER FROM LOW FRONT.

CUT TO:

6. CU PICTURE of youngish man, his
wife and child. Man wears suit. In
scribed on picture is: "Love to Dad
from Ernest, Elsie and Mike." At one
side of picture we have seen LAUBER'S
hand partly holding it. Now the hand
takes the picture out of frame and the
other hand brings another picture into
frame. It is of a man about 35, wearing a doctor's jacket. Printed on the
bottom of the picture is: "Gustave
Lauber, Jr., M.D." Both hands are now
holding the picture. Again, the one
hand takes out of frame the last picture while the other hand brings into
frame another picture: It is of a
young man in World War II uniform.

CUT TO:

7. MS PROFILE OF LAUBER AT
MANTLE WITH PICTURES.

CUT TO:

8. MS DINING ROOM, EMILY
APPEARS IN DOORWAY WITH
PLATTER OF CHICKEN.

> EMILY
>
> We can sit down now, Papa. Every-
> thing's nice and hot.

Lauber moves to his place at table
while Emily puts down platter, goes
back for potatoes and vegetables.

CUT TO:

9. MCS TABLE AT TABLE HEIGHT.
LAUBER is seated at right angle to camera.
He is serving portions onto plates.

> LAUBER
>
> You're as good a cook as your
> mother was, Emily.

EMILY smiles as she comes into frame
with other dishes. LAUBER is finish-
ing serving. EMILY seats herself
across table from father.

LAUBER

And when it comes to gravy, you
know I think you're better!

EMILY looks at her father quietly,
fondly. They bow their heads.

LAUBER

For what we are about to receive,
Father, we thank thee.

EMILY AND LAUBER eat silently
for a few moments.

LAUBER

You . . . er . . . you like that Allen
boy, Emily?

EMILY

Now, Papa, I'm too old to be teased
any more . . . He's a nice boy. I like
him. But there's nothing serious.
After all, next year we'll both be
away at college . . . Different col
leges.

LAUBER

He's going to college, too, eh? To be
a businessman, I guess, or a doctor?

LAUBER glances grimly at
pictures on mantle.

EMILY

What makes you think that, Papa?
He's going to agricultural college.
He wants to be a farmer, like his
father.

LAUBER

(*Snorting*) Like his father! That
man is a farmer? He's a wild man . . .
he's like one of those crazy experi-
menters you see in the movies. Did
you hear the latest thing he's doing?

He's even shooting pills behind the ears of his cattle. Bah!

CUT TO:

10. CU EMILY (at moment when we hear LAUBER'S "Bah!") FROM LAUBER'S VIEWPOINT AND HEIGHT.

EMILY swallows, leans forward.

EMILY

Yes, Papa, I heard about that. Ralph told me.

They're hormones. It's one of the latest scientific developments. Some farmers who have tried it have increased the market weight of their cattle by ten per cent. I don't think that's so crazy!

CUT TO:

11. CU LAUBER FROM EMILY'S VIEWPOINT AND HEIGHT

LAUBER

(*Challengingly*) If Allen's such a good farmer, why doesn't he own his own farm by now? He's no kid any more.

CUT TO:

12. CU EMILY FROM LAUBER'S VIEWPOINT AND HEIGHT.

EMILY

(*Hotly defensive*) Ralph says his father wanted to study and learn ways to be a better farmer first . . . So he went fifty-fifty with his landlord, so he could . . .

Emily hesitates, looks keenly at her father, and plunges ahead.

. . . This is a secret, Papa, but I'll tell you because it's important. Mr.

Allen is going to buy that farm. He
made a bid last week

CUT TO:

13. CU LAUBER FROM EMILY'S VIEW-
POINT AND HEIGHT. LAUBER is sur
prised but covers it by taking a
bite and not looking at EMILY.

> LAUBER
> He did, eh?

CUT TO:

14. OPENING MS OF TABLE AT TABLE
HEIGHT. LAUBER AND EMILY ACROSS
FROM EACH OTHER AT RIGHT ANGLES
TO CAMERA.

> EMILY
> He wants to have a farm he can
> eventually turn over to Ralph. Ralph
> is going to be a good farmer, too!

> LAUBER
> (*A bit sadly*) Strange . . . Allen's
> son wants to be a farmer and my
> sons couldn't wait to leave.

LAUBER looks toward mantle.

> When you were children you all
> loved it here.

CUT TO:

15. MCU FAMILY PICTURE

> Then Gus decided he wanted to be
> a doctor.

CUT TO:

16. MCU PICTURE OF GUS,
JR.

> Mama was very proud of him. I was,
> too.

CUT TO:

17. MCU PICTURE OF BUSINESS
SON AND FAMILY.

> Ernest I thought sure would stay
> with me. Instead he becomes a busi-
> nessman, a salesman.

CUT TO:

18. CU EMILY FROM LAUBER'S
VIEWPOINT AND HEIGHT.

> EMILY
> (*Interrupting*) Vice-president in
> charge of the sales department,
> Papa. And you know you'd never let
> him be in charge of anything here.

CUT TO:

19. MCU OF SOLDIER'S PICTURE.

> LAUBER
> And Victor . . . he never had a
> chance to decide what he wanted to
> do with his life . . .

CUT TO:

20. MS TABLE FROM BEHIND LAUBER.
EMILY reaches out a hand and
covers her father's hand, then
gives it a warm pat. She
releases his hand and reaches
for his plate.

> EMILY
> Some more chicken, Papa? Gravy?

> LAUBER
> Well, a small piece, maybe, and
> some potatoes to go under the
> gravy.[6]

[6] Norman Lobsenz, *Shadow on the Land* (New York: The Office of Communication for the United Church of Christ, Copyright © 1959. Used by
permission.)

The sequence illustrated can easily be played by two cameras. (See Chapter 8 and Glossary for explanations of camera terms.) The scene is planned so it can open on Camera 1, the LS camera. Camera 2 backs 1 for the medium shots of Lauber at the mantle. CUs of the pictures of Lauber's children are achieved by lens changes. Shots 7 and 8 are put in to allow the cameras to be positioned for the scenes at the table. Camera 1 holds on the MS of Lauber in 7 while Camera 2 moves quickly to cover the doorway. This camera can then pan with Emily to the table while Lauber enters the frame from the other side and seats himself. This action and Emily's movement back to the kitchen are timed to allow Camera 1 to be repositioned for shot 9, the MCS at the table. Shots 7 and 8 are excellent examples of action which helps the story to move, but which has been written for the primary purpose of covering necessary camera positioning.

Note the length of time shot 9 is held. The purpose of this interval is to allow Camera 2 to move into position for the CU of Emily in shot 10. The only fast camera move needed in the sequence occurs during shot 10, but here the writer has provided a fairly long speech and Emily's action of swallowing and leaning forward which can be prolonged a second or two if necessary. Three cameras would be useful now, because Camera 3 could be positioned on the CU of Lauber in shot 11. Camera 1 could then stay on the right-angle shot of the table used in shot 9, and would only have to change lens and not be repositioned to get the MS of the table in shot 14.

Except for the repositioning of Camera 1 to pick up shot 14, once the cameras are in position for the reverse close-ups of Emily and Lauber that begin in shots 10 and 11, they stay in place. The close-ups of the portraits are obtained from lens changes on Camera 2, since the pictures are positioned behind Emily's chair. Shot 20 is also made without repositioning Camera 2. At most it will require a slight pull back in addition to a lens change

CHAPTER 6   Your Task as Producer

The producer in television is the person who has over-all responsibility for a program series. He is the business-artistic-talent manager, who has in his hands the administrative oversight of the production process. Primarily, the producer is the watchdog over the budget. This function gives him great power in shaping the course of a program. The title "producer" was borrowed from motion pictures. The position developed in television for the same reason it came into being in Hollywood, to give status to the management representative vis-à-vis the talent—writer, director, cast, technicians. Over the years, the presence of the producer has materially reduced the role of the director in setting policy in both movies and television.

Producers, naturally, have worked assiduously to broaden their own powers. A large number, in both television and the movies, have succeeded in establishing themselves in the enviable role of the producer of a Broadway play or musical. They develop program ideas, commission scripts or buy them in the open market, obtain their own financing (in television by selling the shows to sponsors), hire directors and stars, and personally control the details of production. Producers who work for television networks usually are much more limited in their creative scope than are the independent entrepreneurs. They do not make program policies; the programs they produce are likely to have been decided upon by the management and assigned to them. Their budgets also are set by management. Their writers may or may not be staff members; their directors are certain to be. Seldom do they have the money for scripts and talent to permit them to compete with the big-budget, agency-produced commercial shows.

In the local station it is hardly ever necessary to have producers for programs that are originated internally. Most shows do not have the complications of national productions, and the staff directors can easily handle the details of preparation as well as the on-the-air direction. But religious and other public service programs, most of which originate with organizations that are independent of the station, urgently need producers who will be responsible for every phase of production, including all the work that would normally fall to the director.

The owners and managers of television stations are notoriously indifferent to the fate of public service programs. Many stations callously refuse to schedule any camera rehearsal for public service shows. Some stations provide for a little rehearsal with director and cameras. It is a rare case—if any exists—where a religious program has adequate camera rehearsal. Therefore, if you would avoid utter chaos on the air, you need to work out in detail every visual image, every audio effect, you hope to attain, without counting upon the director, cameramen, and audio engineers to help you. Even the most careful preparation still leaves you with the formidable task of co-ordinating the thoughts and actions of the performers, the director, the cameramen, and the sound engineers when director and crew have not had the opportunity to become fully cognizant of what is to happen before the cameras.

This writer has found that most directors—and their floor crews —have more sense of responsibility for, and take more pride in, public service programs than do their employers. A man becomes a director because he wants to create. His artistic conscience will drive him to turn out the best show he can, against all obstacles. The director usually will welcome all the help he can get to make his show come off well. He wants to know what effects are desired and the best means of obtaining them. The director usually will hold prebroadcast conferences with the producer, and he may even be enticed into taking charge of dry-run rehearsals, especially if he is paid by the religious organization for his services.

THE DUTIES OF THE PRODUCER

Your role as the producer of a religious program is the same as that of the entrepreneur producer of the national commercial show —without the profit motive. You must be the major creative force behind the program, and you must oversee its every detail up to the actual calling of shots on the air. You need not be a professional in television to produce religious programs, but you certainly must know enough about the medium to be able to cope with any of the situations that arise in local broadcasting.

We recommend that in a council of churches, program producers be members of the television committee. They will then be in the strong position of (1) helping to make program policy, and (2) being thoroughly familiar with the ideas and objectives assigned to the series for which they are responsible.

Once the committee has decided upon the type of program, objective, audience, general theme, format, class of performers (i.e., actors, speakers), and the budget for a series of programs, the production responsibility of the committee members ceases. This is where the producer takes over. He can, and probably will, consult with the members of the committee as he works on programs. But he alone must make the decisions. The act of artistic creation is a lonely thing. No committee ever wrote a satisfactory script or preserved the integrity of one rewritten in the image and likeness of the speech rhythms and vocabularies of the committee members. Nor can you, by majority vote, cast a production or determine how a performer shall interpret a role; or decide what share of the budget shall go toward building sets as against buying stock film footage. The committee has every right to evaluate a production and, even if the producer is a volunteer, to take him to task for poor quality and performance. The members have no right to dictate to him or to second-guess him in the making of production decisions. There may be several ways to handle an artistic problem, and they all may be right. Only the producer can decide which one is right for his program.

Following are the tasks a producer may be expected to perform in the preparation and broadcast of a religious program. If you have assistants, you may delegate operations to them, as you do the writing of a script to an author. But you should keep a master list of all the things to be done and should personally make sure each thing has been accomplished before checking it off.

1. When the program series has been firmed-up by the committee, you should outline the individual programs. If you are working on a permanent or long-term series, outline your shows in blocks of thirteen or some smaller number that may be convenient. Your director and the writers who will work on the series can help you in preparing your treatments.[1] So can content experts, such as theologians.

2. The script is prepared. This step should involve conferences between the writer and you as the writing progresses.

3. The script is reviewed, timed, and if necessary, revised.

4. Cast and prop lists are prepared from the finished script.

5. Sets are designed and construction is begun.

6. A shooting script is prepared. The author's script should be broken down into scenes and the shots numbered, as in the sample script at the end of Chapter 5. The example given is a dramatic program. Dramas require the most detailed production descriptions, but other types of programs need to be broken down in the same way. The shooting script should contain all camera and sound directions and cues; instructions for cuts, dissolves, fades; directions for placing and shifting sets and props; instructions for use of pull and drop cards, slides, insert film footage, and other visuals. On the dialogue side, this script should carry all necessary instructions to performers, both for action and for interpretation; all music cues and directions; sound cues and instructions to sound operators.

7. The shooting script is mimeographed and distributed to the director, floor manager, performers, and anyone else who may need it.

8. The program is cast. Casting, at least in dramatic shows, is

[1] A treatment is a précis of what the program is about. In a drama it includes the plot; in a discussion, the subject matter to be covered. The treatment can also describe sets, props, methods of handling action, etc. Treatments may be as short as a single page or may run to many typewritten pages. The more elaborate the treatment, the more understandable your plans will be to writer, director, and other participants, and the more likely you will be to avoid errors and omissions when you finally get into production.

usually the province of the director. In a religious program, it will probably fall to you as producer. You should have the help of the director, if you can get it. Casting means the choosing of participants, whether they be actors, panelists for a discussion program, an interviewer and the persons to be interviewed, a teacher for an educational lecture, or any other performers. Unless you know your performers well, it will always be to your advantage to hold auditions before choosing the persons who are to go on the air.

9. Rehearsals are scheduled. You lay out your set in the hall where they will be held, chalking the outlines on the floor.

10. Props are assembled or manufactured. Title cards and other visuals are prepared. Insert film footage and necessary still pictures are procured. Musical and other needed recordings are assembled. Sound effects are constructed or obtained on recordings.

11. Rehearsals begin and continue until the program is perfected.

12. Publicity is prepared and distributed. This work is not, strictly speaking, the job of the producer, but you will probably have to oversee it to get it done.

13. Camera rehearsal is held.

14. The program is aired. Your job during broadcast is to air-check the program, preferably from a monitor outside the studio or control room, where you may view the production without being distracted by the bustle of the studio.

15. The program is evaluated. Sins of commission and omission are noted, and things that will help in future productions recorded.

THE ROLE OF THE DIRECTOR

In television, the director has more immediate and personal participation in the show than he does in any other medium. The stage director prepares his production and then leaves the actors to fend for themselves once the curtain is up. The motion picture director does half his job on the set, the rest in the cutting room. The television director not only determines the artistic interpretation, he is an active participant in the performance. In fact he gives form, sequence, and pacing to the performance independently of the action taking place on the set. He literally "calls the shots" that make or break the show. His instant decisions are final—once and for all.

In television, every night is a first night. There are no retakes.

The director can be a semiautomaton who sits in the control room calling preset shots designated by the advertising agencies. If such a man is assigned to you, your cause is hopeless. But if your director is a creative person who will search out the meaning in your script and the individuality in the performers and meld the two, the chances are you will have a lively program. In the final analysis, a good director is one who is so immersed in the action that he can feel the flow of movement before it takes place and can hit upon the precise picture at the precise moment it is needed. No amount of advance preparation can substitute for the director's ability to watch the movement and make split-second adjustments to its requirements.

The good director is one who understands the jobs and the problems of all those who work around him—the cameramen, the engineers, the floor manager, the writer, the producer, the performers. But above all, he must be able to *direct*: to inspire and instruct performers so they will understand the motivation behind their speeches and will deliver them in such a way that the ideas they are expressing will communicate with the viewer; to make the performers comfortable and happy under the working conditions he sets for them; to pace his performance so it will have just the emotional quality he has decided it needs; to find the right way to tell his story or to present his arguments or opinions through a succession of pictures that will communicate story content through their flow and continuity.

In good production procedures, the director usually begins to operate as soon as script drafts start coming from the writer. He sits in with the producer and writer on script conferences. When the script is completed and approved, the director prepares the more detailed shooting script, described above. If he can manage it, the director will have an assistant who then takes over scheduling; the procurement of props, sets, films, costumes, and other necessaries; the supervision of set construction; and the oversight of the studio setup.

CASTING

Normally, the director is deeply involved in the casting. Many producers leave all the casting to their directors, requiring conferences only on the filling of major roles. If you can possibly get the station director to assist you in casting, do so. Remember, the cast is anyone who appears before the camera. Your director should be a good judge of whether or not any person being considered for a role will be capable of filling it well. Often the director's professional judgment will be accepted by a committee—or by the potential performer —where yours will not.

Unless he is intimately acquainted with the abilities of a proposed performer, the director will insist upon an audition before approving his appearance in a program. If you, as producer, are fulfilling the director's function prior to actual broadcast, you should follow the same procedure.

Your television committee should develop standards of performance for their programs, and you, as producer, should apply them rigorously. Here are some questions to ask about any prospective performer:

Is he an exciting person? If a minister, for example, is not exciting in the pulpit, he will not be exciting on the air.

Does he have character? Will the viewer, just by looking at him, think, "Here is someone I want to pay attention to"?

Does he have a mobile, expressive face? The close-up is television's chief stock in trade. Here the slightest body or head movement may throw the performer out of frame. Emotions and meanings must be communicated solely through facial expressions. Many successful public speakers, being removed from their audiences, depend almost wholly on gestures to convey meaning and do not use facial expression at all. Many stage actors, because of the broad area of the theater, also depend upon their bodies to express feelings, seldom changing facial expression. Such people have low television potential unless they can adapt themselves to the close-in play of the cameras.

Body movement is important. Can your candidate express feelings with his body and his gestures; and can he adapt his movements to the constricted range required by the close view of the cameras and the smallness of the sets? The broad movements so necessary to pulpit and stage are incongruous on television.

What about voice range and quality? A poor voice may be acceptable to one's friends. It will not be tolerated by the viewers of a television performance. Another speech element of importance is the ability to memorize. A performer who is tied to a manuscript, or even to notes, is handicapped. He can use a teleprompter, but it takes a professional to look natural while reading from one. Prompt cards always give themselves away, because the performer must take his eyes from the camera lens to follow them. He looks as if he is avoiding the eye of the viewer.

Another asset is the ability to speak lines as they are written and to project the motivation the writer has put into them. If almost every line must be rewritten to conform to the performer's speech style and ability, the chances are he will have a hard time interpreting the meaning of his material. (See Chapter 7).

Make a list of the good performers you may be able to use on your programs. Cross-index them according to skills. Study the performances of able actors, preachers, speakers, teachers, singers in public appearances and on television. Catalogue the techniques they use to make their messages come alive. Note particularly their *taste* in their mode and content of expression. A great performance is always one that is in good taste.

Never forget that a good producer or director is constantly growing in his art. He is continually on the alert for new techniques, better ways of saying something. He is an acute observer of the actions and emotions of others. He knows all too well that he never knows enough. He is continually learning, perhaps most fruitfully when he is teaching others how to interpret a part or an idea.

When the Director Takes Control

When rehearsals begin, the director should take control.

Before then, presumably, producer and director will have worked over the script and arrived at a common point of view. You have a cast. All the basic arrangements have been made. From here on it is the director's job to take the disparate elements of the production and to forge them into a show. He will balance your wishes as producer, the ideas of the writer, the skill of the performers and the technical ability of his crew on the scales of his own imagination and interpretative sense; and out of this blend will come the point of view that will be dominant in your program. The director is both the fountainhead and the center of a vast web of activity. Only he can give unity to the show.

Once the director has taken over, you are no longer the boss. You should step aside and assist him in any way you can. It only confuses things for someone to try to give directions to the director when he is working.

Let us warn you again that on the local station you, the producer, will probably have to fill the director's shoes right up to the time the program begins to unfold on the air. But the station will not let you actually call the shots. If you are going to broadcast under such circumstances, take the situation in good grace and do not try to interfere with the progress of the program. Even if the station director is not doing things the way you prefer you will only make matters worse by telling him so while the program is on the air. Wait until afterward and analyze the program with him, in the hope he will do better next time.

THE PRODUCTION CREW

Floor and control room crews vary in number and function from station to station. Be sure you are familiar with the men in your crew and with their duties, so you can prepare your performers for what to expect in the studio.

The *floor manager* is the representative of the director in the studio. He stands between the cameras, wearing a headset. The director gives him orders which he then transmits to performers and crew. He throws all visual cues to the performers and gives them time signals. He is responsible for seeing that the sets are ready and the performers in place before each scene opens. He positions and checks title cards and similar visual props. He may also pull or drop cards in front of the camera.

The *assistant director* sits next to the director in the control room and performs the latter's routine duties. Usually he watches timing and reminds the director of his cues. He may set up shots, previously planned in rehearsal, ahead of the action. During the rehearsal, he takes notes on corrections and changes desired by the director. He may also be responsible for calling the cast, doing make-up, checking sets and lighting before rehearsals and air time, and similar tasks.

The *technical director* handles the electronic switching from camera to camera. He is the boss engineer on the program. Under one system of production, he directs the cameramen on orders from the director. He is then responsible for setting up shots, since the director cannot speak to the cameramen.

Lighting in a local station is usually done by one of the engineers, who may or may not be trained for this tricky work.

Staging, the design, construction, painting, placing, and dressing of sets, also usually falls to the lot of the engineers in smaller stations. For this reason, a good and willing high school youth group can be of inestimable value in preparing religious programs. They can build better sets than the station will bother with, and they can learn television staging and lighting and have a good time in the process.

The *audio engineer* operates all of the microphones used in a program in the same manner as does the studio engineer in radio. He sits at a console in the control room.

The *boom operator* works the microphone boom if one is used. His job is to keep the microphone within proper range of the performers. He takes orders from the technical director concerning placement of the microphone in relation to the camera frame; i.e., keeping it out of frame, keeping microphone shadows off the sets. In placing the microphone for sound quality, he takes orders from the audio engineer.

The *projectionist* operates motion picture and slide projectors which are used to insert filmed material into the program. He works outside the studio, sometimes from the transmitter. He receives orders from the director and is under the technical control of the technical director, who may start and stop the projectors by remote control from the studio.

Make-up is all too often done by an office secretary in the smaller stations. It is well for a producer of religious programs to learn to be his own make-up man. See below.

In the larger stations, there may be other crew members, such as carpenters, grips, graphic artists, dolly and boom pushers to move cameras and microphone booms, and various other floor assistants, but we have listed the most important crew jobs with which the producer should be familiar.

The Cast

Your chief working aids in producing are, of course, the performers themselves—how they look, how they act, the quality of their speech, what they say. The faces of the performers are the most important means of portraying emotions and reactions. Faces also delineate character for the viewer. Therefore, it is a good idea to show a close-up of each performer as soon as he appears, in order to establish identity, and thereafter to use face shots whenever emotion is being portrayed.

Grouping of performers in relation to each other and to the set can also convey ideas and emotion. Place an interviewer and the person he is interviewing side by side in comfortable chairs in a living-room set and, before a word is said, the viewer will get the feeling that this is to be a chatty, friendly conversation. Contrast this decor with the one used by Mike Wallace in his interviews—a bare set with Wallace and his guest facing each other. You get the sense of confrontation, challenge, conflict.

Make-up

Most of your make-up will be for "talk" shows of one sort or another, rather than for dramas, where makeup is used to delineate character. Your objective will be to make each performer look as natural as possible. Make-up is used to eliminate shine and give the skin an even tone, to cover beards, wrinkles, and imperfections, and to darken pale skins to keep the faces from being lost.

A good rule to follow is to use as little make-up as possible. Stage-type make-up, such as heavily darkened eyebrows, mascaraed eyelashes, and rouged cheeks, will appear just as artificial on television as it does in face-to-face encounter. Pancake make-up is used universally in television (Max Factor Panchromatic, usually 1N or 2N for women and 3N or 4N for men). Spread the pancake evenly over the face from the forehead to the clothing neckline, using a slightly dampened sponge. Use a cleansing tissue to smooth the finish. Be sure to blend the pancake well into the hairline. Make up the ears, too. Women should have paste lip-rouge applied with a brush. The lipline should be modeled carefully. Television will require a darker shade of lipstick than is normal for street wear. Men seldom require lip or eyebrow make-up. Most women will need to have their eyebrows darkened. If the eyelashes are light in color, they should be darkened, too. Deep-set eyes should be lightened by applying light pancake to the upper part of the eyesockets.

Be sure to check make-up before the cameras prior to going on the air. Sometimes a make-up that looks satisfactory in the dressing room shows flaws when it is photographed.

With a little practice, you can learn to be a good make-up artist. Try it on yourself before a mirror equipped with lights that will cover your whole face without throwing shadows.

Most people today realize that television requires make-up; but you may run into some persons who object to using it. Explain that make-up is as necessary as is retouching to a portrait—and for the same reason. Strong, direct light overemphasizes angles, wrinkles, and blemishes. It makes the face look stark. Therefore, a person needs make-up (retouching) to soften this starkness and to make him appear natural—as in face-to-face encounter.

Color and Contrast

The appearance of sets and costumes on the screen is related closely to their color values. We will not deal with color television here, but will confine our explanations to the monochromatic system which will probably be standard for some years. While this system is called black-and-white television, actually color is present in shades of gray. Neither hue nor its degree of purity (chroma) has any influence on the shade of gray a color will reproduce on television. Reds, greens, and blues that are in brilliant contrast to each other can all come out the same shade of gray, as many a rueful producer has found when he has dressed a performer in one bright color and put her before a background of another color of the same value, only to have his picture turn out to be an isolated face and two hands engulfed in a sea of uniform gray.

Brightness is the only factor of a color that affects gray value.

The brightness, or brilliance of a color is measured by the amount of light the color will reflect. Brightness is a relative value. It can be altered by varying the amount of light thrown on the object and by the material which carries the color. The same hue of a color will appear as a much lighter gray if photographed from a piece of coated paper than from a soft tweed suit.

Contrast is an important factor in picture quality because the television system is extremely sensitive. On the white side, the system can accept surfaces and objects that reflect up to 75 per cent of the light thrown on them. (Of course, this does not mean an unlimited amount of light may be poured onto a surface.) On the black side, the system can accept as little as 4 per cent reflection. In a single picture, the maximum contrast range is approximately 20 to 1; i.e., the lightest part of the picture can safely reflect twenty times as much light as does the darkest part.

From the foregoing, you will understand why you should avoid shiny materials. No matter what color you may use, too much light will be reflected into the camera lens. Overmuch reflection causes the halos and bright spots that sometimes spoil pictures. Conversely, a material that has no brilliance, such as a piece of rough-textured construction paper, may eat up so much light that the camera will record it as a black blob.

Never put black and white side by side, as when a man wears a black suit and a white shirt. The white will "bloom" from too much reflected light (this is why blue, gray, or other tints are desired in shirts); the black will absorb too much light in proportion. A black-and-white combination is permissible for title cards that are to be used for superimpositions. White lettering is used on a black background.

The surest way to find out if your colors will blend into an acceptable picture is to test them before a camera. In preparing sets and objects, do not put shades of the same gray value next to each other. Work for sufficient contrast by putting light and dark surfaces of the same color in juxtaposition. Some stations have sets of gray-shade sample cards that can be used to check shading and contrast. The easiest way to handle the color problem is to paint all sets and objects in varying tones of gray, using the sample cards as standards.

Costumes

"Costume" is a technical term that refers to all clothing and accessories worn by performers. Street clothes are a costume if they are worn on the air in the course of a discussion program.

Costumes must be chosen to fit the demands of color and contrast described above. Clothing shows to best advantage if it is in the middle of the gray-scale range. The man in a gray flannel suit with blue shirt and solid darker blue tie is just right for television. Collars should be soft because starching increases reflective qualities. Clerical collars should be tinted blue; otherwise, the performer may appear with a halo around his neck.

Women should avoid lustrous fabrics such as shiny silks and brocades. Rough-textured fabric shows to better advantage than does smooth. Tailored suits and dresses that form a trim body line are more suitable than are loose or fussy dresses. Ballerina skirts or dresses billowed out with horsehair slips usually are not flattering in the close confines of a television set.

Clothing should fit well and be carefully pressed. Otherwise, bunching and wrinkling may cause ugly shadows that make the performers appear unkempt. Men should open their coats when they are seated to prevent strain and bunching. Dress necklines should be trim and simple.

Jewelry is a danger because of its high reflective quality. Wrist watches should be removed. Tie clips, lapel pins, rings, necklaces, earrings, and bracelets should be dulled with an antireflective spray. In a pinch, soap or milk can be used for this purpose. Shiny buttons should also be dulled.

Decor

The set and all that it includes, except the performers, make up the theatrical decor of your program. Sets are "dressed" with properties (props), which may be real objects (curtains, pictures, tables, chairs, rugs, an African tom-tom) or mock-ups, fake objects made to resemble the real thing.

The Set. The set itself is the physical construction that places your program in a particular locale. It may be the walls of a room, a city street, a church sanctuary, or merely a plain backdrop against which you will place two chairs for an interview. In discussing script writing, we have explained how the set can be used to foster action. Here we would add the advice to keep the set simple. It is easier for the viewer to comprehend what is going on in a fairly bare set than it is for him to cope with an overdressed, "busy" set. Also, simple sets are cheaper to construct than are complicated ones.

Make your set fit the action you want to portray. If you are presenting a discussion, put your participants in plain, comfortable chairs before a neutral background. It is only what they say and how they look while saying it that has meaning in this kind of a program. If you scatter potted plants, or fancy backgrounds, or bookshelves and library furniture around this kind of set, you will only detract from your center of interest, the performers. If you must hide their feet, put a table in front of them, but do not put flowers on it. Above all, do not build a podium and seat them behind it in solemn, judicial array.

Properties. Make every prop say something, or do not use it. Again, simplicity is the *sine qua non* of communication. Any object you use should be instantly identifiable and immediately comprehendable. If an object you use on the set needs to be explained, it is not a prop; it is a subject for demonstration.

Models and miniatures may be classified as props, although, technically, they are used for demonstration. A model is a representation of something, such as a locomotive, built to scale and made to operate. A miniature is a scale replica which is not constructed to operate. Miniatures are most often used to simulate large sets—such as a whole town—the camera establishing a panoramic view by means of the miniature, then cutting or dissolving to the action which takes place in a full-size set that is supposedly a part of the view shown through the miniature.

Visual Devices. Any object you use to visualize what you are saying or anything that tells your story visually is a visual device.

Title cards are the most common visual device. They are made to the aspect ratio of the frame, 4 wide to 3 high. Most commonly, these cards are 12 by 9 inches or 15 by 12 inches. They may contain lettering or drawings. For good visibility, do not put more than three lines of printing on a card. Allow ample space at top, bottom, and sides for framing. A good color combination for title cards is black lettering on a light shade of gray, non-translucent cardboard.

Titles or drawings can be on individual cards which can be dropped or pulled in sequence. They can also be mounted on a drum turned by a hand crank or a variable-speed motor. Still another device is to draw three or more frames of material from left to right or from top to bottom on a single, long strip of poster board. The camera then pans across or tilts down from frame to frame. These are called pan, or tilt cards.

A simple and useful device is a Lazy Susan. It can be turned to show all sides of a demonstration object. By using vertical partitions on the bed of the platter, you can also prepare two, three, or four miniature stages for the showing of objects.

Still pictures, charts, maps, and graphs are common visual aids in television. Whenever possible, these graphics should be made to do double duty. Each one, of course, should deal with only one subject; but sometimes one can be made to tell several things about the subject. For example, suppose you were illustrating comparative church statistics. Instead of using a simple bar-graph to show gross-number relationships, you could use a pictograph with stick figures. The Protestant line might contain figures of men and women only, with the Roman Catholic line made up of men, women, and children, to show the different methods used in determining membership. Your graph would then show *what kinds* as well as *how much* are being compared.

Since television is *motion pictures*, you are not taking full advantage of the medium if you do not make your visuals *move*. Animation is probably out of the question for the local religious program, but with the exercise of ingenuity, you can probably get some motion into your graphics.

If you were using a map to locate and describe the Navajo Indian reservation, you could heighten interest by attaching pictures of sheep to illustrate the ranching, a cutout of the mission hospital on the reservation, and other similar material. The fact that church membership increases are outstripping church building could be shown in an action graph. One line would contain a pictograph of churches, the other, stick figures of persons. The symbols would be drawn on continuous rolls of paper, then each roll folded to show relationship of members to churches at the start of the graphing period. As the explanation of growth patterns was made, the two paper rolls could be pulled open by an off-screen string, the symbol line of persons being opened rapidly while the church line is opened slowly. Technically, this kind of graph is known as a "pull."

Graphs and charts can also be made three dimensional with movable parts. Among other useful three-dimensional charting devices are flannel boards and metal boards on which you can attach objects and cutouts that are backed with magnetized metal strips.

Finally, do not disdain the schoolroom blackboard as an effective device for keeping information before the viewer. However, on television the board should be green and the chalk, orange or pastel! Be careful of your writing. It should be large and legible or viewers will not be able to read it on home screens.

Projected Aids

Motion picture inserts, either sound or silent, are excellent sources of informational material. They can also be used as part of the action in a program, especially where you want to depict scenes outside the studio. Many stations have motion picture units, and sometimes they are available for public service programs. With the widespread incidence of amateur motion picture photography, it is probable that you can find someone with a 16 mm. camera who will shoot simple film sequences for you. They should be taken on reversal film to save the cost of making a print from a negative. Editing can be done by the photographer or in the station film room.

Virtually all stations are equipped with projectors that will accomodate 2 by 2-inch kodachrome and black-and-white slides. Most of them also have opaque projectors for the transmission of "balops" (also called "telops"), 4 by 3-inch cards containing lettering or drawings. Figure 1 shows a clever balop done by the art department of the educational station in San Juan, Puerto Rico.

REHEARSALS

No religious television program is worth doing without careful rehearsal. Performers who object to rehearsing should not be tolerated, and producers who fail to hold rehearsals should be replaced. The show must be good *before* it reaches the cameras. There is never time in camera rehearsal to replace bad content, brush up a dull performance, or overcome lack of motivation in interpretation.

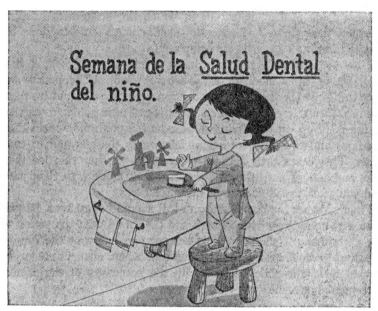

FIGURE 1

Rehearsal really begins with preplanning of the action and interpretation by the producer, in counsel with the director if the latter is available. When the performers are called together for the first time, they should know, in general, what is to be required of them, and the director should know exactly what he wants to get out of each one of them.

The first rehearsal is always a preliminary run through to set the content in the minds of the performers. This holds true whether you are producing a discussion, an educational lecture, or a complicated dramatic show. If there is a script, start off with a reading of it by the cast. Discuss the elements of the program. Describe the sets. Make sure everyone understands the mood of the program; the plot if it is a drama or the theme development or story line if you are dealing with discussion or instruction; the end result you expect to attain from the program. Make any necessary revisions in the script to enhance its capacity to play.

Next come reading rehearsals in which the performers learn to interpret their parts. Any necessary memorizing should be done before the reading rehearsals are completed.

Now you are ready to take your cast into the set itself, if it is available, or into a mock-up of the set if it is not. All properties and everything else needed for the production should be on hand for these dry-run rehearsals without camera, but the cast need not be in costume or use make-up. In the dry-run rehearsals the performers learn their positions and their movements in relation to the sets and to each other. They learn their actions. Over and over they practice their lines and actions until they are thoroughly at home with their parts and you are satisfied with their interpretation.

Finally, comes the camera rehearsal. It should be just that. Its purpose is to co-ordinate the cameras and the sound with the action of the performers. It should not be necessary to interrupt the camera rehearsal to work on interpretation except where changes are necessary to make the action accord with the necessities of the camera and microphone pickups.

A Sample of Rehearsal

Since discussions bulk so large in religious programming, we will describe the rehearsal pattern for discussion programs on *Frontiers of Faith*, the weekly series presented by the National Council of the Churches of Christ in the U.S.A. over the National Broadcasting Company network. Each summer the National Council of Churches produces a number of half-hour discussions in this series. The 1959 discussions afford an example of the way these programs are planned and produced.

Early in the fall of 1958, the *Frontiers of Faith* planning committee decided that the next summer's discussion series would be based on a major contemporary theological issue. A two-day conference to discuss possible themes was called for the week after Christmas and was attended by some thirty theologians and campus ministers from various parts of the country. Out of this conference came the issue for the series: The application of Christian conscience to major ethical decisions being made in contemporary culture, decisions in which people are likely to substitute false gods for the living God in rationalizing self-serving actions.

Later, in further conferences between the committee members and a smaller group of the theologians a title was chosen for the series: "The Gods We Live With"; and the individual programs were planned. It was decided to open the series with a program on the general theme, to be followed by discussions on the family, politics, work, international relations, race, and the lively arts. Each program would have four panelists, with the moderator, Rev. Dr. James W. Lenhart, and one member, Robert Lewis Shayon, appearing on each program. Other panelists would change from week to week.

Two theologians, Rev. Dr. Julian Hartt of Yale University Divinity School and Rev. Alva Cox of the National Council of Churches, prepared background working papers on the general theme and for each program subject. The papers were circulated to all the participants. Meantime, Doris Ann, producer for the National Broadcasting Company, and Martin Hoade, the director for the series, designed sets and had them built, and arranged rehearsal and recording schedules. (The programs were recorded on video tape which was not edited, so each show had the quality of a live performance.)

Each program was recorded in a single day. The participants were brought together for two-and-one-half hours of rehearsal-discussion in which general themes and content were developed. This preparatory discussion was followed by an uninterrupted thirty-minute run-through before the cameras. The camera rehearsal served to familiarize the director and crew with the necessary camera and microphone placement and movement, and the participants with the organization and interpretation of their material.

Following the camera rehearsal, John Gunn, producer for the National Council of Churches, analyzed the good and bad points of the action and criticized the content and the trend of the discussion. Next, the participants were made up. During make-up, and for an hour afterward, they continued their practice discussion, shaping and sharpening the points they would make on the air. Then the program was recorded.

The careful prebroadcast planning and extensive rehearsal for these programs greatly aided the development of lively, interesting discussions, but both producers and participants agreed that more camera rehearsal was needed by crew and performers. These relatively simple productions, like all television shows, proved, in practice, to be hard to get on the air. Television production is so complicated that, it goes without saying, little preparation or sloppy preparation will be fatal to a program's success. On the other hand, the most intensive planning and long hours of rehearsal never seem to be enough. Television, while perhaps not the most demanding, is certainly the most exacting of the performing arts, requiring the mastery of a multitude of intellectual and mechanical details for the presentation of the most simple programmatic material.

BUDGETS

Budgeting is one of the producer's chief jobs. Since he, alone, has all the details of a program in hand, he is the only person capable of estimating and assigning costs. Having made the budget, he is required to live within it, handling the details of disbursements.

It is hopeless to expect to produce religious television programs without spending money. The radio performer can write a script and go to the studio and read it into a microphone at no cost other than his carfare. Television, at the very least, requires a set, title cards, simple props, visual aids, and make-up, all of which require some outlay. For the more elaborate shows, payment must be made for scripts and, often, for the performers.

Plan your budget at the time you plan your programs. Do not go ahead with production unless you have the money in hand to pay essential costs. Air time and station facilities and crew will be provided free to councils of churches by most stations. Your budget should cover the cost of the following items: scripts; sets (if they are not, as they should be, provided by the station); props not available in the station prop room; preparation and construction of visual devices, models, and objects; title cards; rental or shooting costs of motion-picture footage; flat pictures; costumes; rehearsal costs; fees for performers; travel and other expenses of performers; producer's administrative expenses such as postage, telephone, and travel; cost of promotion and publicity for the programs.

Local station production costs need not be high, especially if there is sufficient voluntary help for preparing materials. When *Off to Adventure,* the national children's program distributed by the National Council of Churches, was being tested over WNHC in New Haven, Connecticut, a fairly elaborate production was financed on a budget of thirty-five dollars per week.

One important item that should be in the general television budget of any council of churches is the sum needed to send one member of the television committee annually to a workshop where he can study mass communications theory and television production.

John Lardner, in analyzing the reasons for the success of *Sunrise Semester*, had some things to say about the participants which are pertinent for religious broadcasting.

It seeemed clear to me, that "Sunrise Semester's" entertainment value —its effect on the general audience, that is—was strongly connected with the personalities or idiosyncrasies of [the] teachers. I imagine that the audience tends to exaggerate such personal distinctions, in the same way that viewers exaggerate, wishfully, the differences between one popular singer, or one gunslinger, and another. In other words, I feel that almost any skillful lecturer would be surefire on this kind of program. Just the same, the . . . teachers were a lively and engaging lot.[1]

The personality of the performer impresses the viewers more than does any other single thing in a television program. But the personality that will please the audience is not likely to be just a combination of a pleasant face and manner, a winsome smile and the ability to handle a slick line of patter. The audience may watch such a personality, but they are too sophisticated to be taken in. The personality that will impress them and keep them coming back for more will be a complex and complicated one, compounded of many ponderables and imponderables: A pleasant manner—of course. A mobile and expressive face, but not necessarily a pretty one. Handiness and clarity in the use of words. Modesty, coupled with respect for the ability, the knowledge, and the viewpoint of the audience members. Dignity. A sense of humor. Alertness. Above all—whether the performer be a jazz singer, a dramatic actor, a news commentator, a teacher, or a clergy-

[1] John Lardner, "School Lets Out," *New Yorker*, Vol. XXXV, No. 14, May 23, 1959, p. 144.

man—he must exhibit an obvious and intense respect and love for his subject, revealed in thoroughgoing preparation for the broadcast and reflecting an earnest desire to share this interest with anyone who will pause to appreciate it. This is the kind of personality that will be "lively and engaging," that will wear well on television as do Edward R. Murrow, Ed Sullivan, Dave Garroway, Frank Baxter, Dinah Shore, Bishop James A. Pike, Bob Hope, and the professors on *Sunrise Semester*.

FACTORS IN COMMUNICATION

Communication in television takes place through an interplay between communicator and viewer of a combination of thought, language, action, and voice. Speech, technically, is made up of the last three elements.

Thought

Presumably, the communicator will do his thinking in preparing for his program. He will analyze his subject and develop his central idea in terms of the audience he hopes to reach, the time available to him, and the format in which he will cast his program. He will determine what end he hopes to achieve with the audience; whether he wishes to entertain them, to impress, to instruct, to convince (i.e., to change beliefs), or to lead them to act. He will pinpoint his precise purpose—the new knowledge he wants to leave with the viewers if his end is instruction, the changed belief, the overt action he wants them to take. He will then work out the means he will use to catch and hold the interest of the desired audience and the communication techniques and language that will make them remember his ideas.

Language

Actual communication begins with the preparation of a script. The language of television is a combination of pictures and words. The technique of script writing is treated in Chapter 5. Here we plead for lucidity in expression because of its great importance to successful speech. If you can express yourself clearly and concisely, you can say a great deal more than otherwise in a given period of time. Lucidity will help you to keep your program moving. It will sustain interest. It will help prevent boredom.

Action

In television, more than in other forms of public communication, actions *will* speak louder than words. The intimacy of the television screen, especially in close-up shots, puts the smallest movement, the faintest flicker of expression, under the close scrutiny of the viewer. He absorbs a constant stream of impressions from the action. Some impressions he registers and stores consciously—things like the overt actions of the characters in a drama. Others reach him subliminally, i.e., below the level of his consciousness. These two types of impressions can be equally important in influencing the formation of his conception of the meanings being communicated. There is a continual interplay of these conscious and unconscious images until the viewer has absorbed enough to evaluate the performers and establish an emotional relationship to them. This decisive testing of personal relationships—all done by the viewer, of course—may take place early in the program and result in a decision to stop or to continue watching. If the viewer stays with the show, he will also continue to experience the interlocking conscious-unconscious impressions from the action. But now he is more likely to apply his impressions to decisions about the *content* of the program than to his relationship with the performers.

Actions. Actions that are under the conscious control of the performer can be designed to create a particular impression in the mind of the viewer. They can be either visual or aural acts. The way you stand, sit, hold your body or cock your head in a scene, body movements and gestures, the changing play of facial expressions, the use of props—if these things are consciously employed to advance the action or convey meaning, they will probably register on the consciousness of the viewer. Voice quality that is assumed deliberately, the force of delivery, timing, the emotional tone, the rhetoric used are parallel aural actions.

Conscious actions can do a great deal to further the process of communication. An alert, easy attitude helps keep the viewer alert and interested. The ability to convey the sense that you are in charge of the situation leads to the conviction that you know what you are talking about. Whole stories can be told in subtle, conscious actions.

If you do not believe that, watch a young man and woman carrying on a flirtation in a crowded room. Questions are asked, answers given, and a world of ideas exchanged without an overt gesture or a word being spoken.

There are other, unconscious actions—postures, gestures, and vocal imperfections,—that can easily defeat the ends you hope to achieve with the audience. They are the messages you do not want to send. Glance away from the camera lens for an instant to pick up a cue from the floor manager and the viewer will think, "Aha, he's nervous." Let your body slump, and viewer interest will slump with you. Hesitate in walking or make awkward gestures, and the viewer will think you are poorly prepared. Let your lip twitch in a close-up, and he will be sure you are frightened.

A voice that is technically poor or out of control can cause equally disastrous effects. If you have a vocal scrape, you run the danger of identifying yourself as an unpleasant person, and your subject automatically becomes distasteful. Lack of vocal variety makes your content sound dull. Faulty use of time, force, and pitch make for communication of meanings you did not mean.

Establishing and Maintaining Empathy. Empathy is a "feeling into," the projection of one person's consciousness into another's. It can best be illustrated by reminding you of your feelings at a football game when your team has made a heroic, last-second goal line stand. When it is over, you fall back, exhausted. You are only a spectator, but every muscle aches. You braced yourself, dug in your feet; your adrenalin supply increased. You fought to hold the line every bit as hard as did any of the eleven men on the field. All unconsciously you empathized with the players.

It is usually only after empathy is established that the viewer will be open to persuasion. It is essential, therefore, that you establish empathy in the audience members if you are to touch their emotions. Action has more empathetic emphasis than does speech. Your body can say a great deal, just in the way you hold it erect or allow it to droop or sway, or by the way you walk and gesture. Every dancer knows this. Gestures can communicate ideas directly and can emphasize points of content. In some instances, your point cannot be made *without* gestures. If you doubt this, try telling the story of how you caught a fish, including the description of the size and shape of your catch, without using broad gestures.

Practice gesturing. Try, especially, to get rid of any inhibitions you have about gesturing with your whole arms and body. Forearm and hand gestures with the body held rigid and the elbows close to the sides are jerky and awkward. They make you look foolish. They destroy empathy because no one will react favorably to movement that makes him feel uncomfortable.

Remember that the smallness of the television frame often precludes the use of sweeping gestures. In a tight close-up even a slight movement of the head will throw you out of frame. In waist shots and closer pictures the area of movement is restricted. Therefore, it is wise to practice gestures that will communicate your ideas and that will also fit into the constricted area of the picture. Stand before a mirror and see how much meaning you can convey with head movements and with your hands. A single finger beckoning or pointing accusingly can tell a story.

All movement must be more deliberate on television than it is in real life. Rapid movement, especially in close-up, is speeded up on the screen. It can appear ludicrous and thus shatter emotional illusion.

Vocal utterance also affects empathetic response. Your voice quality reveals your character and emotional state to the viewer with alarming accuracy. The person who can speak with confidence, sincerity, and naturalness has the best chance to break down the barriers between himself and his audience. Your style of speech should be simple and direct. Viewers are quick to detect exhibitionism in the tones and inflections of the voice and in gesture and movement. (Politicians have learned this and have long since ceased parading the flamboyant bravado of traditional party-rally oratory. If anything, they are now erring on the side of being either colorless or "over sincere.") Your voice should have a pleasant quality about it, for as Quintilian has warned speakers, "that which offends the ear will not easily gain admission to the mind." Master the formula: Be natural, be yourself. Speak straight from the shoulder and make it obvious that the way you speak shows how you stand. The audience appreciates this kind of attitude and respects the man who adopts it.

The Voice

Each of us has a habitual norm of voice quality which he thinks of as being the revelation of himself to others—the indispensable expression of his personality. It is, therefore, psychologically difficult to change this norm, even when one's vocal quality is poor, because of the fear that a new pattern of speech habits will be conceived by others to be an alteration in personality. Physiologically, though, good voice techniques can be established with a fair degree of ease, since few of us are endowed by nature with poor voices. Speech habits are acquired by imitation, mostly in childhood from mimicking the voices of our elders. Methods of breathing, so-called voice placement, articulation, pronunciation, and tone quality are learned by the trial and error method. Everything acquired in this way can be unlearned and replaced by superior speech habits; it must be if you are to go on the air, because general American speech is so sloppy that it effectively hides the beauty and flexibility of the natural voice. Viewers will not tolerate in performers on television the provincial dialects, the harsh, strident, or nasal voices, the slurring articulation which they habitually use themselves. You can improve your speech immeasurably if you can identify your problems intellectually, can develop a means of working toward their solution, and can establish an objective standard for measuring progress.

Accent and Intonation. Everybody speaks with an accent. There are three major American accents, Southern, Eastern, and Middle Western. A variant of Middle Western accent has developed on the West Coast and is becoming a fourth general accent. There is no reason to be ashamed of using any one of these accents as long as you speak in the manner of educated persons in the region it represents. A cultured accent helps give individuality to the voice and is preferable to the so-called "general American accent" that has been widely adopted by network commercial announcers. The latter robs the voice of variety and character.

Within the recognized American accents, people speak innumerable dialects. A dialect is a variant from the cultured expression of the accent. It is a corruption of standard English in pronunciation, intonation, usage, and vocabulary. A rich, well-developed dialect may be just the thing needed for a character part in a play, but in general speech it makes English sound like a foreign language to everyone but its practitioners. This fact is easy to comprehend when we deal with foreign dialects in English; but it is often overlooked when everyone around us speaks just as we do. A dialect is a sign of speech provincialism. It is a handicap in public communication efforts.

Individuality in the voice is much to be desired. It is a constructive means of communicating personality through speech. If all of us spoke in the rich, rotund tones advocated by some speech teachers, speaking would be very dull indeed.

Individuality is largely achieved by means of the intonation, your unique combination of melody, force, timing, and pitch into a speech whole. Entire sections of the country use a single intonation. You will probably speak with the intonation you were born into. If it is poor, you can change it by practicing. Create your own manner of intonation, basing it in good vocal quality and patterning it to fit your communication aims.

WORKING FOR VOCAL QUALITY

The Vocal Mechanism

Your vocal quality—how pleasing or displeasing your voice is to a listener—is determined by the use you make of your vocal mechanism (your breathing, your vocal cords, and your vocal resonators) and by the efficiency of your articulation. Speech is not natural to men; it is an overlaid function. All of the speech organs are present in our bodies for other purposes—to take in and distribute oxygen and to expel waste gases, to tear food, to swallow. Each newborn child must, by imitation, master the process of converting these organs to the uses of speech.

Breath Control. The lungs are the motor mechanism of speech. They provide the stream of air that triggers and carries sound. The degree of breath control determines whether your voice will be weak and breathy, forced and harsh, or full and resonant. When you are speaking, you need to have at your command a strong, steady stream of air, controllable as by the throwing of a switch.

There is no one "right" way to breathe for speech, particularly in television where there is seldom a need for maximum volume and projection. But you must breathe in such a manner that you do not tense the muscles of the neck and mouth and so constrict the air flow. In normal breathing, inhalation and exhalation times are about equal. Breathing for speech needs a quick intake of a large amount of air; then there is slow exhalation, the speed depending upon rate of speech and length of phrasing. There is always need for a reservoir of air which is never allowed to run out. Central breathing (sometimes called diaphragmatic breathing) is recommended for all types of public speaking because it is the best way to stay relaxed and still maintain a reservoir of air. The axiom of Shakespearean acting holds good for television: "Pack your tones against your belt."

The Vocal Cords. The cords are vibrating strings that give the stream of air passing between them pitch, intensity, and some measure of quality. This production of vocal sound is called *phonation*. The *timbre* of the voice depends upon physiology. The larger the throat is, the longer will be the cords; therefore, the greater their potential frequency range. (Men have an advantage over women in speech equipment because both their throats and chest cavities are generally bigger than are those of women.) The *quality* of the sound created by the vocal cords can be controlled. If the throat muscles are tense and the stream of air is unduly constricted in passing through the larynx, there will be impurities of tone—harshness, grating, raspiness. Purity of tone is vitally dependent upon relaxed throat muscles and diaphragmatic control of the force of the air stream.

Resonance. The speech resonators are the pharynx, the top part of the throat above the larynx, which opens into the nose and mouth; the nose; and, most important of all, the mouth. They correspond to the box of the cello; they amplify, reverberate, and enrich the tone. In the cello, the size and shape of the resonator are fixed while the lengths of the strings are varied from note to note. The voice is just the opposite. The length of the vocal cords is always the same. Resonance is obtained by quick changes in the size and shape of the resonators. If they do not respond instantly or if they are shaped improperly, the tone will be flat and colorless. To have your resonators under such control that they will respond to their fullest at top speed, you need to have complete relaxation of the muscles of the throat, the jaw, and the mask of the face.

Articulation. This is the release and projection of the tone. The way articulation is handled has a bearing on the pureness of pronunciation. Distinctness of articulation is more important in speech than is volume. Often you can better understand a person who speaks softly and distinctly than you can one whose voice is loud but whose articulation is slurred.

Good articulation requires free, strong, flexible movement of the lips, tongue, and jaws. A tense tongue, tense jaws, and lazy lip movement can negate good tone every time. Nevertheless, some careless speakers achieve rich, resonant tones, then project them somewhat like this: "I wanna hev yuh see this cidy es it oughtta be."

All of us slip into faulty articulation from time to time. We need to test our articulation frequently with exercises before a mirror and with recordings. It is all too easy to miss errors in articulation. We become so used to living with our sloppy speech that our ears miss our mistakes and our brains record the correct sounds, just as if they had been made. How many times have you been corrected for a speech slip and retorted—at least mentally—"I didn't say that at all"? It is important to train your ear to catch every slightest articulatory fault in others and in yourself. Then you will be on your toes to get good vocal quality, whether you are a producer or a performer.

It should be apparent by now how important muscular relaxation is to the attainment of good vocal quality. There are many exercises that will help you relax the muscles used in speaking. They are described in speech textbooks. Find the ones that are most useful to you and practice them before public appearances. They will aid you measurably in improving your voice.

Vocal Techniques

Vocal variety is essential to good interpretative speech. It is the combination of melody, pitch, force, and timing that you employ to give emotional tone to your speaking. Volume is of less importance than these other factors because the microphone pickup requires that volume be held within a relatively narrow range. (See Chapter 9.)

Melody. Speech melody is not a formal combination of sounds, as melody is in music. It is the movement of the voice through the low-to-high range possible for a particular individual without strain. Inflections are a part of the melodic pattern. The function of melody is to express meanings and feelings through tone. Melody is important in conveying subliminal impressions, since it is used to point up shades of meaning, whereas force and time indicate emphasis. A single word or phrase may be capable of communicating several meanings in a given situation. The speaker reveals the right meaning through his melodic pattern. You can quickly comprehend the working of melody if you will do this simple exercise: pronounce the word "Oh!" several times, giving it a different meaning each time—surprise, pain, disgust, joy, comprehension, indifference. Do you see how the melody conveys meaning and feeling?

The vocal technique that will give the widest melodic range is to base the voice in the middle register, which gives room for movement to higher and lower registers to interpret meaning and emotion. Remember that the range of the voice is narrower in speaking than in singing. Do not overreach your normal range and break into a chant.

Pitch. Pitch is the location of a tone on the scale. It is determined by the frequency of the vibration of the vocal cords and is controlled by altering the degree of tension in the cords and, to a lesser extent, by changing the size of the resonators. Variations in pitch are important in the development of melody. Like melody, variations in pitch should move upward and downward from the optimum level for your voice. Pitch changes should be calculated in advance to fit the ideas and emotions being communicated. Random pitch changes are never desirable.

Force. Emphasis is much better communicated by variations in force than it is by changes in volume. Force is the power applied to an utterance. It shows the relative importance of ideas. It holds attention. Sharp stress can pull wandering audience minds back in focus. Subdued stress after a passage of heavy force immediately switches attention to the new emotional situation. Even amateurs are more likely than not to keep stress tied to ideation, whereas it is all too easy to use variations in loudness haphazardly. Furthermore, when loudness is used for emphasis, it loses effect because the electronic system does not transmit well its upper and lower levels.

Timing. The timing in speech includes the duration of sounds and pauses, the rate of utterance and the rhythm. Lack of attention to timing will almost certainly cause monotony in utterance. The elements of timing are rate, pause, quantity, and rhythm.

The term "rate" is applied to the over-all speed of speaking and to the variations in speed of the divisions in the content. Vocal variety is enhanced by thoughtful relationship of the speed of utterance to the ideas in the script and to the emotional meanings you wish to communicate.

Pauses occur between words, phrases, sentences, and paragraphs. They are the punctuation marks of speech. They need to be carefully thought out because they relate the phrasing to the thought structure.

Quantity is the duration of the sound in the speaking of vowels, consonants, syllables, and words. Communication is greatly dependent upon intelligent use of quantity. Certain vowels and consonants have long quantity values and should not be pronounced quickly: ō, ī, ē, l, m, z; others have short values: ĭ, ĕ, ŭ, b, d, k. Similarly, there is long quantity in certain words: vale, coal, heel; short quantity in others: pup, trip, sit.

Passages and whole selections have basic time-quantity values. Some must be read slowly, with long duration on most of the words; others rapidly, with short duration. A line from Walt Whitman's *Leaves of Grass* is an example of a slow passage: "Give me the splendid, silent sun with all its beams full, dazzling." Hamlet's "Speech to the Players" requires speed and precise articulation: "Speak the speech, I pray you, as I pronounced it to you, trippingly on the tongue. . . ."

Speaking such passages without attention to appropriate time values robs them of meaning.

Rhythm is the recurrent pattern of sound sequences created by skillful use of stress and timing. In poetry, the rhythm is regular—metrical. The rhythm is irregular in most prose. In both prose and poetry, proper interpretation of the rhythm is dependent upon causal emotion in the selection. The rhythm, in turn, gives emotional tone to both the written composition and the utterance.

Highly emotional speech is usually rhythmic, whether it be poetry or prose:

> O my son Absalom! my son, my son Absalom! Would God
> I had died for thee, O Absalom, my son, my son!
>
> II Samuel 18:33, AV

> And Ruth said, Entreat me not to leave thee, or to
> return from following after thee: for whither thou
> goest, I will go; and where thou lodgest, I will
> lodge: thy people shall be my people, and thy God
> my God: Where thou diest, will I die, and there will
> I be buried: the Lord do so to me, and more also, if
> aught but death part thee and me.
>
> Ruth 1:16-17, AV

Phrasing

One of the most common faults in speech is rote utterance. Sentences, phrases, and even single words are spoken without linking them together in a conscious thought pattern. Or the speaker falls into a speech tune that repeats itself over and over without regard to the interpretative demands of the script content. What actually happens is that the speaker himself comes to understand the meaning of what he is saying only *after he has spoken the words.* The audience, of course, may not get the meaning at all.

Good television speech requires extensive and painstaking rehearsal. Study your script until you are familiar with every nuance of thought you are trying to express. It is best to memorize the script for everything but impromptu discussion and interview programs. Reading on television is both awkward in appearance and unprofessional.

Before you memorize, phrase your content carefully according to the thought pattern. The phrasing is in large part determinative of your vocal techniques. It will also help you in memorizing.

The phrasing is determined by weighing the relative values of the various word groups in terms of the total idea. It does not necessarily follow the punctuation used in the writing. Punctuation is for the eye, phrasing for the ear.

Ask yourself these questions: Which words clump together to form the meaning groups? Where shall I put the pauses to separate the groups? How long shall the pauses be? What shall be the rate at which single words and word groups are to be spoken? Where and in what degree shall emphasis be placed? What variations in melody, pitch, force, and time will best communicate the meanings? How shall these four speech factors be interrelated?

Finally, practice your part aloud to find out whether you have hit upon the right pattern of phrasing and the best vocal practices for the content. Record your program and play it back before you go into camera rehearsal. By using a recording, you can polish the program a great deal even before you know how the action will look in front of the cameras.

No one can learn to be a good television performer just from reading a book on how to do it. Neither can you hope to be successful on television if all you do is travel to a station and go on the air. Television know-how does not come easily, nor can it be acquired overnight. Its attainment requires, first, practice, practice, and more practice of the techniques of television speech and action. Second, comes the application of these techniques in a carefully planned program produced under a competent director who can correct faults and suggest improvements.

One final word. The intimate quality of television reveals character as does no other form of public communication, with the possible exception of motion pictures. You will be effective and successful in direct proportion to the viewer's judgment of your intrinsic worth.

CHAPTER 8

The Television Camera and
Its Usage

The camera functions in television as the human eye does in viewing the passing scene. Whenever you look at a complicated, fast-moving panorama, such as a large number of dancers on a stage, the kaleidoscope of color and movement is prone to bewilder the senses and to inhibit comprehension of the essential pattern of the scene. Your brain deals with this blockage by directing your eyes to concentrate on a single dancer or on a pair of dancers, thus bringing into focus an apprehensible segment of a whole that is incomprehensible in its entirety. Similarly, when you want to examine an object in detail, you bring it close to your eyes, thus, in effect, making it appear larger and more easily intelligible, and at the same time eliminating surrounding objects that might be distracting. To enjoy the beauty of a landscape, you do the opposite, moving away to give your eyes the opportunity to rove over the widest range and the greatest depth you can encompass. This mental process of visual selection is performed in your behalf in a television program by the camera.

The camera cannot by itself accomplish the visual editing that you do automatically when you are confronted by something to look at. It will faithfully transmit whatever is placed before its lens, but it cannot determine a center of interest or delineate the range and depth of a scene best calculated to transmit comprehensibility. This process can be accomplished only through human planning of a sequence of varied placements of the camera and of the employment, in series, of lenses of varying focal lengths.

Television programs, ideally, are photographed with two or more cameras to give the widest possible variety to this visual editing and to allow it to be accomplished quickly and smoothly. By moving from camera to camera, by repositioning the cameras that are off the air and changing their lenses and by moving the on-the-air camera in pans across the set, tilts up and down and dollys toward and away from the scene being photographed, the director has at his disposal an infinite variety of movements that permit a visual fluidity virtually equal to that of the human eye if it were to have the opportunity to rove about the scene. He has, in addition, the advantage of being able to move from close to far views, narrow to wide, and vice versa, quickly and effortlessly, a thing which the eye cannot do without movement of the body. This editing of action through precise control of a sequence of pictures gives the director the opportunity to tell a predetermined story in such a manner that he can exercise a desired influence on his viewers.

The results of camera usage will always depend upon the artistic competence and taste, the judgment, the orginality, and the ingenuity of the director. But he will be greatly aided in achieving a successful program if you, as producer, understand camera techniques and the available technical facilities of your station so that you can explain to the director what you want to accomplish photographically, over-all and in each scene, and how you want the visual development to progress in relation to the action.

Lenses and Their Properties

If you are to plan your programs intelligently, you must understand what can be done with lenses. Specifically, you need to know what lenses are available on the cameras you will use on your programs and what they can do, so you can work within their capabilities.

Television cameras mount four lenses in their turrets. The cameraman can change from lens to lens in seconds by revolving the turret. The lenses are classified by their focal lengths, designated in either millimeters or inches. The focal length is the distance from the optical center of the lens to the image when the lens is focused at infinity (more than one hundred feet).

It is important to know the focal length of lenses because the focal length determines the angle of view, i.e., the width of scene that can be encompassed in a picture taken with a given lens. The horizontal field of view is an isosceles triangle whose base is the widest scope seen by the lens and whose apex is the lens. The apex angle is the angle of view. (Figure 1.) The vertical field of view is a similar vertical projection.

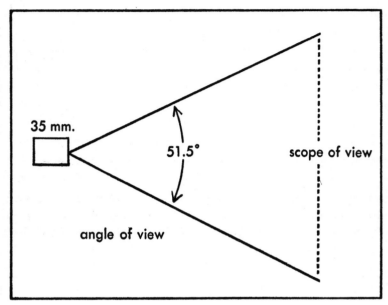

35 mm.

51.5°

scope of view

angle of view

FIGURE 1

The most common lenses found on television cameras and their horizontal and vertical field angles are as follows:

Focal Length	Horizontal Field Angle	Vertical Field Angle
35 mm.	51.5°	38°
50 mm.	34°	27°
90 mm.	19°	15°
135 mm.	13°	10°
8½ inch	8°	6°

The important thing to remember is that the smaller the focal length of the lens, the wider will be the angle of view. The wider this angle is, the more you can include in the picture (Figure 2); but the more there is in the picture, the smaller each segment is (Figure 3). Conversely, the longer the lens, the narrower will be the angle of

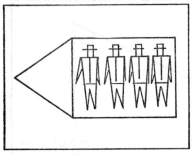

FIGURE 2

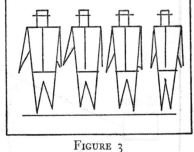

FIGURE 3

view. The narrower angle reduces the amount that can be included in the picture (Figure 4); but makes the image larger (Figure 5). The scope of the picture is always designated in terms of its width, but it is apparent from the Table above that a reduction in width

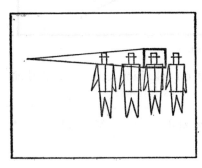

FIGURE 4

FIGURE 5

brings about a corresponding reduction in height. The aspect ratio of the television frame is 4 units wide to 3 units high. The height of the picture is always three-fourths of the width.

Your television station is most likely to have the 50, 90, and 135 mm. lenses in constant use with, perhaps, the 8½ inch lens available because it is the most convenient close-up lens for studio work. With these lenses and two cameras you can safely design virtually any combination of shots needed on a single set. The trick is to avoid booby trapping the director by forcing him to call for the same lens on both cameras at the same time.

CAMERA COMPOSITION AND ACTION

Every picture in your production, whether selected by you or by the director, should be keyed to a definite aim and composed to help accomplish that aim. It should follow the preceding picture, logically and artistically, and should lead naturally into the one that follows. Its composition and duration should be determined by the task it is expected to accomplish in the production as a whole. No shot should be used that does not contribute to the development of the story. No changes in composition or shifting of cameras should take place except as they serve to move the action in the direction and at the pace required. The tempo and content of a scene should determine both picture composition and camera activity. Pace should not be forced by camera action.

For example, tempo can be greatly affected in the comprehension of the viewer by the type of cutting used by the director. Quick and frequent cutting from camera to camera and lens to lens speeds up tempo. In a rollicking comedy scene, short camera holds (frequent cuts) will enhance the sense of a light, fast tempo. A solemn scene will be sustained best with long holds and infrequent cutting.

Elements of Composition and Action

We shall deal here with those aspects of television picturization that will be useful to producers of religious programs, ignoring the detailed technical knowledge that must be exhibited by the television director and cameraman.

Composition. Picture composition begins with recognition of the limitations imposed by the aspect ratio of the television screen—4 to 3. Actually, this ratio is artistically pleasing, although it does not permit the use of tall, narrow vertical scenes or objects. Picture composition within the aspect ratio should follow the recognized standards for artistically designed horizontal pictures.

Be sure your set is so designed and your actors are placed in positions so the horizon line will not divide the picture into equal halves horizontally, and that no vertical line will divide it in half, left and right (Figure 6). Stay away from square and rectangular compo-

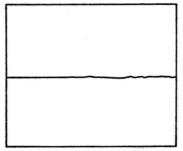

FIGURE 6

sitions. They do not fit well into the aspect ratio of the frame unless they are at an angle in contrast to the plane of the frame. Triangular composition is usually the most pleasing.

WRONG   RIGHT

FIGURE 7

Try to achieve an interesting perspective, just as you would in a still picture. Most objects photograph better from an angle than they do head on (Figure 7). Work to include a variety of horizontal and vertical planes in both your set and your action. Break up your backgrounds, instead of shooting against flat walls or curtains. Show corners. Have your action taking place on several levels; i.e., one person standing and a second seated at a table would give you three levels—table top, seated figure, standing figure.

Groups of people, like objects, usually look better if they are composed for angle photographing rather than faced directly into the camera. For example, discussion programs involving three people are common in religious broadcasting. The lazy or unskilled director of such programs will almost always settle for a composition that places the moderator full face to his long-shot camera and the other two participants at about fifty-degree angles to the central figure (Figure 8). A preferred composition that requires more camera mo-

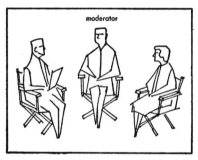

FIGURE 8

FIGURE 9

bility is to place the moderator at right angles to the other two (Figure 9). Another composition with interesting possibilities is achieved by placing the three at a round table and letting a mobile camera ride the table rim. Interesting over-the-shoulder shots are possible with this setup. They can be combined with full-face close-ups and the over-all three shot. The Mike Wallace interview technique of face-to-face confrontation can also be applied to three persons, with the moderator facing the other two. It allows for over-the-shoulder close-ups of all three, a two shot of the panelists and an over-all three shot.

Action should take place at an angle to the horizontal axis of the frame (Figure 10). Movement toward and away from the camera is more dramatic and tends to give the viewer more sense of action than does lateral movement across the camera. Remember in using pans (lateral movement of the camera from left to right or vice versa) that movement of the cast toward the pan speeds the action and movement away from the pan slows it.

When action is taking place, have it fill the screen, with as little background and, especially, side margins showing as possible. This fullness makes for better identification of the viewer with the action. The picture size should be such that the viewer can instantly recognize what is taking place and what objects and people are in the action. Avoid fussy and confused pictures. They will only confuse

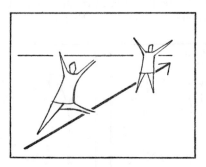

FIGURE 10

the viewer. Except for establishing the scene, close-up and medium close-up shots are always best to ensure viewer recognition of the action.

Camera Angles. Since the camera acts as the viewer's eyes, the camera should be angled in such a way that the scene being pictured looks natural from the viewer's perspective. A shot of a pair of lovers strolling in a park made from a high angle that makes the camera seem to the viewer to be in a tree may give dramatic emphasis to the girl's picture hat; but it will only bewilder and annoy the watcher who would expect to meet the couple at eye level if he were standing or from the angle of a bench if he were sitting.

It is well to vary camera angles from shot to shot in order to give dramatic accent and to prod audience interest. But you can have too much of a good thing. Too frequent cutting from angle to angle, especially if the cameras are aimed from opposite sides of the set, can make the audience lose all sense of the direction in which the action is taking place. By the same token, unusual or distorted angles should not be used just for effect. They are valuable only if they serve to advance the story—for example, the picturing of a man running in fear who glimpses his face distorted in a puddle of water and recoils in horror.

In rehearsal, watch for the angles that set off the performers' features to best advantage. Everyone has a "better side" to his face. Bodies can be made to look gross or trim by the angle at which they are photographed. Watch especially for physical defects or disfigurements that may be unduly emphasized by the close-up television camera. Minor blemishes that pass unnoticed in face-to-face contact become major scars on television if care is not taken.

Basic Camera Shots. Camera shots are identified by the area they cover (long shot) or by the number of persons they cover (two shot, three shot). There are, however, three basic shots and all others are intermediary between them.

The *long shot* (LS) covers the widest scenic area. It is usually made with a wide-angle lens. It can include three or more adults standing in a group plus the scenery above and beside them. Or it can encompass a scenic panorama. Long shots are usually used for "establishing shots," over-all views presented at the beginning of a scene to identify locale or to permit the viewer to become familiar with the set or the participants. Long shots are also useful when the action is to cover a considerable ground space, as in dances or chase scenes or sets where several actions are taking place simultaneously.

The *medium shot* (MS) can include three persons involved in a minimum amount of action and still allow for a clear view of facial expressions and for some of the set to show around the edges of the action. This shot can be "tightened" by moving the camera in to increase the sense of intimacy or to heighten dramatic effect. It can be "opened" by moving the camera away to allow a character to leave or a fourth character to enter the set.

A *close-up* (CU) shows only one person and is designed to catch the most intimate facial expressions. Usually head and shoulders are in view and there is a comfortable amount of space above the person's head. This shot can be tightened to an extreme close-up for dramatic effect. Here only the head shows. Sometimes, for dramatic effect, even a portion of the top of the head is cut off. The extreme close-up is a risky shot, since it will reveal the slightest facial defect or distortion of expression.

On the air, these shots are alternated in accordance with the demands of the action. The camera that is photographing the actual air picture is taking the "action" shot. Your script should be so planned that the director can always hold the off-the-air camera in a "cover shot." This latter is a shot the director can turn to instantly if the action causes trouble in his air shot. Ideally, the cover shot is wider than the action shot and allows for sudden, unexpected action. It is especially important on extemporaneous programs, where the action cannot be anticipated in advance. It is always wise to plan the program so that while one camera is on a close-up the other can be holding a protective wider shot.

Cuts, Dissolves, and Fades. These three elements of camera technique are not used arbitrarily or just to provide variety when the action begins to lag. When used properly, they are carefully keyed to the impressions required by the action.

A *cut* is an instantaneous switch from one camera to another. It provides change in perspective on the scene by shifting the angle of the picture, or by changing the view from long or medium shot to close-up or vice versa, or by combining these two changes. The cuts should follow the logic of the action within a scene. Here is an example of the use of cutting in a dramatic scene:

MCU, BREM IN CHAIR OVER ALICE'S LEFT SHOULDER. PART OF HER HEAD SHOWS. HE REACHES FORWARD AND PATS HER HAND.	**BREM** Stay here tonight. In the morning I'll take you down.
CUT TO CU, ALICE.	**ALICE** I'm afraid to. It's so lonely. If Grant. . .
CUT TO CU, BREM.	**BREM** Even if he comes, nothing will happen.
	SOUND: KNOCK ON DOOR

BREM GLANCES QUICKLY TOWARD
DOOR, LOOKS BACK AT ALICE,
HESITATES, BEGINS TO RISE

CUT TO LS SHOWING WHOLE
ROOM. BREM CROSSES TO DOOR. CAMERA
PANS L AND DOLLIES IN TO FOLLOW
HIM ENDING IN MLS OF BREM AT DOOR
HE OPENS DOOR A CRACK AND PEERS OUT.

CUT TO MLS EXTERIOR, GRANT AT DOOR.

In a discussion program, the cutting should follow the pattern of the talk. It can vary between one, two, and three shots. The camera need not always be on the person speaking. The reaction of a listener can be interesting and important in helping the viewer understand what is being said.

Cutting can be used to heighten the visual interest in a long scene where the action is static, such as that of a person making a speech or a soloist or choir singing. The cuts, to be effective, must follow the content. When a speaker begins a new thought, a cut to a new angle helps to emphasize the transition. But no cut should ever be made in the middle of a sentence or a paragraph. In a song, cuts can be made at the ends of lines or, better still, at the close of stanzas.

The *dissolve* is a blended transmission in which a new scene overlaps and wipes out the preceding episode. It is used to bridge scene changes or shifts in location. If a cut is used when a scene changes, the viewer is apt to believe he is seeing only another shot of the same scene. A dissolve may be fast or slow, depending upon the dramatic effect or time lapse you desire to show.

The ending of a show may be indicated by a *fade* to "black." The picture is dissolved out until all light is gone from the screen. Show openings may be made by starting with a black screen and fading in the establishing shot. The fade is useful, also, to indicate a radical change of scene, such as a long passage of time. One scene is faded to black, then, after a suitable time, the following scene is faded-in. The fade to black is sometimes necessary when actors must move from one scene to another, but it is better to use bridging devices to cover such necessary stage business. A dissolve to a sign, a door, a

chair, or some other object on the new set which can help establish
the meaning of the new scene is more useful and dramatic than a
fade.

A *superimposition* (super) may be used to overlap electronically
the image from one camera on the image from a second camera.
Superimposition is especially useful for overlaying titles, names of
participants, and other informational material on scenes where action
is taking place. It is also employed to lay one scene over another with
a split screen effect, as in a baseball game where the batter is shown
on one half of the screen and a base runner who is out of view of the
plate camera is shown on the other half through a second camera.

Camera Movement. The television camera loses much of its usefulness if it is static. All cameras used on a show should be able to
move freely, both on and off the air. Sets and action should be so
designed that no camera need ever cross the field of view of another.
Allowance must be made for the fact that the cameras are attached
to cable and, therefore, cannot easily cross each other. But on a two-
camera show, each camera can be moved on its side of an imaginary
line running through the center of the studio, and either can shoot
across into the field of movement of the other. Cameras are usually
mounted on booms or pedestals that can be rolled by the cameramen.

Television has technical names, borrowed from motion pictures,
for the movements that are possible with the cameras.

The most common camera movements are *dollys* and *pans*. A
dolly is a steady movement of the camera toward (dolly in) or away
from (dolly out) the scene of action. In the first instance it tightens
the shot to make the action plainer without interrupting the movement of action. Dollying out widens the area of action. Frequently
in opening a program or a scene a long shot is used to establish,
then the camera is dollyed in to a close shot in which the action can
easily be followed by the viewer.

To pan is to move the camera in a horizontal plane to follow the
action. Up and down movement is called a tilt. Pans and tilts do not
require movement of the camera mount, as does a dolly. Any television
camera can pan and tilt.

Boom movements can combine both dollys and pans. A boom
camera is one that is mounted on a mobile crane. The camera can

move up or down and sideways and be dollyed in or out by movement of the crane, all simultaneously.

A *zoom* is a sudden pushing in or pulling away of the camera in relation to the scene. It can catapult the viewer instantly from a distance into the very laps of the players, or vice versa. A zoom is best accomplished through use of a Zoomar lens on the camera. A less satisfactory method is to dolly quickly. Zooms can give striking effects, but should be used sparingly. If your station has a Zoomar lens, beware of the director and crew that are zoom happy.

PLANNING YOUR CAMERA SHOTS

Even if you could have all the camera rehearsal you could possibly want for your program, it would be necessary to plan the show from the standpoint of the camera. In local religious programs, where camera rehearsal is always at a mimimum if it is held at all, this testing of shots is a life and death matter for the success of the program.

The best thing to do is to plan in advance the exact position of performers, objects, and cameras for each shot. This is always done for dramatic programs. It is equally valuable for other program types.

Before you start to prepare sets or go into rehearsal, map out your program on a floor plan of the studio. Make your plan to the scale of one-quarter inch to one foot. Then sketch in your backgrounds and set furniture, and position your performers. Use a lens protractor to determine the width of field of each lens on each camera from the various camera positions and angles you plan to use in the show. You can buy a protractor, or you can make one from transparent plastic by cutting in the lens angles (see Figure 11).

You can work from both ends of the protractor to determine your scope of view. By placing the open end of the protractor against your set, you can determine where the camera must be on the floor to cover the area necessary to the shot. Or you can place the apex of the protractor on the spot where you want to place your camera on the floor; then by observing the field of each lens you can determine whether or not that camera can take the desired shot.

This method of determining camera placement is crucial to the pattern of camera flow on the air. Before you go into rehearsal you will know whether or not your cameras can move in relation to each other to achieve the shot sequence you desire. You will not then make the fatal mistake of placing Camera 1 on your opening cards and finding when you get on the air that it cannot cross the field of Camera 2 to get the necessary close-up after the establishing shot.

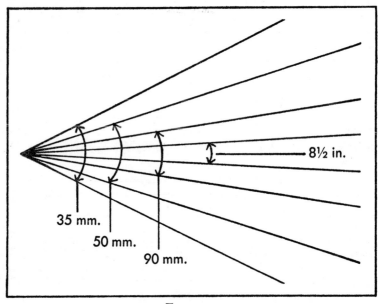

8½ in.

35 mm.

50 mm.

90 mm.

FIGURE 11

Your next step in preparing your program is to hold dry-run rehearsals for the twofold purpose of training the cast and determining whether or not your camera plan will work out in practice. First, on the floor of a church auditorium or gymnasium, lay out the exact dimensions of the studio you will use, chalk in the sets, and place all the furniture and other objects you will use on the air. Then rehearse the cast in the sets, so they will know exactly how to move about when they appear before the cameras. While rehearsals are in progress, use a lens viewer to plan the camera positions and the actual shots. Through the apertures of the viewer you can see everything that the camera will see through its various lenses.

From any camera supply shop you can purchase a viewer that includes apertures for all of the lenses normally used in television. You can also construct a practical viewer. Rudy Bretz has invented a simple, cube-shaped box, known as the "Bretz box," that has windows on all sides. As you turn the box, the window for one lens serves as the peephole for another. The box can be made from six pieces of cardboard or plywood, six inches square. Using a protractor, with the apex placed at the center of the edge of each piece, mark out the scope of view for each lens. The height of each window is three-fourths of the horizontal width of the lens angle, since the aspect ratio is 4 to 3. Of course, each side of the box contains the window for only one lens. Be sure to mark the lens number (i.e., 35 mm.) on both the inside and outside of the box. Assemble the six squares into a box and paint it black for ease in viewing.[1]

In using a viewing box, the size of the hole at which you place your eye is irrelevant. The hole on the opposite side of the box determines your field of view, so if you want to see the scope of a 90 mm. lens, you must hold that opening on the opposite side of the box from your eye.

If you will follow carefully the rehearsal procedures suggested here, you can prepare a shooting script with every camera placement, every shot, cut, dissolve, every action movement in relation to camera clearly marked and timed. Even in stations that commit the unpardonable sin of putting shows on the air without *any* camera rehearsal, such a detailed script will give the director a fighting chance to produce a smooth, acceptable program. Any conscientious director will appreciate this kind of planning and will profit from it.

[1] For detailed instructions on how to make a "Bretz box" see Rudy Bretz, *Techniques of Television Production* (New York: McGraw-Hill Book Company: 1953), pp. 75-76.

CHAPTER 9   The Audio

Sound is television's stepchild. It is the least satisfactory element in a television production, and when measured against the standards of radio, it is very poor indeed. Part of the difficulty with sound is caused by overemphasis of the video over the audio in production; part is due to enormous technical difficulties in relating video to audio.

The audio signal that is broadcast from the television transmitter is technically inferior to the standard radio signal and, especially, to the high fidelity frequency modulation signal, because the audio is allocated so small a share of the television broadcast frequency. A television station's frequency range is quite broad, but most of it is taken up by the video signal. The audio is confined to a band so narrow it is impossible for the station to transmit the full frequency sound range.

Within the television studio, sound pickup is complicated by a variety of factors that radio and sound motion pictures do not suffer from. In radio, the microphone is in a fixed position and the performers are fixed in relation to it to get maximum quality and effect from the voices. Movement in relation to the microphone is for effect only. In television, movement is necessary to action. The performer stays in perspective to the camera, but his speech goes out of sound perspective as soon as he shifts position. Two people walking down a street may be followed in a pan by a fixed camera. They remain constant in size and distance to the viewer, but their voices will be moving away from him unless the microphone moves with them at an unvarying distance from their lips. Motion pictures have this problem, too, but television compounds it by requiring the microphone to be in perspective for two or more cameras, one of which will be photographing a close-up, calling for close sound presence, while the others will be on more distant shots, which require the sound to be farther away from the viewer. A further complication is the necessity to keep both the microphone and its shadow out of range of the lenses of all the cameras.

Sound quality can never be as good in a television studio as in a radio studio. The presence of sets, overhead lighting fixtures, and other objects makes it impossible to have the acoustical perfection of the bare-walled, soundproofed radio studio. The necessary shifting of sets and props, and the movement of cameras and crew members create all sorts of extraneous noises. The microphone also loses focusing power in television, since it is usually placed at greater than optimal distance from performers to keep it out of frame.

Television microphones can be fixed in position if the performers do not have to move around, as in the case of a speech. More likely the microphone will be movable, even in such simple productions as discussion programs. Mobility is obtained by mounting the microphone on a boom that can be moved to follow action, or by placing it on the performer's chest on a neck strap, or on the lapel, or in the hand.

Any microphone movement endangers sound quality. Too rapid a swing of the boom may set up wind noise, a crackling sound. Any movement may expose the microphone to extraneous noises that a moment before were off mike. Get the microphone too close to a hard surface and reverberation (echo) sets in. Reverberation is a bane of television sound. Since television studios are always fairly "live," there are bound to be echoes bouncing about. They are sounds of varying pitches and rates that strike the microphone simultaneously. A certain amount of reverberation is desirable, depending upon the scene being shot; otherwise, the sound will appear to be lifeless. But too much reverberation may make speech sound confused and unintelligible. Human hearing, being binaural, can be exposed to a variety of sounds and focus on a desired segment, disregarding the extraneous ones. The microphone is monaural; all sounds striking it have simultaneous, equal values. There is no focusing power; therefore, echo is much more noticeable than in binaural hearing. The ratio of reverberant to direct sound increases with the increase of distance between the microphone and the sound source. Therefore, it is desirable to place the microphone as near as possible to the source of sound. A directional microphone—one that picks up sound from only one direction and is dead in all other planes—is useful in television.

Working with the Microphone

What do all these audio problems mean to you as a producer or performer in television? They certainly should not lead you to throw up your hands in dismay and leave the sound on your programs to chance and the studio technical staff.

Sound that is as good as you can get with the equipment available, that is natural to the picture being shown, that is, above all, believable and understandable is just as essential as the video in making your program communicate what you want it to. Once your video production plan is completed, it needs to be re-examined and revamped to fit the needs of an acceptable audio performance. In a complicated production, this need will inevitably lead to a compromise between all that is desirable in the video and all that is desirable in the audio. Sets may have to be altered to accommodate the microphone. Positions and actions of performers may need to be changed. Lines and sound effects may have to be revised.

Your relationship of audio to video should always be such that your action is in acoustical perspective and conveys a sense of realism. The audio should include without distortion all sounds that are pertinent to the action and eliminate all that are extraneous to it. Realism in a television program is achieved by blending ideas and dramatic movement in a rhythmic pattern that is believable, using for this purpose the video and all elements of the audio—speech, sounds that arise from the action, sound effects, and music. The sound must be in perspective with the picture. That is, in a close-up shot, the sound must be close and intimate. In longer shots, the sound must have a more distant quality that will make it fit the picture. The picture always determines the perspective of the sound.

Some Tips on Performance

Whether you are producer or performer, familiarize yourself with the types of microphones you will be using on your programs. The audio engineers of your station can explain to you their customary methods for handling various types of programs. By studying their techniques and the responses of the microphones in the studio, you can determine what can and cannot be done in relation to each microphone from any spot on the studio floor.

In rehearsing your program, be sure the cast members practice microphone action as well as camera action.

The *direction* in which a speech is aimed is important. If you are using an overhead microphone, speakers will need to keep their heads up when they are talking, so their voices will be projected as nearly as possible in the direction of the microphone. Suppose, however, the performer must demonstrate something on a table before him. If the overhead microphone is fixed, whenever the performer wants to say something, he will need to pause in the demonstration and lift his head for the explanation. Otherwise, the microphone will be behind his head, and it will be impossible to make a good voice pickup. A microphone hung on a boom is mobile and can be maneuvered and lowered to pick up "head-down" speech. However, the action will have to be planned in such a way that the boom can be moved from position to position without breaking the continuity of the show.

Speakers on television must project their voices as they would do in a public meeting, because the microphone, especially if working from overhead, is usually a good distance away. The volume required is usually less than that needed in a hall, but much greater than the soft, conversational tone that is used in radio, where the microphone is only a few inches from the lips. People who cannot speak up are poorly equipped for television performance. Even intimate scenes calling for quiet conversation—such as love scenes—must usually be played at a higher voice volume than may feel normal, in order to compensate for microphone distance and to override studio noises.

In radio, voices are balanced by placing speakers at varying distances from the microphone. In television, speakers whose voices are at opposite poles in terms of quality, pitch, and normal volume are required to work side by side or face to face with the microphone equidistant from all of them. Balance is achieved through the flexibility of the speakers in controlling their voices. Performers who naturally speak softly are required to raise their volume, those with booming voices to lower theirs to strike an acceptable balance.

Television also demands flexibility in use of the voice, far beyond that needed in radio. An actor who turns away from the microphone must speak louder, as he would in the theater. Otherwise, his voice will fade away. On the other hand, the microphone cannot tolerate sudden shifts in sound and intensity. In radio, they can be accomplished by "working the microphone." The performer can move away from the microphone when he is required to speak loudly and move back in for soft passages. In television, it is often necessary for him to do the same thing while remaining in one spot, as in the case of an actor who is carrying on a quiet face-to-face conversation having to shout an answer to an offstage query, then go on with the original dialogue. It can be done. The method necessary is always to speak somewhat louder than normal conversation would require in soft passages and somewhat softer in loud passages. Volume changes are restricted to a small compass. Variety is achieved by wide ranges of change in the quality, force, rate, and pitch of the voice.

One of the cardinal principles of television is never to surprise your director, cameramen, and sound engineers with your movements. You should always "telegraph" your movements, but in such a subtle way that only the crew and not the viewer will know you are throwing cues. For instance, if you are standing and speaking and you suddenly throw yourself into a chair, you will almost certainly leave the camera pointing at the empty spot where your head was while your voice trails away to a whisper as the boom man frantically tries to lower his microphone, dragging it smack through the middle of the picture in the process. Proper action would be to touch the chair back to indicate you are about to sit down, then lower yourself *slowly* into the chair. Camera and boom will then pan smoothly down with you. When the script is memorized by the performers, action cueing is easy. The director sets certain word cues to indicate the beginning of action changes, and orders his cameras and microphones accordingly.

Even with the most elaborate rehearsal and cueing, rapid movements are undesirable. The camera and microphone boom simply cannot move swiftly enough to keep up with a sudden shift of position. Here, as in use of the voice, the body movement must be adapted from what is natural in real surroundings to what is possible in television.

To Show or Not to Show the Microphone

Some producers and directors make a fetish of always having the microphone hidden from the view of the audience. They believe that the sight of any piece of technical equipment destroys the illusion of reality they are trying to create in the pictures. They will fly the microphone overhead, out of frame, or, if it is on the set, will mask it with flowers or hide it in something, often at the sacrifice of sound quality.

There is ample justification for this point of view in a dramatic program. Think what would happen to the illusion if you were presenting *Saint Joan* and the scene where Joan first meets the Dauphin was played with a microphone standing in full view between the characters. But there are other types of programs where the illusion of reality is not so important, but where it is vital that the spoken word be clear and comprehensible. They include such things as discussions, interviews, speeches, and news broadcasts. Here, the presence of a microphone is not apt to annoy the viewer or to distract his attention. The microphone is, after all, an honest tool of the trade. Everyone knows it is being used to transmit the sound. If placing it in the open, either in fixed position or in the control of the performers, will make for better sound pickup than will a hidden microphone, there should be no hesitation about using it in this way.

For the most part, studio staffs will be sensible about the use of their equipment. They want to get the best possible results out of it. You can usually rely upon the audio engineers to position their microphones, and you should be willing to work within the pattern they set. It is only when you encounter a director who handles video to the detriment of the technical excellence of his sound that you will have cause to protest about the microphone placement.

CHAPTER 10   Promotion

No commercial sponsor would think of investing thousands of dollars each week to pay for time and talent for a television show on a network without including in the budget a substantial sum for promotion and publicity. The local sponsor duplicates this practice on a smaller scale. They both know that the program that has no public build-up attracts few listeners.

The more important the commercial program, the more elaborate will be its promotion. Publicity is the best—and cheapest—insurance against the competition of a rival show in the same time slot and the risk of a consequent debacle due to absence of audience.

If the well-heeled commercials must have extensive and elaborate promotion, it should be obvious that religious programs, which lack the attractive glitter of the stars and which are usually on the air when audience potential is at its nadir, are much more in need of publicity. The time is long past when any program can go on the air and expect to find an audience ready and waiting for it. Viewers have to be wooed and won, and then rewon week by week to keep them as regulars for your program. From the time your program idea is jelled until the last show in the series leaves the air, you cannot afford to falter even once in a relentless public relations drive.

Publicity and Promotion

We have used the terms "publicity" and "promotion" interchangeably up to now. They may be employed that way as generalities, but, although any efforts to attract viewers to a program may be said to be promotional, technically there is a distinction between publicity and promotion. Publicity goes to news media and is used by them without charge because its content is newsworthy. Publicity for a television program consists of newspaper reports and feature stories, pictures and reviews; listing in the newspaper television schedules— especially in the "pick of the air" box—and in *TV Guide*; articles and pictures in magazines; stories and pictures in church papers; stories and pictures in the bulletin of the council of churches; listings in church bulletins used in worship services; news and feature stories used on television and radio newscasts. Even word-of-mouth discussion of a program is publicity. Promotional materials usually cost something to prepare or you must pay to get them used, or both. Advertisements in newspapers and other news media, including television and radio; promotional spot announcements given by the station; folders; posters; direct mail materials; novelty devices; calendars; program directories; mimeographed or printed bulletins; telephone advertising campaigns; billboards and car cards; premiums— all are examples of promotional devices. Both publicity and promotion are needed for an effective build-up of a television series.

Publicity

The most readily available publicity outlets are newspapers, church papers and bulletins, and the bulletin of the council of churches.

Three types of news releases should be written and distributed to these outlets: (1) an announcement story which may go out as much as two weeks before the start of a program series; (2) a feature story, timed to run the day before or the day a program starts on the air; (3) weekly stories detailing the subject to be aired and participants in each program. The latter should be distributed *at least* a week in advance of the broadcast.

All press releases should be typed, double spaced, with wide margins, on one side of a 8½ by 11 inch sheet. If more than two or three copies are going out, the release should be mimeographed. If carbons are used, be sure they are clean and sharp. A newspaper editor will throw a story into the wastebasket rather than take a chance of misspelling a name because a carbon is smudged. The copy should begin about one-third of the way down the first page to leave room for the insertion of a headline. Use newspaper punctuation and capitalization, so the city desk will have to make as few alterations as possible in the story. In the rush of getting out a paper, perfect copy has a much better chance of being used than does a story that must be edited extensively. The name, address, and telephone number of the person responsible for the release, i.e., the person the editor is to call if he wants further information, should be placed in the upper left-hand corner of the first page of the story. The release date and time should be placed in the upper right-hand corner in capital letters.

Except in feature stories, follow standard newspaper practice and write your story with all the important facts in the lead paragraph, the first paragraph of the story. Answer as many as you can of the usual questions posed for the lead: who, what, when, where, why, how? Paragraphs following the lead should be written in descending order of importance, with the last paragraph carrying the least important material; so editors can shorten the story by cutting from the bottom up.

Following are sample stories of the types you should prepare for your programs. The first is the announcement story taken from the publicity kit for *Off to Adventure,* which is distributed by the National Council of Churches to all stations that carry the programs and to all church councils that sponsor them. In the kit, each story is accompanied by an appropriate photograph. Note how this story can be cut at the end of any paragraph without losing the essential facts of name and time of broadcast or the sense of narrative continuity.

Name of your organization
Address   OFF TO ADVENTURE
Telephone number   ANNOUNCEMENT STORY
Name of person responsible for publicity

FOR IMMEDIATE RELEASE

THE REAL AFRICA IN NEW "OFF TO ADVENTURE" SERIES

The people behind the front page news from Africa will come to life in 13 weekly "Adventures in Africa," the children's television series scheduled to premiere on Station ——, Channel ——, on ——,
                                                                                                (day)

———— at ————.
(date)   (time)

The latest in the National Council of the Churches of Christ's "Off to Adventure" programs for upper elementary and junior high school children, "Adventures in Africa," is being presented by Station ———— as a public service in co-operation with ——————————.

(Council of Churches)

Each quarter-hour program in the series presents a new real-life adventure filmed on the spot in the most explosive parts of the African continent. Children of Africa act out their own stories in modern industrial cities and primitive villages, in hospitals, in schools and on athletic fields.

There is real danger when a witch doctor terrorizes a village. There is comedy when a grapefruit used as a soccer ball explodes under the impact of a hearty kick. There is pathos as a crippled boy struggles to walk with new braces. There is the excitement of watching new nations coming into being in Ghana and the Congo.

The young viewers' guide to African adventure is the "Skipper," the Rev. Dr. Gibson I. Daniels, minister of Saugatuck Congregational Church, Westport, Connecticut. In preparation for the authentic documentary series, the Skipper traveled thousands of miles through the countries of south and central Africa studying the lives of the people and the work of Christian missionaries among them.

The filmed programs were produced on location in Ghana, the Congo, the Union of South Africa and Angola.

"Adventures in Africa" is geared to an interdenominational study theme used in Sunday schools of Protestant churches in the United States and Canada. The series is sponsored in Canada by the United Church of Canada.

The Africa series was a joint effort of more than 40 American and Canadian educators, researchers, African experts and film technicians.

The following release is a shorter, more coldly factual announcement story that also describes an entire series of programs.

VARIOUS RELIGIONS PRACTICED IN AFRICA ON "SUNRISE SEMESTER" DEC. 5-7-9

African religious practices, including Islam, Christianity, and the work of missionaries, will be the subject of Dr. Elliott P. Skinner's lectures in "Sociology 26" on "Sunrise Semester" during the week of Monday, Dec. 5 (WCBS-TV, Channel 2, 6:30-7:00 A.M., Mon., Wed., and Fri.),

Monday, Dec. 5: Christianity and the missions in Africa. (Assignment: Pages 489-503 in "Cultures and Societies of Africa," by Ottenberg.)

Wednesday, Dec. 7: Religions in modern Africa. (Assignment: Pages 1102-1119 in "American Anthropologist," Vol. 60, No. 6; Chapter 3 in "Nationalism in Colonial Africa," by Hodgkin.)

Friday, Dec. 9: Labor migration. Assignment: "Africa," October, 1960 edition.)

"Sunrise Semester" is presented jointly by the WCBS-TV Public Affairs Department and New York University. Associate producer for "Sociology 26: Peoples of Africa" is Richard Goodman. John Musilli directs. Dr. Skinner is Assistant Professor of Anthropology at N.Y.U.

The next two releases go out on a weekly basis and are designed to publicize individual broadcasts. Both are short, as befits this kind of release, which cannot be expected to get much space.

Note the differences in style. *Off to Adventure*, being aimed at children, attempts to whip up excitement by stressing the strangeness and mystery of far-off places. *The Way to Go*, which has a fairly constant audience of educated adults, couches its release in terse, matter-of-fact style and language.

FOR RELEASE ON (day and date)

SURF BOATS AND STEAM CRANES SHOW
AFRICAN CONTRASTS ON "OFF TO ADVENTURE"

Passengers for Accra, capital of Ghana, land from their ships by surf boat and are carried ashore on strong African backs. But not for long.

The story of fast-moving change in Africa will be told on "Off to Adventure," the religious series for children, on Station ———, Channel ———, ——— at ———.
(day)   (time)

With the Skipper as their guide, young viewers will watch great cranes at work building the breakwaters of a new port for Ghana. They will see the building of a giant dam for hydro-electric power to refine aluminum from the country's plentiful supply of bauxite.

The program includes visits to the jungle to see the growing of cocoa, Ghana's most important crop, and to an open-air market and a fishing village. Viewers will join a class of Ghanaian school children on a trip to the Parliament building of the young nation.

The new "Off to Adventure" series is designed to help children of the United States and Canada understand the people of Africa struggling to find their place in the modern world. Titled "Adventures in Africa," it is geared to a study course on Christian missions used in Protestant Sunday schools. The series is produced by the National Council of the Churches of Christ in the U.S.A. and presented as a public service by Station ———— in co-operation with ————————————.

(Council of Churches)

JAPAN'S CHANGING ATTITUDES DISCUSSED BY REV. ALOYSIUS MILLER ON "THE WAY TO GO" SUNDAY, NOVEMBER 27

The Rev. Aloysius Miller, s.j., will examine the contrasting attitudes of the Japanese in the 1940s with those held today when he looks at "The Changing Face of Japan" on "The Way to Go," Sunday, Nov. 27 (WCBS-TV, Channel 2, 9:30-10:00 a.m.).

Father Miller, who has lived in Japan since 1947, is Director of Development at Sophia University in Tokyo. Among the topics he will pursue are the change in the attitudes of Japanese youth and the growth of Catholicism in that country. He also will discuss his work at the university.

"The Way to Go" is a WCBS-TV Public Affairs Department presentation. Robert Goodman directs. Host for the series is Ormond J. Drake.

These sample stories carry suggested headlines. Their purpose is more to call attention to interesting content than in the hope they will be used. A busy radio-television editor may have his eye caught by a head when he would not take the time to read the lead.

Send your news stories to the television editor, the religion editor, and the city editor of your papers. Do not worry about this duplication. It is your insurance that somebody on the paper will read your release.

Even if you are on the best of terms with the editor and staff of your local paper, do not expect them to write your stories for you from telephoned information or from a letter giving a résumé of the highlights. They are too busy to do this, and there is too much other news available. The publicity director who prepares a neat, clearly written press release will always have his story accepted if there is a choice between that and a story on which the facts have been telephoned to the paper.

If your program is newsworthy enough to justify the printing of an advance release about it, it may also be worth a follow-up news story that reports what was said, or even worth a review by the television editor. Ideally, follow-up stories should be prepared and delivered to the newspaper in advance of the broadcast. Reviews, of course, have to be written by someone who has seen the show. This person can be your publicity director, especially in places where there is no television editor on the paper.

One of the most important publicity devices for a television program is "pick of the air" listing. It is an assurance that the viewer who is looking for something to see—maybe your program—will know when you are on the air. The best way to make sure of a "pick" listing is to plan for it in advance. Prepare a series of short statements about the programs, one for each show, and send them to the television editor before the programs go on the air. Then, each week, call him and remind him of the next program and of the fact that he has information on it. All commercial shows follow this practice.

Here are some sample highlight listings.

From *Off to Adventure*:

Program: Station ———, Channel ———, $\overline{\text{(day)}}$, $\overline{\text{(date)}}$ $\overline{\text{(time)}}$.

VILLAGE   *Off to Adventure*: Premiere, "Adventures in Africa"
BEWITCHED   series. "Village Bewitched"—When a witch doctor gets
                    control of a village, misery and fear grip the villagers.
                    Here's the story of how the witch doctor "took over,"
                    and how he met his match.

Program: Station ———, Channel ———, $\overline{\text{(day)}}$, $\overline{\text{(date)}}$ $\overline{\text{(time)}}$.

GATEWAY   *Off to Adventure*: "Gateway to Africa"—Accra, the
TO AFRICA   thriving port city of Ghana, one of Africa's newest nations, is typical of the new life Africans are making for themselves. Program reports new industries, improving living conditions, and education of children.

From a local station, WGAL-TV, Lancaster, Pennsylvania:

Omnibus opens New Season with Story of the Presidency, "He Shall Have Power"

In the free world, the most important office in terms of power is that of President of the United States. For a searching and dramatic study of the Presidency since the time of Washington, see the premiere of *Omnibus*. "He Shall Have Power" turns a probing eye on the meaning of the office of President, and the changes that have been wrought in it by the shifting course of world affairs. (Sunday, November 13, 5:00 P.M., WGAL-TV, Channel 8)

"Sub-Killers" Report on Navy Hunter-Killer Exercise on *"The Twentieth Century"*

"Sub-Killers" chronicles the hunt by the U.S. Navy for "enemy submarines." The program was filmed on location 200 miles off the coastline of the Carolinas during an exercise by the Navy's Task Group Alpha. (Sunday, November 13, 6:30 P.M., WGAL-TV Channel 8)

Highlight listings of religious programs as they appeared in the *New York Times*.

> 9:30-10 A.M.—The Way to Go: "Nature of Today's Protestant Church"—The Rev. Dr. Robert W. Spike, guest —(2).
>
> 10-10:30—Lamp Unto My Feet: "Racial Conflict and the Church"—The Rt. Rev. Richard Ambrose Reeves, Bishop of Johannesburg, Transvaal, Union of South Africa, guest—(2).
>
> 10-10:30—Protestant Heritage—(4).
>
> 10-11   —Religious Hour—(13).
>
> 10:30-11—Look Up and Live: "Children and Christmas," Part I—(2).
>
> 1- 1:30—Directions '61: "This, My Son," play about the general theme of rebirth and redemption—(7).
>
> 1:30-2 —Eternal Light: "The Tree Lives," by Clyde Ware. Theodor Herzl's efforts to secure Palestine as a homeland for the Jews—(4).

The highlight listings you prepare for the newspapers should also be sent to all of the churches in your community for inclusion in their bulletins. Bulletins are one of the most valuable and most neglected of the publicity media available to religious broadcasters. The bulletin offers the best means there is for informing the church constituency of the religious programs available in a given community. Your radio-television committee should make a determined effort to get each church to reserve some space for the weekly listing of programs. Be sure that Church A lists *all* of the council's programs in a given week, not just those in which representatives of that church are to appear. Weekly listings help everybody—including the representative of Church A when he broadcasts. Such listings help to create a continuing audience that is loyal to the *program* and will tune in week after week. Periodic listing in bulletins tends to attract a haphazard viewing response. Often the people of a given church forget to see a program when their own church is represented, because the time and day of the program has not been fixed firmly in their minds by frequent repetition.

Promotion

There is general agreement in the television industry that self-promotion is the best kind. All networks and stations use promotional spots to advertise their own shows. It is routine for an announcer to say at the end of a show, "Stay tuned for X which follows immediately."

Religious programs should come in for their fair share of these promotional announcements. When you make arrangements for a station to carry one of your series, try to get an agreement that it will also give you a stated number of spot announcements calling attention to the programs. You will probably have to write these announcements yourself and prepare the accompanying visual material. But if you can get the station continuity staff to help you, do so. They are probably more skilled than you are at preparing spot copy.

Following are some sample spots from the *Off to Adventure* publicity kit that may help you design your own announcements.

BOY SCOUTS Hey, all you Scouts! The drums of the Congo have
OF a message for you. Join Skipper for a camping trip
THE CONGO with African Boy Scouts on *Off to Adventure*, ————
                                                      (day)
              at ————.
                  (time)

VILLAGE AT WORK	Come sing along with the people of Africa on *Off to Adventure* ———— at ————. See how African boys and girls work and play to the rhythm of music on *Off to Adventure*.

VILLAGE
AT WORK

Come sing along with the people of Africa on *Off to Adventure* ———— at ————. See how African
(day)   (time)
boys and girls work and play to the rhythm of music on *Off to Adventure*.

MISSION
OF MERCY

Don't watch *Off to Adventure* this week unless you want a lump in your throat. An African boy crippled with polio learns to walk again. There'll be tears and laughter, too, in *Off to Adventure* ———— at ————.
(day)   (time)

Many church organizations now prepare printed or mimeographed folders telling about their television programs. These folders can be distributed in churches, and in meetings of civic groups; left in stores, offices, schools, and libraries; and mailed broadside. Mailings should not be limited to church membership lists. Advertising folders afford an opportunity to reach unchurched people at little cost per impression. They can be sent to persons on commercial mailing lists, telephone subscribers, families listed in city directories, members of labor unions and professional groups, women's clubs, parent-teacher associations, luncheon clubs, residents of the Y.M.C.A. and Y.W.C.A., and similar groups. All are valuable potential audiences for religious television programs.

A bulletin service for viewers is worthwhile. It may also be distributed by mailings to more general groups and by placement in literature racks. A government postal card containing program listings may suffice. A more elaborate bulletin may have descriptive items about the programs, personality sketches of participants, letters from viewers, questions and answers about programs, and appeals for funds for program support.

Newspaper advertisements on the television page are well worth the small cost they entail. They need not be elaborate, may merely list the name of the program, time of broadcast, and sponsoring body. Naturally, it helps if the name of a well known performer, promise of important subject matter, and a catchy title can be included. Newspaper readership surveys show that television advertisements are read with regularity by viewers in search of their programs for the day. Advertisements may add some prestige to the programs, too, the viewers acting on the theory that what is worth spending money to advertise may be worth watching.

Do not use the church page for television advertising, even though its rates are cheaper than those in the rest of the newspaper. Exposure will be almost solely to persons who might be expected to tune in anyway; the advertisement will not reach the unchurched. There will also be a higher proportion of non-set owners among church page readers than will be found in the general readership of the paper.

Letters mailed to persons who might be expected to be interested in a particular series of programs are an inexpensive and dignified means of announcing the inauguration of a series. They are especially useful when sent to teachers, librarians, lodge secretaries, ministers, and other persons who may be expected to pass on the word that a new program is in the offing.

Following is a letter sent by the American Broadcasting Company network to opinion leaders throughout the country to call attention to *The Valiant Years*. Letters of this sort will be most effective if they bear a salutation and are personally signed.

November 21, 1960

On Sunday, November 27, at 10:30 PM New York time, the first of a series of 26 half-hour programs, WINSTON CHURCHILL: THE VALIANT YEARS, will be telecast over the ABC Television Network. Based on Sir Winston Churchill's epic six-volume study of the Second World War, the series is an ambitious project in visual history. It features a special musical score by composer Richard Rodgers, famous for many hits from *Oklahoma!* to *The Sound of Music*.

We hope the enclosed bookmark, containing a selected list of books about Churchill and World War II, will serve as a reference for further reading on the man and the time. We hope that this series—another step forward in ABC Television's expanding activities in public affairs programming—will make an important contribution to America's understanding of the world we live in.

Two days before the Churchill premiere, on Friday, November 25 at 8:00 PM, we will present another in ABC's BELL & HOWELL CLOSE-UP! series. The program, entitled "The Money Raisers," will deal candidly with the vast enterprise that charity collections have become, covering both the legitimate and the questionable aspects of fund raising.

We believe that both the CHURCHILL and the CLOSE-UP series will be stimulating and rewarding television fare.

Sincerely,
(signed) *Oliver Treyz*

Posters, billboards, and car cards are known as display advertising. Posters are the easiest of the three to acquire and to distribute. If you have the money, they can be elaborate, multicolored pieces, which are always the most effective. But good posters can be done by hand or printed from a simple one-color type layout. Usually it is easy to find public places to display them. Churches, store windows, theaters, hospitals, Y.M.C.A.s, libraries, and schools are a few of the places where posters can be useful aids in recruiting an audience for your programs.

Most transportation companies reserve a generous amount of space in their vehicles for car cards advertising the work of nonprofit organizations. The advertisements in buses and commuter trains attract thousands of eyes each day. They are excellent promotion aids, both for your program and for the station that carries it. Usually you must pay for the printing of the cards.

Sometimes stations use car cards as one of their promotional devices. If your station does this, be sure to ask for space on some of them to advertise religious programs.

The cost of preparing simple three-sheet billboards is not prohibitive for religious organizations. Outdoor advertising companies often provide boards, rent free, to nonprofit organizations that will defray the cost of designing and printing the posters. Such boards are one of the most useful forms of display advertising. The Missouri Synod of the Lutheran Church has found it profitable to buy billboards to advertise their *Lutheran Hour.*

The offer of a premium will always attract mail from audience members. Premiums can range from copies of an address to elaborate novelties. *Off to Adventure* mails out copies of Indian sign-language symbols and colored pictures of places visited and filmed in Japan. On the back are listed missionary education books which the children who write in for premiums are urged to read. Premiums are an excellent device for local religious broadcasters to use to put them in personal touch with viewers for purposes of recruitment and research.

Managing Publicity and Promotion

Publicity and promotion for television should be the responsibility of one person or, at most, of a small committee. The publicity director should make it his business to get to know newspaper publishers, editors and reporters, television and radio news broadcasters and editors, and any other persons in the community who control news media. He should work hard to gain the reputation of sending in only stories that are newsworthy and that are strictly accurate in every detail, including, especially, the spelling of names. Nothing will kill promotional efforts more quickly than the substitution of press agentry for news reporting, or careless handling of names, dates, and other factual material.

Always remain on friendly terms with the news outlets. Do not complain when they kill a story that is of supreme importance to you. Do not make invidious comparisons between the amount of space your programs get and that given to broadcasts of other groups. Remember, for the most part editors make an honest effort to judge stories solely on the basis of their news value and to give priority to those items that are of most vital interest to the public. They always have too much copy for the space to be filled. Something must go out.

When you do get a story in the newspaper or on radio or television, no matter how small it is, do not fail to write a letter or to telephone or to stop in to thank the editor and the reporter who were responsible for it. They like to know you appreciate them, even though they are only doing the jobs they are paid to do. Visit the same courteous treatment on ministers and church staff members who run your material in their church papers and bulletins.

Call upon the news people and the promotional staff of the station for help when you are not sure how to handle a story. They know the right way. They will seldom refuse to give advice.

When you have an important story coming up, be sure to call the news outlets in advance to let them know they are going to receive it. Then they will be on the lookout for your release. It does not hurt, either, to check to make sure your story was received. Releases have a disconcerting habit of disappearing in the litter of a news room.

Above all, be dependable. If you promise to turn in a story, or to check a name or a fact, or to bring someone around for an interview, do not fail to deliver as and when you agreed to. Go to any ends to help a reporter who is working on your story; and do it cheerfully.

As long as you are responsible for publicity, keep on your desk in plain sight Joseph Pulitzer's famous news-room motto: "Get it right! Get it now! But get it right!"

Christian Perspective
on Mass Communication

Do the American People Think for Themselves?

Throughout this book we have sought to present methods that may be used to get the American people to think about religion and to make decisions about themselves and their society that are consistent with the teaching of the gospel of Christ. But many serious thinkers have in their minds a disturbing question that challenges these aims: Does the individual living under the impact of the mass media any longer have the freedom to make up his mind?

Hendrik Kraemer speaks of the "demonic potentialities and realizations" of these instrumentalities, and of their "culture-destroying tendencies."[1] It is absurd to argue, as some do, especially in the industry, that the mass media only mirror the culture, that they are shaped by the tastes of the people and are thus the epitome of the expression of "cultural democracy." These media under their present managers exist to arouse desires, shape tastes, reorient values. If they had no influence, or even little influence, their commercial support would quickly fade away and they would no longer be either powerful or profitable. Roger Shinn has pointed out that there is a duality in the relationship of the mass media to the culture; they cannot be

radically better than the culture at large, but they will elevate or degrade the culture in important ways. Ours is not a monolithic society with a fixed ideology and scale of values. In the diversity of American life all sorts of interests and purposes compete. It makes a great deal of differ-

[1] Hendrik Kraemer, *The Communication of the Christian Faith* (Philadelphia: The Westminster Press, 1956), p. 11.

ence whether mass communications appeal to prejudice or to understanding, whether they reinforce our cheapest or our most discerning values.[2]

Among the complex political, economic, and social revolutions that have riven the fabric of human relations in the twentieth century, the communications revolution is far from the least important. It has been spawned by the scientific and technological advances in optics, electronics, chemistry, and mechanics that have made possible the mass-circulation newspapers, magazines, paperback and comic books; the cinema; and radio and television. These instrumentalities, coupled with radical industrial advances and readjustments, have imposed severe tensions upon both Western and Eastern cultures. Their effects on whole cultures are as yet unclear. When it comes to assessing their impact upon individuals—especially upon their freedom of thought—the obstacles are well-nigh insurmountable. This much we do know, however. Virtually every individual is being subjected to a new congeries of institutional pressures—not the least of which are being exerted by the mass media of communication—all of which are designed to reduce his individuality and to bring him into conformity with the institutional objectives. Elaborate technology and heavy capital investment seeking return demand that there be *mass production* and *mass consumption*. To keep this cycle going, a determined effort is made to capture whole populations and to hold them continuously under high-powered sales exploitation.

Here is the point at which mass production and the mass media of communication fit together like hand and glove. Modern technology has given birth to a gospel of "gracious living" with production-consumption as the means to salvation. There is an evangel of "something for everybody" and nobody can ever get enough. The communications instrumentalities are the evangelists. Their aim is to mold thoughts and feelings so people will end up as passive puppets to be used to the best advantage of the managers of the production-consumption process.

This convenient union of industry and communication has been made possible by still another aspect of the technological revolution,

[2] Roger Shinn, statement to the Mass Media Standards Committee, Broadcasting and Film Commission of the National Council of the Churches of Christ in the U.S.A., January 22, 1960.

the urbanization of American society. Mass communication did not spring full-grown upon us with the blooming of the television tube. Printing has always had mass appeal, but it was unable to achieve mass distribution until its potential readers began to be concentrated in cities, where mass circulation was economically feasible. Similarly, radio and, later, television gained their present power in American economic and social life because (1) there were concentrated audiences available and (2) the commodity distribution system was able to give these audiences easy access to the products advertised over the air. Thus, it was possible to meet the enormous costs of the mass media because they, in turn, served an indispensable function in the process of meeting the even more enormous costs of mass-producing consumer products.

The inevitable result of the partnership between the mass media of communication and mass-produced commodities has been the employment of the communications organs for petty purposes. Motion pictures, radio, television and, to a lesser extent, magazines and newspapers have been devoted to providing entertainment and relaxation. For countless people they have been a narcotic that dulls the pain of empty hours. The quiz and payola scandals have uncovered an evil conspiracy in television and radio to subvert the good and the beautiful. Even so, in none of the mass media (comic books excepted) does one seem to find much that is consciously vicious. It is more a matter of the mediocrity that results from sterile imitation, of a drift into what is easiest and cheapest to do. Of course there are bright spots—inspired writing, superb drama and music, knowledgeable reporting and commentary. But these things are so much the exception! The rest, rather than increasing public maturity, is largely inhibiting it. Communication of serious thought and artistry is not only not striven for in mass communications, it is thought to be downright subversive to the objectives of the "big sell."

One of the worst apparent effects of our petty use of the mass media is standardization of taste. Every idea, every object is reduced to the status of something that will sell. Religion is no exception. Each person in the audience is visualized only as a consumer, is valued only in terms of what he can be persuaded to buy.

Our culture is dangerously subservient to its economy. Hundreds of millions of dollars are spent in advertising each year to convince us it is our duty to maintain a high level of personal consumption; that if we do not live as luxuriously as possible, the whole productive process will break down and leave us with nothing to consume at all. "Treat yourself right. You owe it to yourself," we are told. When people speak out against the abandonment of thrift and modesty in personal display, when they argue that there are social goods that are at least as important as private self-gratification, they are branded as virtual traitors. No less a personage than the president of General Motors, the world's largest corporation, has called such dissenters "hair-shirt philosophers" who are "exponents of a new austerity, a new puritanism, a new spartanism," who consider "the American way" to be "a sinful way." Under "the free enterprise system" social goods and services are a mere "by-product" of individual consumption, he says.[3]

Religion poses the question: "What is man?" and the mass media reply: "Man is a consumer." The churches can hardly close their ears to this answer and still pretend to an interest in the welfare of persons. If the churches are to attempt to witness to the Gospel through the mass media, they cannot ignore their resultant involvement with the philosophy expounded by those organs and, therefore, the crucial necessity to struggle against its demonic elements. By not speaking out to show both the mass communications industry and its audiences that the pursuit of self-gratification does not account adequately for the sources of human action, the churches ally themselves by their silence with the forces that are substituting shallow and trivial meanings for great objectives and great convictions.

Standardization of Programs

Broadcasters claim they are working in an art form, but they call themselves an "industry." Actually, the close tie between television and mass-production industry has inevitably transformed television from an art to an adjunct of industry, governed by industry's goals and following industry's methods of standardization, interchangeability and mass distribution of a limited number of products.

[3] John F. Gordon, president, General Motors Corporation, address before the Society of Automotive Engineers, Detroit, January 11, 1961.

Television broadcasting has trapped itself in a circle of standardized views that lead to the production of standardized programs that,
in turn, reinforce standardized views.

First, there is the argument that the television we have is the
television we *ought* to have. Then, because it is as it ought to be, it
would be folly to try to make it anything else. Finally, because television is so expensive, even if it were not what it ought to be, no one
could afford to try to change it. All that can be done, all that *ought*
to be done, is to stick to the tried and true formulas that have sold
commodities in the past.

"Network broadcasting," a network vice-president explains it, "has
to have something . . . for everybody. For the fact is that broadcasting is a truly mass medium; it has to be. Unless it can enlist and
hold the interest of most of the people a good part of the time, it
is just too expensive a medium to survive.[4]

The fiction that the United States is dependent for television
service on the profit-seeking activities of the broadcasters and advertisers is implanted widely by industry spokesmen. As long as this
fiction remains substantially unchallenged by the government and
the general public, the networks, stations, and advertising agencies
will continue to produce programs designed not to "enlist and hold
. . . most of the people," but to attract in each case that audience
which might be expected to do the most buying of the commodity
being advertised. Usually this selected audience is women, as will be
demonstrated below. Large numbers of viewers are of primary importance. The more people that can be drawn to a show, the more
likely the sponsor is to capture a substantial number of the audience
class that is really wanted. Individual programs, especially at night,
are downgraded by the networks' drives for "circulation," a constant
audience of great size that can be held throughout an evening against
the competition of other networks. In the topsy-turvy values of television, the "carry-over" audience is more important than the one that
actually watches a program. If a program—no matter how good it
is, no matter how loyal or influential its audience may be—has a
comparatively low rating, it will be dropped by the network because

[4] Richard S. Salant, vice-president, Columbia Broadcasting System, address to
the Rotary Club of St. Louis, Missouri, June 26, 1958.

of the fear it will jeopardize the schedule for the entire evening. Religion and other serious subjects have no chance to break into night time under this system where not even an advertiser is permitted to present a program that might cut down on the audience for the advertisers that follow it. Jack Gould concludes that

so long as it is necessary to avoid the prospect of even a single soft "link" in a chain of programs, there is a built-in, automatic limitation on what type of programming can be done in an evening schedule. The consequences of this approach to programming—not weighing the individual show as an entity but as part of a complex mosaic—is readily apparent. No single presentation can break very far out of the established pattern of popularity without theoretically dragging other shows down with it. The over-all pressures for a sustained audience of great size at all times, accordingly, dictate adherence to sameness.[5]

This standardization of programming in television, which also exists in others of the mass media of communication, tends to foster standardization of taste in viewers. Since program fare, from all the outlets, is uniformly the same, the audience members have no yardstick with which to judge the artistic merit of what they see. It is virtually impossible to prove scientifically that television has *lowered* standards of taste, since we have no criteria to determine what the standards were before television came on the scene. But in the light of the objectives the broadcasters themselves have enunciated and of the shows they produce, informed social critics are worried about the effects television may be having on cultural standards and relations. Edward R. Murrow confesses to "an abiding fear" about what both radio and televsion may be doing "to our society, our culture and our heritage."

There is no question but that television is consciously trying (1) to have people visualize themselves primarily as consumers and (2) to establish conspicuous consumption as a mark of good taste. Television looks upon the middle income family as the prototype consumer. It therefore works hard at plugging what the advertising agencies conceive to be middle class desires, habits, morality, and social concepts as the ultimate standards of public taste. And since the advertisers are well aware of who controls the purse strings in the

[5] Jack Gould, "Victim of Ratings," *New York Times*, April 19, 1959, p. xii.

purchase of mass-produced commodities, programs shamelessly pander to the power sense of women. Commercials, even for beer, are meant to sell women. The daytime serials frankly portray the dominance of women and inveigh against their unjust suffering at the hands of callous males. In the evening, with men watching, the programs dare not be so bold; so the sponsors fell back on such programs as *The Life of Riley* and *I Love Lucy*. Father is pictured as a nincompoop, bad-tempered, flighty, unpredictable, the deserved butt of every joke, and the victim of an endless variety of female conspiracies. But, it may be argued, in the westerns, the most numerous of all the show types, males are dominant. However, these heroes are not men of the community who make decisions and solve problems in democratic fashion; they are supermen from without who impose their wills on society. They are not dominated by women, but neither do they dominate. They preserve their romantic appeal and hero remoteness by avoiding entanglements with women, while at the same time treating these most precious consumers with kid-glove politeness. The heroes of television are just as much stereotypes as are the hapless fathers. To top it all, the audience members also loom as stereotypes in the minds of the people who create the programs and the commercials.

This kind of stereotyping not only sets false and unattainable standards for family living, it also drives out programming that has artistic integrity. Of course, television has some outstanding programs that attempt to portray life realistically or that deal in tender humor and fantasy. *Play of the Week* and *Father Knows Best* are examples. But, as Walter Lippmann writing in the wake of the television quiz scandals noted, Gresham's Law operates in television as surely as it does in monetary affairs. Bad programming tends to drive out the good. The reverse is never true. Good programming must be consciously sought after. It is much more difficult to achieve than is bad. Paradoxically, once good programming exists, it is also much more vulnerable to attack than is bad programming. The good show consciously expounds a point of view in which some elements will be unique or uniquely treated; it strives for high artistic standards; it makes reasoned judgments concerning such things as truth, righteousness, and beauty. These things are the stuff that critics deal with.

They can be discussed and are worth disscussing. Judgments can be rendered concerning the ideational values in the show, its technique, its artistic merit. The good show raises expectancy in both audience and critics. It aspires to a worthwhile goal. When it fails to achieve it the consequent disappointment of both audience and performers is serious and may mitigate against another try. The bad show escapes this rigorous process of intellectual discipline. It does not pretend to say anything and nothing is expected of it except the idle filling of the time between commercials. Its stereotyping of ideas and characters leaves nothing to discuss; so critics are silent, or merely dismiss it as trash. No critic would bother to review *Hawaiian Eye*, but *Playhouse 90* had to rejustify itself week after week against the opinions of all the critics.

Treatment of Public Issues

Another dangerous form of standardization exists in the handling of public issues by the mass media, and again television is a principal offender. The American constitutional system is predicated upon the submission of issues, policies, and candidates to public examination and criticism and to the making of deliberative choices between parties and candidates. An informed citizenry is assumed to be capable of rational choice in the election of public officials. Mass communication may be on its way to subvert these fundamentals of our conduct of government, substituting for them a commodity view of politics.

Both major political parties now use the advice and services of advertising agencies and other mass media specialists. There is nothing pernicious about the desire of the politicians to use television to help them get elected. We would want them and their views seen and heard by as many voters as might be willing to attend to them. But the method of exposure is of major importance. Heretofore we have depended upon direct access to the candidates and their declarations to aid us in making up our minds about how to vote. There has been a great deal of buncombe, of course, but a voter can discount a lot of it when he meets the candidate face to face or reads his words in cold print. The advertising agencies have introduced into politics the same theories and practices they use in commercial advertising. They merchandise a candidate for public office in the same manner that they do any other salable product. Moreover, they are wedded to the celebrity testimonial as a sales technique and are deeply suspicious of reason and argument, looking upon them as obstacles to successful selling. They are convinced that in politics, too, the public will buy on the basis of names, faces, personalities, and slogans; that platforms and issues should be kept well in the background, if they are worth mentioning at all. When political argument is presented through spot announcements and domestic dramas, or when a candidate is surrounded by the trappings of a political spectacular where the emphasis is on stars and testimonials, not issues, it is questionable whether any sort of rational judgment on the part of the voter is possible.

The Political Power of Television. After his election President John F. Kennedy freely admitted he could not have won the Presidency had it not been for the television debates he held with Richard M. Nixon. Most pundits rated the debates as decisive because they gave Kennedy "exposure" to an enormous audience he would not otherwise have reached. Actually, they were decisive for a much more important and complicated reason.

These confrontations were, of course, not debates. There was no measured presentation of views and issues and rebuttal. When issues were introduced, they were handled badly by both men more often than not. What the public experienced was the opportunity to study two faces at closer range and over a longer period than had ever before occurred in political compaigning. We made our decision on what we saw in those faces, not on the basis of a reasoned flow of ideas, or the defense of issues or of party platform. Personality, *as revealed from the peculiar perspective of the television camera,* was the decisive factor in choice.

The television camera emerged from the presidential campaign as an actual wielder of political power. It is bound to be used regularly in the future to reveal candidates in intimate personality detail. The critical question whch remains to be answered is whether the intimate camera close-up merely favors a good performer who can project a pleasing image of himself or whether it probes beneath whatever image a man is wearing to reveal the true personality.

The Handling of News and Events. When day-to-day public issues are dealt with by the mass media, they are often oversimplified. Delusively simple answers are given for complex, but comprehensible, questions. There is a tendency to treat complicated issues in black-and-white terms; to explain things like our disagreements with President Gamal Abdel Nasser as if they arose only as a phase of the struggle between the West and Communism, ignoring the causative factors in the tangled and far more pertinent ambitions of Arab nationalism. Distortion in the interpreting of public issues may occur because of hasty or faulty editing. In television it often results from the practice of capsulizing—the compression of an important news item into a few words and a picture. A story that might occupy a column in the *New York Times* typically becomes a thirty-second bulletin on television. There is no room for interpretation or for the filling in of background. There is also little sober, responsible editorial comment on television, although it is permitted by the Federal Communications Commission.

Recently television has been taking its role as an agency for news reporting and interpretation more seriously than in the past, as is witnessed by the excellent coverage given the Khrushchev visit to the United States, the 1960 presidential campaign and similar major stories, and documentaries on such issues as the population explosion and Negro student "sit-ins" in the South. But there is still vast room for improvement in both the bulk and the quality of news and public affairs programs. The churches, which are concerned with nurturing informed persons who will act responsibly in the community, have an important stake in the character and the amount of interpretation of public issues that reach the public through the mass media. Here is a place where the influence of Christianity might be brought to bear in behalf of the informational needs of all the people.

Manipulation

A critical and sensitive issue in the ethics of mass communication is the use of these media for the manipulation of people. The typical reason for manipulation is commercial—to sell commodities—but political manipulation is increasing and instances can be documented of the use of these media to gain influence, power, and control. The absorbing moral question, however, is not so much what the purposes of the manipulation are. It is whether, from the standpoint of the Christian doctrine of man, the dignity and integrity of the individual are being compromised by the steadily growing arsenal of manipulative techniques being made available to the mass media by clever students of human behavior. We have already pointed out the danger that religious groups who unquestioningly employ accepted mass media practices may also become involved in this sin of manipulation.

A fundamental principle of Protestantism is respect for the integrity of the individual. Protestantism concedes him the right to make decisions in the light of his understanding of the faith which he holds and of the best judgment of which he is capable. The Christian sanction against manipulation extends specifically to the manipulation of people for what is presumed to be their best interest.

WHAT CAN THE PEOPLE DO?

There is no question as to where legal control of broadcasting rests. It is in the people, administered by means of legislation passed by the Congress. The Communications Act of 1934, by stating that broadcast licensees must operate "in the public interest, convenience, or necessity," makes it clear that the welfare and the wishes of the people should be paramount in programming. The Federal Communications Commission itself has stated "the Communications Act as a whole clearly reveals that the foundation of the Commission's authority rests upon the public interest, convenience and necessity."[6] The Supreme Court delineated this principle in a noteworthy case, NBC vs. United States by ruling:

An important element of public interest and convenience affecting the issue of a license is the ability of the licensee to render the best practicable service to the community reached by broadcasts. . . . The Commission's licensing function cannot be discharged, therefore, merely by finding that there are no technological objections to the granting of a license. . . . Since the very inception of federal regulation by radio,

[6] Federal Communications Commission, Report and Statement of Policy Re: Commission En Banc Programming Inquiry (Washington: FCC, July 29, 1960), p. 10.

comparative considerations as to the services to be rendered have governed the application of the standard of "public interest, convenience, or necessity."[7]

In view of this apparently clear-cut policy and of support of it registered by the legislature, the courts, and the agency charged with administering the law, why have broadcasters been able to flout at will their statutory responsibilities to afford reasonable opportunity for issues of public importance to be discussed, for local self-expression, for public interest groups such as churches to air their views, and for program service to minority groups?

First, because there is genuine and widespread disagreement as to just how far the Federal Communications Commission may go in applying the public interest provisions of the Communications Act to specific programming. Section 326 of the Communications Act, as amended, provides that:

Nothing in this chapter shall be understood or construed to give the Commission the power of censorship over the radio communications or signals transmitted by any radio station, and no regulation or condition shall be promulgated or fixed by the Commission which shall interfere with the right of free speech by means of radio communication.

The Supreme Court on several occasions has made it clear that freedom of expression on radio and television is protected by the First Amendment. In *United States vs. Paramount Pictures* the Court stated:

We have no doubt that moving pictures, like newspapers and radio, are included in the press whose freedom is guaranteed by the First Amendment.[8]

In *Superior Films vs. Department of Education* Justice Douglas in a concurring opinion said:

Motion pictures are, of course, a different medium of expression than the radio, the stage, the novel or the magazine. But the First Amendment draws no distinction between the various methods of communicating ideas.[9]

[7] 319 U. S. 190.
[8] 334 U. S. 131, 166 (1948).
[9] 346 U. S. 587 (1954).

As recently as 1959 the Court warned that ". . . expressly applying this country's tradition of free expression to the field of radio broadcasting, Congress has from the first emphatically forbidden the Commission to exercise any power of censorship over radio communication."[10]

Obviously, the line between evaluation of public interest performance and censorship is thin. But the Federal Communications Commission has never attempted to clarify the extent of the very real power Congress expected it to exercise over programming, preferring to let broadcasters operate as they please without hindrance from Commission regulation over anything but obscenity, profanity, indecency, lotteries, or programs designed to incite to riot or to induce the commission of crime.

Second, the Federal Communications Commission has failed dismally to enforce the Communications Act in the interest of the public. Since 1945, at least, the Commission has been generally conceded to be almost completely subservient to the industry it is supposed to regulate. One Commission chairman has been forced to resign because he took gifts from broadcast licensees. Other Commissioners have been shown to have all-too-intimate relationships with licensees and industry representatives.

James M. Landis in his report to President John F. Kennedy on the Federal regulatory agencies said:

The Federal Communications Commission presents a somewhat extraordinary spectacle. Despite considerable technical excellence on the part of its staff, the commission has drifted, vacillated and stalled in almost every major area. It seems incapable of policy planning, of disposing within a reasonable period of time the business before it, of fashioning procedures that are effective to deal with its problems.

The available evidence indicates that it, more than any other agency, has been susceptible to ex parte presentations, and that it has been subservient, far too subservient, to the subcommittees on communications of the Congress and their members. A strong suspicion also exists that far too great an influence is exercised over the commission by the networks.

[10] *Farmers Educational and Cooperative Union of America* vs. *Day, Inc.*, 360 U. S. 525.

The quality of its top personnel is, of course, primarily responsible for these defects. . . .

Third, even in the face of the quiz program scandals, the payola scandal, the widespread outcry for reform of the Federal Communications Commission and its procedures, it is apparent that the opinions of individuals or of small groups concerning the content of television programs carry little weight with networks and stations. While letters of praise or protest to stations, to networks, and to sponsors, and public resolutions and testimony are not without value, they cannot be expected to bring about radical improvements in an enterprise that reaps the tremendous financial harvest that television enjoys, just for doing what it now does. America is growing in numbers, wanting more, consuming more all the time. Stations and networks are well aware that television audiences will grow inexorably just through the increase in population. The broadcasters can unconcernedly shrug off protesters and suggesters. They are a mere drop in the bucket among the millions of persons who do not know how to—or who just do not—articulate their feelings and choices.

Fourth, the people's abiding disadvantage is the absence of any effective system of feed-back. The huge communications empires are so powerful as to be practically autonomous, and their policy makers are many echelons removed from the consumers of their programs. Television viewers can neither determine the content of programs themselves, nor tell the purveyors of content just what they want. The argument is advanced by the spokesmen of commercial television that it is the people who have given television its immense stature and power, that they have raised it to its present importance because it serves them to their satisfaction. This is at least partly true; television would not have the audiences it does if a majority of the people were wholly dissatisfied with what it has to offer. It is also true that in a pluralistic society such as ours, there are many standards of taste and desire, and critics are apt to lose sight of the fact that what they do not like may suit someone else's taste. Yet these facts must be considered: People will often accept something less than what they would really like to have, if nothing else is available to them. The public has never been asked, either by government or by the television interests, what services they might reasonably desire and expect from television. The people have never indicated that they are satisfied with television as it now is.

The producers of television programs have the ability and resources to do a variety of things they are not doing to give the public many things it *may want*. They need to be persuaded to *try*. Bitter criticism of television abounds and is spreading, but the majority of the men who control the outlets and the programming do not seem to be willing to heed it. They will not chance the sacrifice of profits to open even just a little time in the prime evening hours for programs that will raise the public's awareness of important issues, that will educate, that will help in the slow advance toward a higher cultural level, that will weigh spiritual issues and elevate spiritual values. Yet, Jack Gould says, were they to do this "with predictability and regularity it's a fair guess that 90 per cent of the criticism of the medium would evaporate overnight."[11]

Even such a small change can be expected only as the result of vigorous, widespread public action. There is need for the development of standards for the ethical conduct of mass communications, standards that the public comprehends and will support, as the Canadian people have upheld the recommendations of the Fowler Commission. There is need, also, for a voice, clear and insistent, that will demand that all phases of radio-television broadcasting, from government licensing and oversight to the volume of advertising, shall be accommodated to the public enjoyment and welfare rather than to the sales designs of commercial advertisers.

The task of making and supporting standards is one for which the church, with its own ethic to use as a yardstick, is eminently fitted. It is to the credit of the National Council of Churches that as soon as the quiz scandals were revealed, it spoke out before the Federal Communications Commission for strict enforcement of the Communications Act and a cessation of practices of broadcast licensees and advertisers that are inimical to the public interest.[12] It was quickly joined by other concerned and powerful interests—the

[11] Jack Gould, *op. cit.*, p. xii.

[12] Testimony of James Wine, Associate General Secretary of the National Council of the Churches of Christ in the U. S. A., before the Federal Communications Commission, December 7, 1959.

Attorney General, committees of Congress, the Federal Trade Commission, much of the nation's press, women's organizations, parent-teacher associations, many conscientious station and network executives, uncounted private individuals and, finally, the Federal Communications Commission itself. But the struggle has just begun. The practices that are being universally condemned as they are uncovered in radio and television are not isolated moral lapses. They are of a piece with the moral looseness that is endemic in our culture. They will not be rooted out of television and radio in a flurry of publicity and condemnation by broadcasting's competitors of the press, but will require years of calling to account the whole of the mass media for their stewardship. If the churches are serious about their responsibility for this task, they will have to settle down for the long pull and develop objectives which they will strive to attain.

As far as television and radio are concerned, the churches might well join with other responsible elements in society and in broadcasting to achieve needed reforms and improvements such as the following:

1. Appointment to the Federal Communications Commission of men of integrity and ability who will administer the Communications Act impartially. Mr. Landis pointed out in his report to the President that there can be no solution for the situation in the commission "other than the incubation of vigor and courage in the commission by giving it strong and competent leadership. . . . Good men can make poor laws workable; poor men will wreak havoc with good laws."

It is the last condition that has existed in the commission. The Communications Act has never been tested against a determined effort to enforce it.

2. Divestment by congressmen and senators who are members of the communication sub-committees of the Congress of their stock holdings in communications media.

3. Amendment of the Federal Communications Act to provide for the licensing of networks for stated periods by the Federal Communications Commission, and for renewal of the licenses only after a public hearing in which the Commission shall determine that such renewal is in the public interest. The economics of television make

it virtually impossible for a local station to survive without a network affiliation. The Commission itself has admitted publicly that, while the station licensee is legally responsible for everything broadcast over his facilities, "in practical operation" he has no control over network program offerings. Networks select and supervise the programs "which, of course, are the principal broadcast fare of the vast majority of television stations throughout the country."[13] Since the networks control the programming, they should be held publicly accountable for the material they disseminate.

4. Divorcement of advertisers and their agents from the power to control program content or to stipulate that their advertising shall be associated with a particular program or shall not be placed adjacent to a particular program. It would be naive to think that whoever pays the bills will not always have a great deal to say about programs, no matter who produces them; but newspapers and magazines have always successfully resisted advertiser dominance of editorial content. Radio and television got off on the other foot and have lived to rue it, since the advertising agencies determine what shall and shall not go on the air. It will probably require Federal legislation to remedy this situation, although a firm stand by the networks probably could clear it up. Jack Gould points out that "it is a tradition of advertisers that, once they know what a medium's regulations are, they will conform. If the networks can summon up enough courage to let the world know who is boss in fact as well as publicity release, then sponsor dominance will begin to ebb."[14] Licensing and close oversight of networks would help attain this end.

5. Publication by the Federal Communications Commission of the criteria it uses in granting and renewing licenses. These standards have never been made a matter of public record. They are reported to be based upon maximum allowable number of commercial announcements, percentage of commercial to sustaining time, proportion of live to taped programming, and percentage of time devoted to public service programs. But whatever criteria may be articulated in broadcast license cases, James M. Landis reported to the President,

[13] Federal Communications Commission, *op. cit.*, p. 14.
[14] Jack Gould, "Forgotten Clues to the TV Crisis," the *New York Times Magazine*, December 13, 1959, p. 92.

"they are patently not the grounds motivating the decision. No firm decisional policy has evolved from these case-by-case dispositions. Instead the anonymous opinion writers for the Commission pick from a collection of standards those that will support whatever decision the Commission chooses to make."

6. Establishment by the Federal Communications Commission of guidelines as to what constitutes the public interest under the Communications Act. Standards would be set only after extensive public hearings in which both the broadcasters and the public—including the churches—might have an opportunity to testify. The networks, in particular, as the main program source should be required to blue-print evening schedules that would provide a diversity of programs but would still leave room for the big entertainment shows that are surely wanted by a majority of viewers. The objective of the Federal Communications Commission in setting guidelines should be to preserve what is good while providing for fulfillment of the obligation to broadcast in the public interest. Once such standards become known and understood by both broadcasters and the public, it should not be hard to judge a network or a station by the sum total of its programming without in any way interfering with its freedom to schedule whatever programs it sees fit to carry.

7. Prohibition by Federal legislation against trafficking in station licenses. A person or corporation that receives a license grant should be required to construct and operate the station for a minimum period of years or to turn the grant back for assignment to another applicant. After the minimum operating period, no transfer of the station should be permitted without a public hearing by the Federal Communications Commission in the community where the station is located.

8. Expansion of publicly supported educational television into a national network with coverage equivalent to that of the largest present network. This educational facility is not suggested as a competitive service—as the British Broadcasting Company and the commercial network are in Britain and the Candian Broadcasting Company and private stations are in Canada—but as a necessary service to the burgeoning schools and colleges with their shortage of teachers and to adults who wish to have educational services

similar to *Sunrise Semester*. The development of educational stations and an educational network should not be allowed to become a means whereby the commercial outlets can shirk their public service responsibilities.

The Thorny Problem of Codes and Censorship

No matter what system of oversight might be developed for television production, there is bound to be tension between the demand for freedom of artistic expression—to say nothing of freedom to do anything a producer might want to try—and the demand that the intimate family circle in the home be protected from the intrusion of ideas and acts that are inimical to cherished moral values. Any society has the right and the duty to protect itself and its institutions from onslaughts that threaten to destroy its moral fabric. Yet, once one has granted this principle, he must still face the question of where to draw the line. In a democracy, and especially a pluralistic one such as ours, it would be surprising if any two people agreed exactly upon just what should be allowed and what prohibited in any particular situation.

Codes are easy to draw up, harder to enforce, impossible to depend upon as the means of shielding people from exposure to the things prohibited by the codifiers. "Codes by their nature deal with externals. Some externals are important, but they usually miss the main points," says Roger Shinn.[15] A code that was rigidly enforced would make the same prohibition concerning violence in *Macbeth* that it would on violence in *Have Gun, Will Travel*. It is impossible for a code to exercise aesthetic judgment in such a matter. A single idea, act, or manner of dress in a production also cannot be evaluated in isolation. Only an understanding of the whole intent of the piece, of the way it handles human emotions and situations, of the quality and integrity of its revelations can afford an adequate basis for judgment.

Honesty and moral uprightness in the producer are the only things we can count upon to protect the public from salacious, immoral content in television programs. No code can discriminate between what is morally and aesthetically valid and what is merely salacious trash.

[15] Shinn, *op. cit.*

The producer with artistic integrity can and will discriminate, without a code. The irresponsible producer will ignore or slink around the code.

Censorship poses the same problems as do codes with the added difficulty of the authority granted to the censor. Who is so moral and incorruptible that he may be vested with the power to control another man's thoughts and utterances? Even the most wise, the most restrained, the most upright man exercising the function of a censor will create more abuses than he solves. A faceless government agency acting in this capacity is even less to be desired.

Justice William O. Douglas has aptly characterized the inherent dangers in censorship:

> The music selected by one bureaucrat may be as offensive to some as it is soothing to others. The news commentator chosen to report on the events of the day may give overtones to the news that please the bureaucrat but which rile the . . . audience. The political philosophy which one radio sponsor exudes may be thought by the official who makes up the programs as the best for the welfare of the people. But the man who listens to it . . . may think it marks the destruction of the Republic. . . . Today it is a business enterprise working out a radio program under the auspices of government. Tomorrow it may be a dominant, political, or religious group. . . . Once a man is forced to submit to one type of program, he can be forced to submit to another. It may be but a short step from a cultural program to a political program. . . . The strength of our system is in the dignity, resourcefulness and the intelligence of our people. Our confidence is in their ability to make the wisest choice. That system cannot flourish if regimentation takes hold.[16]

Is the foregoing an argument that we can and must accept without protest whatever the people who control television production choose to create and broadcast? By no means! Constant vigilance is necessary. The viewer is just as much responsible for upholding moral and aesthetic standards as is the producer. The church shares in this responsibility at two levels, since its people are both producers and viewers of television programs.

Robert W. Spike has defined the task of the church in relation to television content in words that bear repeating.

[16] *Public Utilities Commission* vs. *Pollak*, 343 U. S. 451, 468, Dissenting Opinion.

The church has the obligation to go on in its own teaching and preaching ministry to do explicit moral teaching based on its heritage and its faith. It does not have the right to insist on this in the . . . industry. It does have the obligation to work for the presentation of the full range of honest representation of modern life, its dilemmas, its tragedies, its choices, its joys. What it works against is cheapness, exaltation of the raw sense experience, vulgarity disguised as sentimentality or piety or religion.[17]

The churches need not—in fact should not—have a monolithic, unanimous opinion on every issue of morality posed by the mass media. But it is incumbent upon their leaders that they exercise a conservative influence for the preservation of the moral and spiritual values which we cherish in our culture by speaking out in practical terms to guide their millions of constituents in making discriminating decisions about what to accept and what to reject from these instrumentalities.

In Summary

Christians have ethical responsibilities toward the functioning of the mass media of communication, just as they do toward other institutions of modern life. In the struggle to understand and master these instrumentalities, they have not always taken note of their demonic qualities. Many Protestant broadcasters, at least, have tacitly accepted the communications industry standards: that communication takes place through the merchandising of personalities; that values can be treated as commodities. Religion is also viewed as a commodity, something that can be sold by the same technique and using the same degree of truth that the mass media apply to the selling of soap.

Furthermore, there has been too little effort to relate mass communication to the concerns and viewpoints of the Christian Church —especially to the thrust of evangelism and missions—and to evaluate results of its use scientifically. Nor has religion developed an aesthetic attitude toward the media, relating itself to the *arts* of communica-

[17] Robert W. Spike, statement to the Mass Media Standards Committee of the Broadcasting and Film Commission of the National Council of the Churches of Christ in the U. S. A., January 22, 1960.

tion rather than to the methods used for the commercial sale of products.

One step toward a serious consideration of the modern communications media would be for the churches to join with the most responsible elements engaged in communication to set minimal aesthetic and moral standards where no adequate standards now exist, yet where good citizenship demands that they must exist. Criteria can be evolved which imply no censorship in individual cases, yet which require that what is seen, heard, and read shall bear some recognizable relationship to the meaning of Christian ethics. In television, the churches can fruitfully use their own programs to illustrate such standards.

The churches can best attain their aims by refraining from punitive action against the communications industry, from harassing it with investigations, and, above all, from advocating censorship of program content. They should, however, act intelligently to discover and make public the facts about how mass communications are being conducted and to develop public understanding of the ethical implications of the various courses of action being taken by mass communications media.

Perhaps the most important task of the churches is that of awakening the consciences of the men who control the communications instrumentalities and of the public to the appalling results that can stem from the misuse of mass communications. It is too much to say that these media have become all-pervading and are the prime taste setters and arbiters of American culture. It is nevertheless true that they can influence tastes, change opinions, motivate action. If they are to operate forever only on a commodity-sell basis, they may all too soon become a literal "opiate of the people."

In questioning the ethics of mass communication, as in all questioning of the social order, the churches dare not strike a self-righteous pose. They are deeply involved in every social process. Neither can the churches derive benefit from something for which they will not assume responsibility. They cannot, in conscience, make widespread use of television, as they do, without assuming a large share of the burden of the struggle to employ it in the interest of all of the people all of the time.

Glossary of Television Terms

ACOUSTICS.   The science of sound. It deals with the creation of sound, its transmission, and its physical properties. The term is also applied to the resonant qualities of studios and concert halls, and to the characteristics of microphones.

AMPLITUDE MODULATION.   See *Modulation*.

ANIMATION.   Filming static objects such as cartoon drawings or puppets by stop motion (the exposing of one frame at a time) so the finished film will give the illusion of motion.

ANNOUNCER.   The person who introduces and closes a television program. Not to be confused with *Narrator* (which see).

ANTENNA.   A cluster of conductors supported high above the ground to radiate from a transmitting source or collect at a receiver the electromagnetic radio or television waves.

ART DIRECTOR.   The person who designs studio sets and props and supervises their construction.

ASPECT RATIO.   The ratio of the width of a television picture to its height. The picture is four units wide by three units high.

AUDIO.   Descriptive term for the sound portion of a television program (voice, sound effects, music).

BALOP.   See *Telop*.

BARN DOOR.   Term for a hinged, adjustable fitting, like a blinder, that may be attached to a light to vary the size of a beam and its direction.

BG.   Abbreviation for background. May be applied to *sound*, as in the case of background music and effects, and to *staging*, where it refers to scenic backdrops, photos, etc.

BILLING (OR BILLBOARDING).   Naming of participants and those responsible for production of a program, usually at the end of the show. Also credits used in publicity about the program.

BLACKOUT. Usually called "going to black," this is the practice of blacking out the television screen from the control panel to denote passage of time or change of scene in a program. Often used when an actor must make an instant change from set to set.

BLASTING. Overloading a camera with light or a microphone with volume to the point where distortion occurs.

BLOCKING. The breaking down by the director of the action called for in the script into separate floor set-ups in the studio and individual camera shots.

BLOOM. The glare seen in a picture as the result of reflection of light from highly polished surfaces. May also be caused by maladjustment of the camera control mechanism.

BOOM. A movable, extendable arm for suspending a microphone in mid-air and permitting its movement from place to place on set. The boom operator is called the *boom man*.

BREAKAWAY. A prop constructed to disintegrate easily, such as a paper-thin wall a performer can break through.

BRIDGE. Any material used to indicate transition from one scene to another. In sound a bridge is usually music or effects. In video it may be pictures, text, or similar devices.

BURN. Image retention by the tube of a camera that has been held immovable on an object for too long a time.

CAMERA TERMS AND DIRECTIONS. Cameras usually are numbered, with corresponding numbers appearing on the monitor screens for quick identification. Camera *direction* is taken from the viewpoint of the monitor tube; that is, *camera left* or *camera right* are the left and right of the person viewing the screen. This is the reverse of theatrical directions which are determined by the left and right of the actors.

Camera shots are described in terms: (1) of the number of persons appearing in the picture—one shot, two shot, three shot, etc.—and (2) of the apparent distance of the viewer from the camera subject:

LS—long shot
MLS—medium long shot
MS—medium shot
CU—close-up
XCU—extreme close-up

Camera movement: A *dolly* is movement toward or away from its subject; that is *dolly in* is toward, *dolly out* (or *back*) is away. A *truck* is movement of the camera parallel to the scene or to the movement of performers. A *pan* is movement of the camera from left to right. The director tells the cameraman, "Pan left" (or right). A *tilt* is vertical up and down movement of the camera.

Camera angle: The angle of variance, measured at the subject, of the placement of the camera to left or right of a line on the floor bisecting the set.

Camera chain: The mechanical and electronic facilities needed to operate one camera. Included are the camera and lenses, power supply, cable, and video control unit.

CANS. Slang term for headphones worn by technicians.

CAPTION. A title. A statement shown on the screen for explanatory purposes.

CHANNEL. The electromagnetic frequency assigned to a television station by the Federal Communications Commission.

CIRCUIT. The closed path followed by an electric current. May also be a network of such paths. *Closed circuit* is used to describe a television program seen on monitor screens, but not broadcast.

CLIP. A segment of motion picture film introduced into a television program.

COMMERCIAL. Term applied to the advertising material on a program. Often used as slang for identification used by public service organizations.

COMPATIBILITY. Color television transmissions that may also be received on black and white (monochrome) sets without distortion.

CONTINUITY. The process of carrying the attention of the audience smoothly from scene to scene in a production. The term is also applied loosely to the spoken portion of a script.

CONTRAST. The variation between tones in a scene or in a picture. The *contrast range* is the ratio between the brightness of the brightest tone and the darkness of the darkest tone.

CONTROL PANEL. A desk or table fitted out with the electronic controls necessary to transmit picture and sound from the studio floor, make the necessary mix and quality control of the two, and send them on to the transmitter.

CONTROL ROOM. A room, usually adjacent to and most often overlooking the studio floor, from which the artistic and operational control of a television program is carried on.

COPYRIGHT. The exclusive right to publish, reproduce, and sell a literary or artistic work. Material protected by copyright may not be used on television without permission of the copyright owner.

COVER SHOT. A wide-angle camera shot, usually overlooking an entire scene, to which a director may cut while repositioning his closer-in cameras or in case a camera is obstructed or some other fault appears in a scene. The cover is a "protection" shot.

CRANE. A movable platform containing a crane arm on which a camera is mounted. The crane can be moved up and down and to right and left, and the whole body pushed to any desired place in the studio.

CRAWL. A term applied to a title that moves slowly up the television screen, usually controlled by a motor-driven drum device.

CUE. A signal, given verbally or by hand, to cast and crew members directing them to begin a program, a sequence, or a particular act.

CUT. To delete a scene or passage from a script or program. To terminate a program or a particular action by ordering: "Cut."

CYCLORAMA. A semi-circular screen or backcloth, encircling the back of a set to provide neutral background.

DECIBEL. A unit of the measurement of the volume of sound; one-tenth of a bel.

DEFINITION. The degree of fineness of detail in a television picture. Definition depends upon focus and depth concept of the cameraman.

DIORAMA. A miniature of a large setting—such as a whole town—used for panoramic and "establishing" shots.

DIRECTOR. The person in charge of the artistic presentation. He works with the script writer, translating script into action on the studio floor. He auditions and chooses performers, conducts rehearsals, decides how cameras are to be used, and is in control of the entire production on the air.

DISSOLVE. An electronic transition from a scene to the next in which the picture in the upcoming scene is superimposed on the closing scene and the new view gradually replaces the previous one.

DOLLY. 1. Moving a camera steadily toward or away from its objective. 2. A wheeled mount for a camera.

DOWNSTAGE. The area nearest the footlights on a stage. In television the term is used to indicate the area closest to the camera and to move downstage is to move toward the camera. (Upstage: away.)

DRUM. See *Crawl*.

DRY RUN. A full-dress rehearsal without cameras.

DUB. To re-record a sound track.

ECHO. Repitition of a sound after an interval of time, usually because of reflection of the sound waves. In radio and television echo may be caused artificially in an "echo chamber"—a room with a speaker in one end and a microphone at the other through which the sound from a studio is passed.

ELECTRICAL TRANSCRIPTION (ET). A recording on a disk.

ESTABLISHING SHOT. A long shot used at the beginning of a program or a scene to show an over-all view of the set and the performers, preliminary to subsequent closer shots of details and individuals.

EXTRA. An actor who stands, sits, or moves about on a set to furnish atmosphere, but who speaks no lines.

FADE. 1. Gradual change of a television picture from light to dark to indicate the end of a scene or a program. 2. Gradual lowering of the volume of sound.

FEDERAL COMMUNICATIONS COMMISSION. The Federal regulatory agency established by Congress to grant licenses for use of radio and television frequencies, and to police the operations of the broadcast licensees.

FEED BACK. Whine or howl in a speaker caused by kick-back of sound waves from a speaker into a microphone being used in the system.

FILM STRIP. A series of 35 mm. pictures printed sequentially on a single strip of film and projected as stills.

FILTER. Glass or gelatine of varying color and density used in front of a camera lens to correct color balance or the amount of light entering the lens.

FLARE. A bright circle of light on a picture caused by light being flashed directly into the camera's lens.

FLAT. A rectangular piece of scenery used for walls and backgrounds. Usually a wooden frame with paper or canvas covering.

FLOOR. The working area in the studio where a program is played.

FLOOR MANAGER. The director's representative on the studio floor. Using a telephone link with the control room, he relays the director's instructions to cast and crew by means of hand signals and written directions.

FLOOR PLAN. Scale layout of the studio floor showing location of cameras, microphones, sets and their details—door, windows, furniture, props, etc.—and other information essential to the planning of a program.

FLUTTER. Rapid fluctuation in the intensity of a sound or rapid variation of frequency in the reproduction of recorded sound. (See

Wow.) Flutter in a picture is fluctuation in its brightness on the screen, caused by interference.

FLY.   The lifting and lowering of scenery from above by means of ropes and pulleys. Also the platforms from which the scenery is controlled.

FOCUS.   When an object appears sharp, it is said to be in focus. Focus in television is dependent upon the aperture of the lens setting and the depth of field.

FOOT CANDLE.   A unit of measurement of light intensity.

FOOTAGE.   A term applied to any given length of motion picture film.

FRAME.   The area contained in a television picture as seen through the camera finder. Used by the director as a command to the camera, frame means: "Compose the picture."

FREQUENCY.   The vibration rate of an oscillation, measured by the number of cycles performed in a second.

FREQUENCY MODULATION.   See *Modulation.*

GAIN.   Technically, the amount of increase an amplifier can impose on a given signal. Loosely, in programming, often used when volume is meant.

GHOST.   A fuzzy secondary image on a television screen, caused by electronic disturbance.

GOBO.   A solid piece of cloth or wood used to cast a shadow or shield the camera lens from light.

HALATION.   See *Flare.*

HAND PROPS.   Small, movable articles placed on a set to dress it or used by actors in the course of their performance.

HEAD ROOM.   The space from the top of the performer's head to the edge of the frame in a television picture.

HEADSET.   A combination telephone transmitter and headphone receiver worn by crew members to take direction from the director and the technical director and to talk back and forth.

HIGHLIGHT.   See *Lighting.*

HITCH-HIKE.   An announcement attached to a program after the content and the production credits have been completed. Usually used to advertise a product, an organization, or an event not included in the main program. A hitch-hike comes within assigned program time, as compared to a station-break announcement which follows a program.

IDIOT BOARD.   A prompting device consisting of material written on large art board sheets that are held near the lens of the camera within range of vision of the performers. See also *Teleprompter.*

IMAGE ORTHICON. The television camera tube used most widely today. It has extremely high light sensitivity.

INSERT. Any material—cards, photos, etc.—exhibited in an on-going program from a source outside the performers.

KILL. An order to stop or eliminate. "Kill the lights." "Kill that scene."

KINESCOPE. The filming of a television program from the tube for use in repeat broadcasts.

LAP. A form of dissolve.

LENS TURRET. A revolving mount on the front of a television camera. The turret contains a series of lenses which can be quickly switched by the cameraman.

LEVEL. The intensity of a continuous light or, in sound, of a continuous tone used for test purposes. Also loosely used to indicate volume.

LIGHTING. The illumination of a set to produce a realistic interpretation of the scene—place, time of day, mood—in the camera. *Flat lighting* gives a uniformity to the scene, everything having about the same value and with sense of depth lacking. *Back lighting* is applied from behind, usually from a concentration of lamps, and sharply outlines the performers against their background. *Front lighting* is done from above or beside the camera and gives a diffused effect, but with more highlights than in flat lighting. *Hard lighting* is a concentration of light that causes sharply defined shadows to create strong contrast between light and shadow. *Soft lighting* is diffusion of sources to avoid strong shadows. *Foundation lighting* is the over-all general light needed on a set. It must be augmented to produce artistic effects. *High key lighting* produces scenes that are predominantly light in tone (i.e., daylight). *Low key lighting* emphasizes dark tones (i.e., night scenes). The *key light* is the main source of illumuination, all other lights being related to it. A *highlight* is the brightest spot in a scene. *Spotlighting* is the concentration of a narrow beam of light on a single object to highlight it. *Cold, or blue, lighting,* usually produced by fluorescent bulbs, is cooler but less efficient than are incandescent lamps.

LIMBO. A scene shot against neutral background outside the regular locale of a program.

LINES PER INCH. The electron beams that unite to form a television picture. The beam scans from left to right 525 times to the vertical inch. The resulting combination of single electron lines is seen by the eye as a formed picture.

LOCATION. A place, outside a studio, where a television program is produced.

LOOP. A segment of film or tape which has been spliced into a loop so it may run continuously, repeating its content with every cycle. Usually used for background sounds or pictures.

MICROPHONE. An instrument for converting sound waves into mechanical vibrations in an alternating current. (Slang: *mike.*)

MICROPHONE BOOM. See *Boom.*

MOBILE UNIT. Control and camera equipment mounted in a truck for remote pickup and transmission of television programs.

MODEL (OR MINIATURE). Any small scale replica of an object used in rehearsal or production. A miniature is usually a whole set reproduced to scale and photographed to appear full size on the screen.

MODULATION. A variation from a mean. In amplitude modulation this variation is made by increasing and decreasing volume on a single frequency to overcome interference. In frequency modulation the sound is transmitted across a wide frequency band which permits interference to be bypassed.

MONITOR. A television screen in a control room or on studio floor, used to check progress of a program.

MONTAGE. Short scenes that quickly dissolve from one to another to give the effect of coverage of a great many times, subjects, or places.

MOOD MUSIC. Background music that supposedly intreprets the atmosphere of a scene.

NARRATOR. A person, on- or off-screen, who comments on the action or explains action in a program.

NEMO. Slang for a pickup outside the studio.

NETWORK. A number of television stations joined by coaxial cable or relay stations and transmitting the same program at the same time (e.g., the National Broadcasting Company). The networks own some stations, but most of their outlets are affiliated with them by contract.

OFF-CAMERA (-MICROPHONE). 1. A sound source not before the camera. 2. A sound (on- or off-camera) directed away from the microphone to convey a sense of distance.

PACKAGE. A filmed program, self-contained, for showing on television.

PERSPECTIVE. The apparent spatial relationship between objects viewed on the screen, or between different sources of sound.

PRE-EMPT. To take the time granted to one program for the broadcast of a substitute.

PRODUCER. The executive in over-all charge of a program or series.

PROPERTIES. Articles—furniture, bric-a-brac, etc.—needed in the design of a set.

RATING.   Measurements of audience size by interviewing of a small sampling of viewers and projection of the results to the whole population.

REAR PROJECTION.   A method of projecting still or moving pictures onto a screen to provide background for a scene.

REMOTE.   An out-of-studio pickup.

REPEAT.   Rebroadcast of a program by means of tape or kinescope.

REVERSE SHOT.   The placing of two cameras front and back to the action so actors can be seen in reverse to each other. A difficult thing to do in television, since cameras may be in each other's viewing range.

RIG.   To hang flats or overhead lights.

RUN-THROUGH.   A rehearsal.

SCRIM.   Gauze or a mesh screen placed before a light to diffuse its rays.

SCRIPT.   The written program that is the basis of a production. The script contains all material to be spoken, directions for action, and descriptions of music and sound effects.

SEGUE.   Blending of one musical phrase into another to denote change of mood or scene.

SET-UP.   Preparation of a studio and the sets for a production. (Set-up man.)

SIMULCAST.   Broadcasting of a program simultaneously on televison and radio.

SLIDE.   A still picture or title, usually mounted in a 2 x 2 inch frame.

SOUND EFFECTS.   Any sounds used in a production, other than spoken words or music.

SOUND ENGINEER.   The technician who controls the audio portion of a program.

SPECIAL EFFECTS.   Miniatures, models, dioramas, and certain electronic trick devices that give the illusion of large settings.

SPOT ANNOUNCEMENT.   A short announcement inserted between programs.

STAGING.   Arrangement of a set on the basis of a previously drawn diagram.

STILL.   A photograph used in a program.

STOCK SHOT.   Film rented from a film library to fit the needs of a production.

STORY BOARD.   An illustrated plan of the sequence of a program.

STRIKE.   To break down and remove a set.

SUPERIMPOSITION.   Overlapping the image from one camera with the image from another, as in the showing of titles over action.

SUSTAINING PROGRAM. One for which a station receives no fee for air time or facilities for production.

SYNCHRONIZATION. Linking together of action and sound in films.

TALK BACK. A monitor circuit which allows the director in the control room to talk to the cast and crew on the studio floor.

TAPING or TAPE RECORDING. The recording of a program on magnetic tape for broadcasting at will.

TECHNICAL DIRECTOR. The technician who, from the control room, controls the switching of cameras at the order of the director.

TELOP. Also known as *Balop*. The telopticon projector for opaque slides, drawings, and pictures. Telop is also used for the material projected.

TEST PATTERN. Schematic design of lines and circles used to test television receivers and to align cameras electronically.

THROW. The distance from a projector to a screen.

TITLES. Consist of name of program, its sponsor, cast, director, producer, technicians.

TRANSCRIPTION. 1. Recording of a live program for subsequent use. 2. Verbatim report of program content.

UHF. The ultra high frequency band of broadcast channels.

UPSTAGE. See *Downstage*.

VARIABLE FOCUS LENS. One in which the focal length can be changed during shooting to accommodate camera movement in and out. See *Zoom*.

VHF. The very high frequency band of broadcast channels. VHF channels are assigned mostly to commercial stations.

VIDEO. The visual or pictorial portion of television as contrasted to the audio or sound phase.

VOLUME. The magnitude of sound at a given moment expressed in decibels.

WIPE. Transition from one scene to the next in a moving, two-dimensional pattern such as a circle or diagonal. Also the term applied to the erasing of sound from a tape.

ZOOM. A fast move into or out from a subject by means of continuous change in focal length in a special lens, the camera appearing to move rapidly when, in fact, it is stationary.

Index

Abstract sets, 102-3
Abstract truths, word pictures to communicate, 96
Accent, 157-58
Accuracy, 113-14
Acoustical perspective, 182
Action, 154-56
  composition and, 169-77
  cueing of, 184
  editing of, 166
  fitting the set to, 144
  as result of religious communication, 28
  as test of faith, 27-28
Actions, conscious and unconscious, 154-55
  and words, 99
Activism, 22
Adolescence. *See* Teen-agers
"Adventures in Africa," 188-89, 190-191; *see also Off to Adventure*
Advertising, 27, 203
  addressed to subcultures, 10
  of community events, 88
  control of program content by, 216
  display, 197
  folders, 195
  newspaper, 195-96
  and political parties, 207-8
  of programs, 187, 195-97
Aesthetic judgment, 218, 219
Alcoa Playhouse, 48
Alfred Hitchcock Presents, 48
American Broadcasting Company, 85, 196

American way of life, popular concept of, 8
Anderson, Phoebe, 58
Andersonville Trial, 70
Angle of view, 167-68
Animation, 145-46
Ann, Doris, 149
Announcement story, 188-89; *see also* Spot announcements
Anti-intellectualism, 20
Aristotle, 14
Articulation, 160
Artistic forms of program, 24
Artistic integrity, 219
Aspect ratio of screen, 169, 179
Assistant director, 138-39
Attitudes, 7 n., 43
Audience, analysis of, 39-42, 72, 74
  carry-over, 204
  children, 43, 46-47, 57-60, 88
  complexities of, 23, 24
  effects of television on, 42-44
  families, 55-57
  getting reaction of, 41-42, 84
  men, 54-55
  numbers and quality of, 38-39
  passiveness of, 4, 5
  potential, 44-47
  and process of communication, 4
  ratings by, 40, 64-66, 69
  relationship between communicator and, 40-41
  for religious programs, 47-50
  selection of, 49, 50-66, 78, 88
  as stereotypes, 206